Collective Knowledge Management

NEW HORIZONS IN INTERNATIONAL BUSINESS

Series Editor: Peter J. Buckley, *Centre for International Business, University of Leeds (CIBUL), UK*

The New Horizons in International Business series has established itself as the world's leading forum for the presentation of new ideas in international business research. It offers pre-eminent contributions in the areas of multinational enterprise – including foreign direct investment, business strategy and corporate alliances, global competitive strategies, and entrepreneurship. In short, this series constitutes essential reading for academics, business strategists and policy makers alike.

Titles in the series include:

Collective Knowledge Management

Foundations of International Business in the
Age of Intellectual Capitalism

Haruo H. Horaguchi

Professor of International Business, Hosei University, Japan

NEW HORIZONS IN INTERNATIONAL BUSINESS

Edward Elgar
Cheltenham, UK • Northampton, MA, USA

First published in Japanese as *Shūgōchino Keiei: Nihon Kigyō no Chishiki Kanri Senryaku* © Bunshindō 2009

Published by
Edward Elgar Publishing Limited
The Lypiatts
15 Lansdown Road
Cheltenham
Glos GL50 2JA
UK

Edward Elgar Publishing, Inc.
William Pratt House
9 Dewey Court
Northampton
Massachusetts 01060
USA

A catalogue record for this book
is available from the British Library

Library of Congress Control Number: 2013951856

This book is available electronically in the ElgarOnline.com
Business Subject Collection, E-ISBN 978 1 78347 323 6

ISBN 978 1 78347 322 9

Typeset by Servis Filmsetting Ltd, Stockport, Cheshire
Printed and bound in Great Britain by T.J. International Ltd, Padstow

Contents

Figures

Tables

Preface

Human beings create knowledge as a result of interaction with others. Although knowledge is understood as an act of personal knowing, it is created through interactions among human beings. In the field of business management, these interactions can be strategically promoted. The ways in which firms adapt knowledge management may decisively impact their competitiveness. This book is devoted to focusing on this proposition and identifying the keys for collective knowledge management.

We will see that understanding the theory of collective knowledge creation provides us the answers to certain questions, such as the following: how can one lead innovation in a country while manufacturing companies are shifting their production bases to foreign countries? What methods are implemented by multinational firms to accumulate knowledge resources or dynamic knowledge competence? Why are there many competent multinational enterprises proliferating in some countries while people are suffering from a lack of basic human needs in other countries?

During the 1990s, the dichotomy of tacit and explicit knowledge was prevalent in the social sciences in Japan, and the concepts were embedded in both cluster promotion policy and open innovation policy. In 2004, Professor Tadao Kiyonari – then president of Hosei University – suggested that I engage in ongoing observation of business–government–university alliances in Japan, which had been institutionalized as a cluster-creation policy. I organized a series of teams for our field research projects as the director of the Research Institute for Innovation Management, Hosei University. I am thankful to those professors who participated in the research projects: Hisashi Yaginuma, Shigeru Matsushima, Junji Fukuda, Yongdo Kim, Yoshinori Konno, Seiki Yukimoto, Ruixue Li, Toshio Kimura, Ken Nittono, Yasushi Kodama and the late Tomofumi Amano. We conducted research on inter-firm collaboration and business–university alliances in various parts of the world. I also benefited from the valuable advice obtained in the Business School of Innovation Management, Graduate School of Hosei University. For this, I would like to thank Professors Hiroyuki Fujimura, Kosuke Ogawa, Fumihiko Mori, Yoshiro Fukuda, Yoshiharu Okamoto, Kazuo Ohmura, Yoshiyuki Okamoto, Kenji Ohmori, Atsunori Matsumoto, Masaru Udagawa, Koichi Shimokawa and Toshiyuki Yahagi.

One thing I noticed during our field research was the existence of habitats for knowledge. I observed an ecosystem of knowledge-creating patterns and noticed theoretical links between knowledge management and cluster-creation policy. The workplace, inter-organizational relationships, industrial agglomeration and the national economy create knowledge in distinct patterns of concentric circles. I compared this observation internationally by speaking with collaborators overseas. I want to thank Professor Jean-Louis Mucchelli, Dr René Haak, Professor Dr Holger Ernst, Professor Dr Thorstein Teichert, Mr Carl-Ernst Forchert, Mr Henning Hetzer, Professor Henry Oinas-Kukkonen and Dr Yoshikatsu Shinozawa, with whom I learned how European industrial clusters function and how manufacturing industries have historically developed in different countries.

In 2009, I published a Japanese version of this book, *Management of Collective Knowledge*. That was the year my colleague and I celebrated the 50-year anniversary of the Faculty of Business Administration, Hosei University. Professor Kenji Kamiya was the dean then and devoted himself to organizing a series of events. We invited Professor Michael E. Porter for a special lecture and held a wonderful event to celebrate the anniversary. Professor Richard E. Caves, now emeritus, was my advisor at the department of economics at Harvard University, where I spent two years as a Fulbright Scholar from 1994 to 1996. By then, I had encountered the concept of industrial clusters in Professor Porter's book. Professor Caves kindly introduced me to Professor Porter during my days at Harvard. This book is written to broaden the applicability of the cluster concept into which I have been inquiring since that time.

My special thanks go to Professor Emeritus Susumu Hagiwara and Professor Emeritus Nisaburō Murakushi, who highly praised my Japanese book; they gave me the 2010 Mori Kahei Award for the best book. It was an impressive occasion to have a round-table discussion with Professors Kazuo Koike, Yutaka Suzuki and Akio Kondo. I also want to thank those who participated in our international workshops on collective knowledge in Tokyo and in Kyoto: Professors Dongyoub Shin, Jonghoon Bae, Yasuo Sugiyama, Akira Takeishi, Naoki Wakabayashi and Masato Itohisa.

The translation into English for this book was essentially completed while I was a visiting scholar at the University of Washington from 2012 to 2013. I want to offer my sincere gratitude to Professor Marie Anchordoguy, the Chair of the Japan Studies Program at the Henry M. Jackson School of International Studies; she and her husband, Mr Leslie Helm, were very generous with their time and hospitality for my field research on the aircraft manufacturing industry in and around Seattle.

I am happy that I included references to research papers I published in 2013 in this book. With those inclusions, numerous omissions and rewriting, this English version is different from the Japanese version. Nevertheless, I would like to thank Mr Takashi Maeno, on behalf of Bunshindō Co., who granted me official permission to translate my Japanese book into English and to publish it. I am also grateful to Professor Patrick Q. Collins for his generous support in editing the English manuscript and Ms Hiroko Kubo for preparing English versions of the figures.

In the spring of 2013, a Chinese version was published in Beijing. I would like to thank Professors Xinxin Hu and Xuan Liu for their efforts to translate it into Chinese. This English version was realized through the recommendation of Professor Peter J. Buckley. I am most grateful for his generosity. It was at the end of the 1980s that we met at the office of Professor Tetsuo Abo at the University of Tokyo. I am honoured that my book is included in the New Horizons in International Business series edited by Professor Buckley.

I dedicate this book to my family.

The author acknowledges that this work was supported by JSPS KAKENHI grant number 22243032 and SEI Group CSR Foundation.

Haruo H. Horaguchi
Chiyoda-ku, Tokyo
December 2013

1. Knowledge and capabilities in business management: the risks of tacit knowledge

"Knowledge" is becoming a key component of management studies. Knowledge management has come to be viewed as the sixth administrative field after production management, sales management (marketing), financial management, human resource management, and information management. This is the newest emerging field in the studies of management since Frederick W. Taylor proposed the first field of administration in production management 100 years ago.

The study of management has tackled the production management of products. It has been equipped with an arsenal of scientific engineering research accumulated over more than 100 years. If we can clarify principles of knowledge management, as has been achieved for the concepts of production control, we shall be able to correctly position knowledge management within the process of business management. The field of knowledge management itself requires a skill set. This skill set is as technical as production, marketing, financial, human resource and information management.

Knowledge management is still in an embryonic stage and has the potential to flourish into a full-fledged occupation in its own right. At present, there is ongoing recognition of the work of knowledge management, and it essentially falls within the responsibility of managers as one of the ubiquitous tasks with which they are entrusted. Interestingly, managers may themselves recognize such work on a tacit level, or they may handle it without being aware. This is the reason why knowledge management is not yet considered as an applied technique for managing organizations. Building an intra-company local area network (LAN) system and the databases stored within this system are examples of information management within an entire organization, but there is no clear recognition of the difference between the building of information systems and the actual implementation of knowledge management as a task for managers.

We will show in this book how a company manages its organization while keeping an eye on knowledge. The research on this process reveals that innovation and productivity are substantially influenced by the way people are managed. Knowledge management and its consequent creation play a significant role in influencing the competitiveness of enterprises and ultimately the affluence of a society. Here I mean the competitiveness of enterprises in terms of the quality of the tasks carried out by workers and I mean the affluence of society in terms of how enterprises bring about innovation in society.

So how are we to produce knowledge in business? To this end, what appropriate management techniques should we consider? There are already plenty of studies discussing knowledge management techniques.[1] In particular the study of tacit knowledge is relevant. However, we need to be aware of certain risks associated with the concept of tacit knowledge while understanding that knowledge management is important. This point will be elaborated further in the second section of this chapter and thereafter. In the first section, I will present a survey regarding the theory of knowledge management and state the conclusions at which existing theory arrives.

1   HOW TACIT KNOWLEDGE IS MAPPED AMONG THE THEORY OF KNOWLEDGE

Signs, Information and Knowledge

Human beings think with signs. Whether the signs comprise an oral language or a literal one is not essential. The thinking process requires the acquisition of some forms of signs. Peirce (1868) proposed the needs of signs for human thinking and Eco (1976) argued that codes, sets of signs, are transmitted by people who wish to understand meanings with connotations. But what signs convey is information and not necessarily meaning. For example, the sequence of DNA does not have any meaning in and of itself. In fact, Saussure (1916) pointed out that the information conveyed via signs does not necessarily contain meaning. He proposes that the difference between societal "langue" and personal "parole" is the difference between oral speech and the connotations given by the context there.[2] Parole is classified into either the category of signifier (*le signifiant* in French), which is transmitted through speech, or the category of signified (*le signifié* in French), which receives the signifier as an idea. In other words, the first category is representative of the intention to convey meaning and the second category is representative of the interpretation when speech is received.[3]

Take a three-digit number as an example. The sequence of numbers such as 110 does not contain any meaning. The sequence of these signs is transmitted as information arranged as single numbers. When signs are transmitted between people, they become information. The question here is how the human being who has received 110, a string of signs, as information goes on to make sense of it. Making sense is extremely subjective behaviour. In Japan, for example, 110 is the number used to call the police at times of emergency. In the world of informatics, the binary 110 means 6 in the decimal base system. The act of vesting meaning into 110, which was received as information, is what is known as the function of knowledge.

Knowledge is what facilitates the matter of grasping 110 as an emergency number or converting it based upon the terms of the binary base system. Knowledge facilitates the act of interpreting 110, received as information. If you have knowledge of the binary code, you are ready to translate it into the decimal system. The number 6, which is the output of the decimal base conversion, is merely new information and nothing more. It is feasible to release information without knowing who receives it. The quantity of information conveyed by the mass media and billboards cannot be estimated as long as the receivers of this information remain indeterminate. Information can overflow. On the other hand, quantity of knowledge depends on the comprehension of the receiver of that information. Knowledge can only exist up to the point where information is understood by human beings. If you cannot understand a given sentence, however, the sentence is merely information.

This argument leads to a simple but important proposition: knowledge can only exist within relationships between people. It is not possible to transmit knowledge in isolation. The activity of reading a book and understanding it is a personal act that is performed alone. However, the book has to have been authored by someone else before it is taken by the reader's hand. Knowledge is born as a result of exchanging information. Exchanged information between people is construed as knowledge. Therefore knowledge is inherently brought about by a plurality of people. Consequently, by extension of such an understanding, we can see that knowledge is transmitted in the following ways: one to one, one to many, many to one, and many to many.

Knowledge and Management

Paradigm is defined as knowledge shared by scores of people and tacit knowing typically represents individual knowledge. These two concepts were proposed as a response to Popper (1957). Popper (1957) criticized historicism's theory of developmental stages, and attached great importance to the process of presenting and testing a hypothesis as a procedure to be followed through in scientific research. For Popper (1957) science should be composed of refutable propositions. Subsequently, two other scholars presented convincing arguments against Popper's proposition. The first was the concept of paradigm raised by Kuhn (1962), and the second was the concept of tacit knowledge raised by Polanyi (1966a).

According to Kuhn (1962), in the historical development of science, large scientific breakthroughs were achieved when a paradigm shifted due to conflict played out between generations, rather than through the logical process of refuting the validity of a hypothesis by experiment as advocated by Popper. This paradigm, or a worldview, is believed by a group of scientists. Research which is being performed within an existing paradigm is usually labelled "normal science" with institutional settings such as academic journals and merely contributes to realizing step-by-step advances. Popper (1957) grasped scientific work as the consummation of the unending cycle of proposing and then testing hypotheses, whereas Kuhn (1962) emphasized that paradigms exist on a macro level of thought above this cycle.

Polanyi's (1966a) concept of tacit knowing helped broaden the definition of knowledge. By clarifying that human beings know matters in a way that goes beyond words, and that this state of mind is one form of intelligence, he asserted the existence of indefinable knowledge as a form of knowledge that differed from knowledge expressed through the written word. Furthermore, he argued that the existence of such indefinable knowledge led to the "emergence" of new knowledge.

The attention given to the concept of tacit knowledge made the study of knowledge management seem promising. Tacit knowledge is defined as knowledge that could be known but is inexplicable via the medium of words. Polanyi states in his seminal work, *The Tacit Dimension*, that there is a sense of physicality incorporated in the concept of knowledge. Physicality refers to the fact that some forms of knowledge become the kind we are unable to express through words because they represent skills we have learned through experience. The definition of tacit knowledge includes the recognition and memory derived from possessed skills, acquired technology, physical strength and inherent functions such as the senses of tasting, touching, smelling, and hearing. This is inherently personal.

In contrast to tacit knowledge, the type of knowledge that can be explained through language is called explicit knowledge. A concrete analogy for explicit knowledge can be found in the language of computer programming. What can be expressed in a programming language is explicit knowledge, and whatever is impossible to express, or whatever needs to be altered from the intended expression in a programming language, is tacit knowledge. Tacit knowledge, like recognition of the human face (Polanyi 1966a), is a form of knowledge that cannot be expressed in an objective fashion. For example, when people communicate via email and telephone, facial expressions and emotions are not conveyed well. However, when people actually meet face to face, or when people use Skype, they are able to establish a mode whereby they can exchange information in a very in-depth manner. A slight hesitation in conversation is transmitted through face-to-face communication. This is because on such occasions tacit knowledge can be conveyed through facial expressions.

The concept of tacit knowledge was applied by Nelson and Winter (1982) in the field of evolutionary managerial economics. In the context of explaining evolution of management, they attributed tacit knowledge as a driving force to put forward routine operations in a firm. In Chapter 4 of their book they discuss skills as the one requirement of tacitness. As long as tacit knowledge is not shared with others, it is the manager who executes managerial decisions to combine the tacit knowledge of employees. Emergence of innovation is induced through useful questionings which often arise from anomalies relating to previous routines (p. 128).

Some studies applied tacit knowledge to the analysis of workplaces in the manufacturing industry. Inoki (1985, 1987) and Koike and Inoki (1987) adopted the concept of tacit knowledge as a principle that explains the formation of skills. They carried out an empirical study on the formation of skills in workplaces of the Asian manufacturing industry. Inoki (1987) argues that executives cannot completely accomplish the task of collecting and managing such knowledge and skills since tacit knowledge may not be appropriately defined. Knowledge and skills possessed by individuals at workplaces are indefinable knowledge (p. 213). Therefore, as it turns out, executives do not manage knowledge itself, but manage an organization's individuals who are believed to have knowledge. Here one can see a form of kinetics is advocated that we can comprehend knowledge through a common experience in the workplace. The common experience makes workers undergo acquisition of knowledge beyond description by job instructions and understanding of what words can transmit.

Theory of Knowledge Creation

Nonaka (1990, 1991) and Nonaka and Takeuchi (1995) claim that knowledge is generated in the process of converting tacit knowledge to explicit knowledge and, as case studies, they studied the process of developing an automatic electric baking oven, and the process of designing an automobile. The theory of knowledge creation proposed by Nonaka and Takeuchi (1995) attaches great importance to the concept of tacit knowledge.

In 1995, Nonaka and Takeuchi published the book *The Knowledge-creating Company* and began disseminating their theory of knowledge

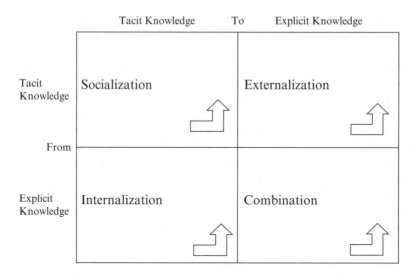

Note: Arrow directions are shown to clarify the explanation.

Source: Extracted from Nonaka and Takeuchi (1995), p. 62, Figure 3.2.

Figure 1.1   Knowledge conversion modes by Nonaka and Takeuchi (1995)

creation. Prior to this, Nonaka (1990, 1991) had already put into place a theoretical framework of knowledge creation, but this book added some case studies to their research with clear disposition. Amid the rise of uncertainty and complexity in the environment surrounding business enterprises, the theory of knowledge creation answers the question of how organizations should go about creating knowledge. At the heart of this theory lies the basic assertion that organizations that operate on the basis of the theory of knowledge creation are innovative.

Figure 1.1 illustrates the theory presented by Nonaka and Takeuchi (1995), showing how knowledge is created in the course of the conversion from tacit knowledge to explicit knowledge. The left side of Figure 1.1 shows the input, and the upper side shows the output, as in input-output analysis in economics. When an input of tacit knowledge yields an output of tacit knowledge, the process is called "socialization". When an input of tacit knowledge yields an output of explicit knowledge, the process is called "externalization". When an input of explicit knowledge yields tacit knowledge, the process is called "internalization". When an input of explicit knowledge yields explicit knowledge, the process is called "combination".

Nonaka and Takeuchi (1995) cite the development of the automatic electric baking oven by Matsushita Electric Industrial (which changed its company name to Panasonic in 2008) as a case study of this process. In 1984, the Rice-Cooker Division, the Heating Appliance Division, and the Rotation Division were integrated to form the Cooking Appliance Division. Thirteen middle managers from various posts of new divisions gathered and carried out a three-day training camp, launching an attempt to share tacit knowledge. "Easy & Rich" was suggested as a concept of the automatic electric baking oven development, and a prototype was made accordingly. However, this prototype ended up overcooking the outside of the bread, while leaving the inside uncooked. Nonaka and Takeuchi (1995) refer to the sequence of events up to this point of the process as the first cycle of knowledge creation.

The second cycle involved a trial and error process that lasted approximately one year. Specifically, this cycle saw Matsushita Electric's female managers take up an apprenticeship under the chief baker of a hotel and subsequently relating the expression "twisting-stretch" to engineers of Matsushita Electric in reference to a kneading skill. According to Nonaka and Takeuchi (1995), the training in the hotel was described as "socialization", and the act of conveying this to the engineer was interpreted as "externalization". Furthermore, they claimed that a successful prototype was completed when the technological knowledge of engineers was "combined" with the "twisting-stretch" way of thinking, and thereafter the process shifted to the third cycle.

In the third cycle, the development objective of keeping the cost below 40 000 yen was set. This objective was achieved through the socialization and externalization carried out by team members. In particular, this involved removing the refrigerator and adding yeast during the kneading process. The product, the Home Bakery, was launched in February 1987 for 36,000 yen, and went on to become a hit, attaining sales of 536,000 units in just the first year alone (Nonaka and Takeuchi 1995, p. 108).

The spiral passes through the four quadrants of socialization, externalization, combination, and internalization. Figure 4.9 in Nonaka and Takeuchi (1995, p. 109) shows that five phases are repeated three times. Specifically, these five phases consist of "sharing of tacit knowledge", "concept creation", "criteria of justification", "prototype construction", and "transfer of knowledge".

When comparing both, we see that socialization corresponds with the "sharing of tacit knowledge", externalization corresponds with "concept creation", and combination corresponds with "prototype construction". However, where internalization is concerned, no corresponding concept appears in Figure 4.9 of Nonaka and Takeuchi (1995, p. 109). In addition, it should be noted that "criteria of justification" and "transfer of knowledge" do not appear in their Figure 3.3 (p. 73).[4]

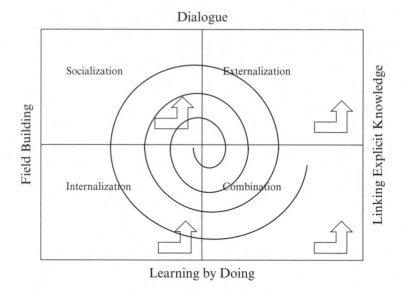

Note: Arrow directions have been added by the author.

Source: Extracted from Nonaka and Takeuchi (1995), p. 71, Figure 3.3.

Figure 1.2   Knowledge spiral

2   THE RISKS OF TACIT KNOWLEDGE

Criticisms from Europe and America

The theory of knowledge creation proposed by Nonaka and Takeuchi (1995) has clarity and is appealing. Additionally, it has served as the framework for many subsequent studies.[5] However, some scholars have already criticized the theory. Snowden (2002) condensed the four quadrants of socialization, externalization, internalization, and combination to refer to them as the SEIC model, and judged the research carried out by Nonaka and Takeuchi (1995) to represent second-generation knowledge theory.

According to Snowden (2002), first-generation knowledge theory is grounded on the concept of business-process re-engineering, which requires speedy conveyance of information necessary for decision-making. In this first-generation theory, neither the importance of tacit knowledge nor the importance of "place" was pointed out. Responding to what he calls the second-generation theory of knowledge conceived by Nonaka and Takeuchi (1995), Snowden (2002) insists on the appearance of a new, third-generation theory of knowledge.[6] In other words, he says that second-generation knowledge management techniques ignore the fact that knowledge is ephemeral. This oversight is apparent in the depiction of the spiral, which implies that knowledge is something that needs to be accumulated like a set of stocks. The cost is high as a company forms and maintains an intra-company group for the purpose of knowledge creation, which Nonaka and Takeuchi (1995) propose as a case study. Furthermore, such a group also entails the risk of giving rise to idle personnel after the work of knowledge creation ends. In the third-generation model that Snowden (2002) advocates, there is integration of a self-organizing sphere of activity maintained by an informal community, and transfer of new knowledge generated there to the formal sphere of activity. Snowden (2002) calls such a process "just-in-time knowledge management".

The criticism by Gourlay (2006) is more elaborate.[7] One part pertains to terminology. Specifically, he points out that there is a distinction to be made between the expression "tacit knowledge", as used by Nonaka and Takeuchi (1995), and the expression "tacit knowing", as used by Polanyi (1958, 1966a). According to Gourlay (2006, p. 1422), the latter is a concept that attaches great importance to the process,[8] and he points out, in particular, that Polanyi (1966b) himself had written that while tacit knowledge can be possessed by itself, "explicit knowledge must rely on being tacitly understood" and applied.[9]

Gourlay (2006) also raises the question of whether a difference exists between "explicit knowledge" and "knowledge" in the view of Nonaka and Takeuchi (1995) and concludes that there is no such thing. While Nonaka and Takeuchi (1995) define knowledge as "justified true belief", according to Gourlay (2006), this definition is not different from the definition for explicit knowledge. Furthermore, Gourlay argues that the manager's role is one of approving explicit knowledge. In effect, he argues this by pointing out that the automatic electric baking oven, which had been formed into a product after it became explicit knowledge through a process of externalization, was sold after it met the approval of the manager of Matsushita Electric. This becomes estranged from Nonaka and Takeuchi's (1995) definition of knowledge as "justified true belief". In other words, Gourlay (2006, p. 1423) points out that an idea or plan approved by the manager may merely be what Nonaka and Takeuchi (1995) refer to as explicit knowledge.

Awareness of Ignorance

It is appropriate to add the following two points to such criticisms. The first is lack of awareness of ignorance. There is no scope for ignorance in the theory of knowledge creation conceived by Nonaka and Takeuchi (1995). There is no room for setbacks such as loss of a unit of tacit knowledge due to being ineffective, or there is no room for degeneration of an item of knowledge into a rule of thumb due to falsification of an item of explicit knowledge. Figure 1.3 incorporates an area of ignorance in the knowledge creation theory of Nonaka and Takeuchi (1995).[10] If there is an area of ignorance, knowledge may not always increase in the shape of a spiral. At times, it may fall into the domain of ignorance and thereafter resurface from there. However, there will be other times when it fails to escape from the darkness of ignorance.[11]

Peirce (1868) attached great importance to the process of forming a hypothesis, or retroduction by way of estimating through the contrapositions of deduction and induction against each other.[12] Figure 1.3 shows the process of retroduction in the event that tacit knowledge is acquired on the basis of explicit knowledge. The process by which one acquires tacit knowledge from explicit knowledge resembles the process whereby a researcher accidentally discovers a phenomenon that is impossible to explain using the existing hypothesis while the researcher is trying to validate his research.

In addition to retroduction, two other patterns can be found in the way the intellect upgrades, or becomes sophisticated. The first pattern, as indicated with the label "Zen" in Figure 1.3, is one in which tacit knowledge advances to a higher level of tacit knowledge. As for whether it is possible to acquire tacit knowledge as tacit knowledge of a higher degree, the matter may be debatable. However, judging from the fact that the process of acquiring tacit knowledge from ignorance is named "experience", the complement of this that remains is the behaviour of "understanding without experiencing anything". While "Zen" may not be an appropriate metaphor, this upgrading of tacit knowledge is similar to the practice of "Zen".

Secondly, as the label "ramification" suggests, there is the case of explicit knowledge becoming recognized anew as explicit knowledge of a higher level. Illustrative examples of this process of ramification are easy to point out. For instance, by showing annual data for "number of days when a heavy snowfall warning was issued" in terms of a monthly breakdown, it can be claimed that this item of explicit knowledge has been ramified as quantitative data. Nevertheless, there remains a possibility that an actor who starts from ignorance may also end up remaining ignorant. In Figure 1.3, I have named such a process as the process of imbecility.

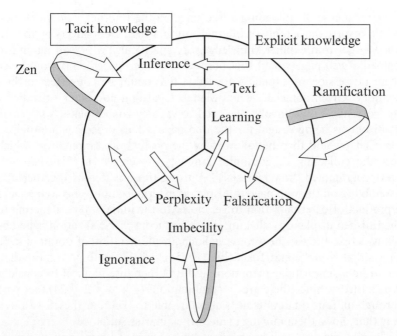

Figure 1.3   The classifications of intellectual work

Questions Regarding the Conversion from Tacit Knowledge to Explicit Knowledge

The second issue peculiar to Nonaka and Takeuchi's (1995) knowledge creation theory pertains to the conversion from tacit knowledge to explicit knowledge. The first point is in respect to the assertion that the deferred externalization of tacit knowledge may be beneficial to an organization. There are cases when management becomes easier by neglecting to convert tacit knowledge to explicit knowledge. The reason why a sushi chef does not create a manual on how to prepare sushi, for example, is because this allows him to maintain his position as the master of his art, and also maintain a level of income commensurate with such a position. As long as a pupil working at a sushi restaurant attempts to imitate work that is not written in a manual, the sushi chef can retain power over the pupil. In addition, he can evaluate and direct the motivation of the pupil.

Secondly, a crossover between tacit knowledge and explicit knowledge may not necessarily spiral rightwards, as in Figure 1.2. It is likely that movement through each quadrant will occur at random. One can even assume, for example, a case of a leftward spiral occurring: for instance, consider a case of uploading a web page on the Internet. The initial step would involve the activity of internalization, which sees conversion to tacit knowledge from explicit knowledge. So, specifically, a person aiming to upload a web page would first browse other web pages. This would give them possession of explicit knowledge that could be converted in their memory. Given some basic knowledge regarding computer operations, the next step would involve the need to vaguely contemplate "what form of display is being sought for the web page". This process is internalization. This would then be followed by the process of combination, which sees the collecting of computer languages, such as HTML and Java, and programmed "raw materials". Putting those materials together and assembling on the web page to display is externalization. This web page is a product of externalization to get closer to the initial image. Reacting to the finished displays by clicking on chosen icons is socialization, whereby many people browse the web page. Such an enumeration of doubt in logic shows that Nonaka and Takeuchi's (1995) clockwise path is no more than an ad hoc, simplistic explanation, and it is therefore illogical to consider it as a theory. Since there are 24 combinations ($4 \times 3 \times 2 = 24$) that pass through all four quadrants, it is also possible to consider these cases in a way that shows them moving in an anti-clockwise spiral.

Thirdly, the way tacit knowledge can be expressed may vary according to whether the person who externalizes the tacit knowledge is the holder of the tacit knowledge or whether the holder and the externalizer are different individuals. How tacit knowledge is externalized will depend on the intended action. This point directly relates to the creation of collective intelligence, and is elaborated upon in Chapter 2.

When enumerating such various problematic points, theories of knowledge creation through conversion from tacit knowledge to explicit knowledge appear to have an issue they share in common. This issue concerns the theoretical prerequisite that humans possess the ability necessary for understanding explicit knowledge, acquiring tacit knowledge, and then converting tacit knowledge into explicit knowledge. Tacit knowledge is meaningful only if human ability is sufficient to utilize it. This prerequisite of having capability is, however, not assured to be in existence in business settings.

3   KNOWLEDGE AND ABILITY

The Risks of Depending on Tacit Knowledge

There are several dangers associated with tacit knowledge, including dangers of carrying out management practices that place too much emphasis on tacit knowledge. The first such danger is the danger of corrupt tacit knowledge.[13] Allowing tacit knowledge to remain tacit seems like showing respect for the skill of the artisan. However, it is, in fact, a risky business approach: if tacit knowledge disappears from the artisan, recognition of this fact will be delayed.

There are at least two scenarios in which tacit knowledge can disappear or become corrupt. The first scenario is when profits are pursued via ethically unacceptable means. For example, there was a case involving a high-class restaurant in which it had been discovered that leftovers from a customer's dish were being re-served to the next customer.[14] In this incident, what was noteworthy was that customers did not realize that this was happening for a long time. In other words, even if tacit knowledge is a corrupt kind, you can hide it for a certain period of time. The second scenario is the problem of transmitting tacit knowledge to the next generation due to the ageing and eventual death of the holder of the tacit knowledge. Since human beings are alive, they inevitably die: if tacit knowledge is not passed on before this happens, it will vanish.

In management that depends on tacit knowledge, there is a second danger, that "the level of explicit knowledge that exists prior to the realization of tacit knowledge" becomes downplayed. This is the danger that the cognitive ability of self-awareness will underestimate the power of thought. While we refer to tacit knowledge as the ability to know through various senses, this also depends on something expressed through words. For example, the expertise of an artisan kneading dough with the delicate use of their fingertips is tacit knowledge, and it is said that digitizing this tacit knowledge and using it in an automatic electric baking oven is turning tacit knowledge into explicit knowledge. However, this knowledge creation process, for the most part, omits the logic behind kneading, since it does not pay sufficient attention to the thought process involved. To understand a certain sense that words cannot express, awareness of the concrete materials found in one's surroundings is necessary. A bread artisan who has no grasp of the difference between wheat flour, strong flour, soft flour and yeast will not be able to create delicious bread no matter how much he or she depends on the dexterity of his or her fingertips. As for technical knowledge required for the design of an automatic electric baking oven, explicit knowledge regarding technology elements is imperative. Such knowledge includes the development of heat sensors, the design of power-saving circuitry, customization of LSI, calculation of the internal resistance in a power circuit, drafting mould design, use of computer-aided design (CAD) software for container moulding, and design and selection of materials that take into consideration coefficient factors of thermal conductivity. In effect, these elements require a level of prior knowledge, which a designer of an automatic electric baking oven needs to have.

The third danger of attaching too much importance to tacit knowledge is the undervaluation of mental arithmetic. In the Japanese-English dictionary, there are three English terms corresponding to the Japanese word *Anzan*. That is, *Anzan* can be translated as mental arithmetic, mental calculation, or mental computation depending on the level of difficulty of what is being calculated.[15] When a human being calculates, it is possible to express this process as one involving explicit knowledge. However, when obtaining explicit knowledge from another form of explicit knowledge via *Anzan* (mental arithmetic), it is not always clear whether the thought process involved is based on tacit knowledge or explicit knowledge.

For example, when performing a differential calculus operation, will the necessary thought process be based on tacit knowledge or on explicit knowledge? Unlike arithmetic operations of natural numbers, beginners find it difficult to understand differential calculus and integral calculus, because these fields partly rely on mental calculation and do not readily offer explanations that appeal to the sight. When performing the operation of $5 + 4$, one can visualize it by adding five stones to four stones and then counting the resulting total number. In contrast, in the case of differential calculus, offering a visual explanation proves difficult. For example, if $e^{(\mu - x)^2}$ is differentiated with respect to x, the operation will yield $-2(\mu - x)e^{(\mu - x)^2}$, but the thought process of performing this logical process without turning it into words is open to question. Is this process in the end tacit knowledge? Is it explicit knowledge? Or is it neither?

If you attempt to explain through words an *Anzan* (mental arithmetic) operation that seeks the solution, $-2(\mu - x)e^{(\mu - x)^2}$, it becomes necessary to explain derivatives stipulated by Newton's formula and define their chain rules and exponential functions. However, an operation carried out by a person accustomed to making such a calculation is a form of applying a type of formula and not an explanation using words. A mathematical calculation, in the end, regardless of who performs it, yields the same solution and supposedly does not permit unevenness of data such as data relating to hardness of dough. In this sense, it can become firm knowledge. However, there is room for doubt regarding whether the process of carrying out an operation to attain explicit knowledge in the end is solely dependent on explicit knowledge. Part of the process of mentally carrying out an operation, or *Anzan*, may be dependent on tacit knowledge, which cannot be expressed in words.

In Japan, there is a tradition of *Anzan* (mental arithmetic) as manifested in the games of *Go* and *Shogi* (Japanese chess), and in the practice of using the abacus. Under such a tradition of carrying out "tacit calculations", the process of calculation is not put into words. Still, calculations are clearly being carried out through some form of logical thinking based on intuitive selection of moves. The contents of the calculation consist of the rules of the games, the unfolding intense battle between white and black stones in the case of *Go*, and the functions and movements of the *Shogi* pieces. In the case of numerical computations with the beads of an abacus, the arithmetical processing takes place when reconfiguring the beads by fingers. In the sense of being nonverbal, the baker's dexterity in using his fingertips is tacit knowledge. However, the thought process of a master of *Shogi* is also tacit knowledge. But to lump together both haptic sense through fingers and logical thought processes with heuristics under the single label of tacit knowledge is to trivialize the diverse aspects of the knowledge creation process.

As forms of thought processes similar to *Anzan* (mental arithmetic), there are three more examples to consider. These are the process of understanding a foreign language without the aid of translations, the process of summarizing prose, and the process of performing a musical instrument via recalling a memorized musical score. The work of reading a sentence of a certain length and condensing it is the work of creating explicit knowledge from explicit knowledge, and, according to Nonaka and Takeuchi (1995), this work is the work of combination. According to Figure 1.2, in this work of combination, tacit knowledge is not included as input. However, if ten people were each to write a summary, there will be ten different results, showing that the criteria for selection vary from person to person. These criteria may not be verbally explainable by the individuals themselves.

Ways to help understand explicit knowledge must not be downplayed in the course of emphasizing tacit knowledge. To acquire higher-level tacit knowledge, it is necessary to have higher-level explicit knowledge. A person who understands forms of explicit knowledge, such as a piece of writing, mathematics, and musical notes, can recognize more subtle differences than a person who does not understand them. Explicit knowledge works as a prerequisite to the acquisition of tacit knowledge. In other words, if innovation occurs in education methods used for understanding explicit knowledge, tacit knowledge is also heightened. Efforts to understand explicit knowledge and the educational skills required for achieving this are not rendered unnecessary by attaching too much importance to tacit knowledge.

Just to be clear, let me point out that it is possible to feign comprehension without having explicit knowledge. Such a state may be referred to as the corruption of explicit knowledge. For example, a straightforward case would be a university professor or PhD student who operates a package program that performs statistical analysis, and presents a thesis while being ignorant of its mathematical structure.[16] A research paper's primary aim is to explain through language, and for this reason, explicit knowledge in such a paper is a pretext, attesting to the fact that a hollowing-out of knowledge is occurring in this case.

The Concept of Ability

In considering ability as a prerequisite for acquiring tacit knowledge and explicit knowledge, a summary of what is actually meant by general human ability is presented. Firstly, ability is often roughly classified into native ability (or talent) and acquired ability. Not just anyone can succeed in such occupations as pianist, baseball player, or Sumo wrestler. Clearly, native, physical, and cerebral sensitivities are demanded. In such occupations, in addition to native ability, acquired effort is also necessary. In fact, in such occupations, it is often said that "ability to make an effort" is also necessary. In other words, it can be said that the act of making an effort depends partly on an innate ability to do so.

Secondly, while the expression "problem-solving ability" exists, there is no expression such as "problem-solving knowledge". However, it is clear that in problem-solving, the ability to make use of knowledge is necessary. Problem-solving cannot be accomplished by just having knowledge. In this case "ability" means the ability to choose from a full array of knowledge so that one can usefully solve a problem. In other words, problem-solving is believed to be dependent upon ability to decide which knowledge is being used.

Thirdly, expressions such as "growing ability" and "extension of ability" refer to situations where an individual may understand multiple facets of knowledge at the same time. The expression "to extend the ability of a junior high school student" implies the idea of endowing the student with the ability to find out necessary knowledge when it is necessary and to promote its understanding for the purpose of applying such knowledge towards solving problems and creating solutions. Problem-solving ability entails the ability to process a problem by recalling divergent units of knowledge at the same time and linking them together.

Fourthly, the act of evaluating ability is subjective. For example, every pianist playing Chopin would have their own interpretation of Chopin, each differing in the way they play Chopin. In effect, the same piece of music will vary in mood by how an individual pianist strikes the keyboard.[17] Other instances that illustrate the subjectivity of evaluating ability include a baseball player or a Sumo wrestler. We see sometimes that a baseball player being discharged from a former team going on to actively participate in another baseball team a year after. In the world of Sumo, expert opinions differ on whether a Sumo wrestler should adopt a muscle-training programme or a traditional training programme. The performance of the Sumo wrestler is not yet dependent on the training programme.

Is It Knowledge or Ability?

Above, I have contrasted ability with knowledge. Doing this has led to the following proposition: to acquire "tacit knowledge", you need to have the ability to do so. Ultimately, tacit knowledge refers to that which is brought about by one's ability, and that which is mastered through ability. To have "mastered some technique" implies having acquired the ability to carry out this technique anytime or to have acquired the ability to make appropriate decisions regarding this technique.

Referring to Plato's "Meno", Polanyi (1966a) pointed out a well-known paradox regarding the act of searching for a solution to a problem. According to Plato, if one knows what one seeks, there exists no problem, and if one does not know what one seeks, one cannot expect to find a solution. The solution to this paradox that Plato proposed, according to Plato himself, can be found in the knowledge that all discoveries recall an act that took place in the past. Polanyi rephrased Plato's answer and stated that problem-solving is carried out through discoveries of what we know but cannot yet put into words. In other words, the key to solving the paradox that Plato showed in "Meno" is, for Polanyi, tacit knowledge (p. 22). In the final chapter of this book, I give another answer to this paradox in relation to collective knowledge management.

According to Polyani (1957), only when a problem troubles someone does it become an issue that should be solved. For example, even if you ask an ape what is the correct way to play chess, the ape will not understand what the question itself means. On the other hand, a correct chess move that appears brain-wracking to an ordinary person may be a simple problem for a grandmaster. Therefore, according to Polyani (1957), true discovery occurs when there is a huge logical gap between problem and solution and ideas overcoming this gap come to light. A person who achieves this is called a genius. If an instance of problem-solving proves to be either too easy or insolvable, it becomes meaningless. And meaning only arises when it is recognized that there is value commensurate with the talent, effort, and financial resources invested in its solution. The intuitive heuristic effort is effort that articulates what is being solved as well as the type of route a solution demands.[18]

Simon and Lea (1974) discuss the derivation of problem-solving and regularity, citing the example of deciphering a code. For example, if DONALD + GERALD = ROBERT is given as code, and if D = 5, the first digit moves up, T = 0. Then since L + L = R in the tens place, it becomes clear that R is an odd number. Furthermore, in the sixth place, since D + G = R, it follows that 5 + G = R, or in other words, R must be an odd number and it is a number larger than 5. Consequently, logic shows that R is 7 or 9.

Carrying out such a line of thought is the problem-solving ability. The only knowledge supporting this problem-solving ability, as shown by Simon and Lea (1974), is the rule of addition. Just as the computer incorporates the function of storing memory (RAM) and the function of processing (calculations and operations), the knowledge that the human brain memorizes can be understood as being analogous to RAM, and the ability that the human brain possesses can be understood as being analogous to the processor. The act of externalizing tacit knowledge is analogous to the act of printing out the results of computer operation after stored data is processed. Giving a new set of programming to the computer to carry out a new task, the processor has to have a capacity to handle the data. If the level of problem-solving ability is low due to the obsolescence of the processor in the computer, there can be no outcome born as a consequence of responding to a difficult problem.[19] Such a speculation leads again to the proposition: to acquire tacit knowledge, it is necessary to have the ability to do so.

The Ability of the Business Enterprise

So far I have discussed an ability of human beings in general. I need to proceed from the above-mentioned proposition to an inquiry on how corporations hold ability. Chandler's (1992) "Organizational Capability", Hamel and Prahalad's (1996) "Core Competencies", and Teece and Pisano's (1994) "Dynamic Capability" are differentiated versions of referring to the abilities possessed by a company. Fujimoto (2003) argues that "competitiveness of depth (production competitiveness)" and "surface competitiveness (product competitiveness)" are born from an organization's "organizational capability". "Competitiveness of depth" is a form of competitiveness that is not directly visible to a corporation's clients and is indicative of productivity, production lead-time, development lead-time, and quality of manufacture. "Surface competitiveness" is an indicator that the clients of a corporation can recognize directly, and refers to cost, time to delivery, appeal of the product, and appeal of advertising.

Fujimoto (1997) classifies the competitive ability of corporations into "static capability", "improvement capability", and "evolutionary capability". "Static capability" refers to productivity and manufacturing quality at a certain point in time, as well as production patterns that affect them. "Improvement capability" refers to routine patterns of activity that raise static-ability levels. "Evolutionary capability" is explained as the ability to bring about change in the routine activity patterns of improvement ability. Alternatively "evolutionary capability" (p. 325) can be expressed as "ability-construction ability" (Fujimoto 1997, p. 12) and can be understood as the ability to bring about Fujimoto's (2003) "surface competitiveness" and "competitiveness of depth".

Based on such an understanding, the next question we should ask is how to construct "organizational capability" itself. There is the serious question of whether a corporate structure is sufficient to enable an organization to build capability and produce new knowledge. What kind of qualitative difference emerges between the case when only employees of a corporation build organizational capability, and the case when a corporation collaborates with outside abilities it can find?

For example, a pianist is a sole proprietorship, which earns income from his or her acquired ability. The appeal of a concert and the musical pieces performed are surface competitive edges, and behind the scenes disciplined practice, which is a form of competitiveness of depth, is necessary. For another example, let us assume that Toyota carries out continuous improvement initiatives, and has "evolutionary capability", which includes the emergence of the production system. This would mean that at Toyota the "competitiveness of depth" will be developed continuously by its employees.

Besides these examples of a pianist and of Toyota, are there no other mechanisms that could organize abilities of individuals and thereby generate new knowledge? The next chapter of this book asks the following: what kinds of patterns can be found in the methods used to acquire competitiveness by collectivity of individuals who cooperate to develop abilities and generate knowledge? In this book, this pattern is referred to as collective strategy, and the following chapters take a closer look at this subject.

A corporation's competitiveness may not only be sustained by mutual cooperation of its employees. It may also be affected by relationships that go beyond the framework of the corporation, or by the specificity of the field in which the corporation operates. With this book, I wish to clarify these points. Apparently, each country has corporations with distinctive abilities. Corporations of some countries excel in manufacturing, others in financial services, and yet others in hotels and tourism. For example, regarding car production, countries with manufacturers operating on a global scale are those such as the USA, Japan, Germany, France, Korea and Italy. Car production in China and in India is still confined in domestic markets. Thus, car production all over the world is dominated by introducing the technology from those countries. If you examine passenger plane production, you will see that Boeing and Airbus compete with each other for ascendancy, in effect, creating a rivalry between the USA and Europe.

When contemplating why such uneven distribution of corporate ability comes about, it can be understood that this is because there are limits to the way people convey their expertise. Consequently, this would mean that globalization is born from the uneven distribution of corporate ability. For instance, when a certain corporation maintains rare management know-how that another company in a foreign country does not possess, international business opportunities are born for the former. It may be said that ability to differentiate products and services and ability to discover niche markets exist because opportunities and abilities are unevenly distributed.

Converting into Organizational Ability

The growth of organizational ability reveals a paradox. When an entrepreneur launches a company, the entrepreneur can sustain this company alone. It may be said that the level of personal ability is equal to the level of the company's ability. During the initial stages of establishing business, it is the individual who sustains the company. However, when a company develops into a large enterprise, there are cases when even replacement of a director or president will fail to have any sizeable impact on the financial results of the company. For example, it is hard to imagine that the resignation of one employee of McDonald's will alter the competitiveness of the company. When a company grows into a large enterprise, the replacement of its director may not cause any significant change in organizational ability.

So how does the transition occur from personal ability to organizational ability? And furthermore, how do the participating members begin to give priority to the interests of the organization over their own self-interests? To answer this question, there are some hints to be found in the game theory's concept of the prisoner's dilemma. The situation of the prisoner's dilemma exposes the inanity of human collective behaviour. Is there no way in which two players can realize their mutual benefit and escape the prisoner's dilemma?

Existing studies have offered the following solution.[20] This is the line of thought that evaluates the value of a one-time betrayal at a low level of pay-offs by assuming a discount rate *vis-à-vis* future payoffs. In line with the explanation of Gibbons (1992), I explain the logic behind cases when the choice of cooperation, in the course of an unlimited period of time, emerges as a rational one.

Consider the situation where two players have two strategies. Given an unlimited period of time, the players consider carrying out a trigger strategy. Consequently, the choice is made for the {R1, R2} combination, which helps acquire at first the payoff of 4. The payoff

Table 1.1   Prisoner's dilemma

	R2	L2
R1	4, 4	0, 5
L1	5, 0	1, 1

Note: The table has been partly rearranged.

Source: Gibbons (1992), pp. 88–92.

to be gained in the event that cooperation constantly continues is $V = 4 + \delta 4 + \delta^2 4 + \cdots = \sum_{t=1}^{\infty} \delta^{t-1} \pi_t$. After the second term, evaluation is made on the basis of discounting only the discount factor δ *vis-à-vis* the payoff. Then, you can arrive at the following formula:

$$V = 4 + \delta(4 + \delta 4 + \delta^2 4 + \cdots) = 4 + \delta V$$

$$V = 4 + \delta V \Leftrightarrow V = \frac{4}{1 - \delta}$$

This is the net present value of the discounted payoffs acquired in the event two players continue cooperating.

Next, consider the trigger strategy. This is the strategy of betraying your partner after he has betrayed you. The trigger strategy is presumed to change in the following ways. In the case of the t-period strategy, when the partner adopts cooperation Ri (i = 1, 2) at a point in time in the past (t−1), the same strategy is adopted. If that is not the case, the player adopts the strategy of betrayal, which is denoted as Li (i = 1, 2) in Table 1.1. Therefore, if we assume a player betrays from the outset, then we arrive at the following equation:

$$S = 5 + \delta 1 + \delta^2 1 + \cdots = 5 + \frac{\delta}{1 - \delta}$$

From here we can make the comparison $\frac{4}{1 - \delta} \geq 5 + \frac{\delta}{1 - \delta}$ and acquire $\delta \geq \frac{1}{4}$. In other words, if the discount factor is larger than 3 (300 per cent), a higher payoff can be acquired through cooperation than through betrayal. This point becomes clear by rewriting the equation as $\delta = \frac{1}{1 + r} \geq \frac{1}{4}$.

Even if no mutual communication exists between players, if there is a discount rate high enough in a game without any time limit, the situation called the prisoner's dilemma can be avoided. This is also the case when the payoff to be gained by betrayal is low. Consequently, cooperating for an organization is beneficial in a situation where the calculation of a long-term payoff is possible.

4   PRESENTATION OF THE RESEARCH THEME

Knowledge Is Created Collectively

In games such as *Go*, *Shogi*, and chess, in their early through middle stages, we can foresee a plethora of potential moves. This differs from the end game, where the number of outcomes is limited, as in a decisive "life and death problem of *Go*" or a "*Shogi* problem of checkmate". Computers can now analyse this aspect and arrive at the correct sequence of moves much faster than a human being. The problem arises when the number of potential moves becomes considerably greater, making the computational load much larger as well. Logically speaking, while such a situation is computable, a move made by human intuition becomes preferable since the load is high. When the move is proven to be effective, it would turn out that "the correct answer was discovered".

Despite the fact that games such as *Go*, *Shogi*, and chess pit a single player against another single player, a number of people can examine the ongoing state of play. Thus, in these games, individual thinking can be replaced by collective thinking. In the case of mathematics, verification can be carried out by a number of people. In the world of professional *Shogi*, a player's moves are conveyed to another room through what is known as a "discussion board". In this room, a number of other players observe and discuss the moves. This is an established practice in the world of professional *Shogi* in Japan. While the two players silently make moves, the intent and significance of those moves, and even decisions related to formations, are analysed and explicated by a number of *Shogi* players gathering in another room.

It is easy to understand the proposition that knowledge creation is carried out by individuals. Knowledge is commonly associated with such an image. Polanyi (1958) emphasized the intellectual work of the individual and its intrinsic properties of tacit knowing. This involves an individual explaining the contents of what they understand to another individual. Knowledge moves between individuals. The person who accurately and quickly understands the knowledge written in a book explicates this knowledge to the person who is unable to understand it. Knowledge is commonly associated with this image of one-to-one correspondence.

Simon (1945), the creator of the concept of "bounded rationality", called attention to the fact that human ability to process knowledge is limited. Even Ansoff (1965), known for his management strategy theories, speaks of what he calls "partial ignorance", to explain that the knowledge of executives and their powers of rational decision-making are limited. The bounded rationality concept proposed by Simon explains the limitations of the human decision-making process. At the same time, Simon explained that the decision-making carried out by organizations, in effect, allowed organizations to override the decision-making carried out by individuals. In other words, this is a case of collective knowledge seen within an organization where the limitations of individuals vary from person to person in terms of quality. While each individual is limited in their ability to process information, this limitation can be surpassed by combining individual abilities. If this is the case, each individual should be making a form of "bounded contribution" to the organization. In other words, in the event a new contribution to an organization is demanded, it is possible to see this organization's collective knowledge at work within the organization.

Individuals convey the knowledge they understand and acquire to other individuals. This is called technology transfer, and many studies have been published in the areas of economics and business management. However, the creation of knowledge, which is the starting point, is in the first place carried out through collective effort. In such a case, knowledge is not a matter of transference. There are various means of creating knowledge in a collective fashion, and while individuals may not notice this, it is becoming commonplace.

Collectivity creates knowledge. That is, a number of human beings engaged in the act of ability construction create a single unit of knowledge. Organizations that are able to skilfully manage such a collective approach to creating knowledge are strong organizations and will be able to survive in the marketplace. Nonaka and Takeuchi (1995) argue that in the West, tacit knowledge and explicit knowledge cross-circulate entirely at a personal level, whereas in Japan, the interaction between tacit knowledge and explicit knowledge tends to occur at the group level. As for knowledge creation, the authors point out that "middle managers lead knowledge-creating project teams, which play a key role in sharing tacit knowledge among team members" (p. 198).[21]

So how can people create knowledge collectively?[22] They create knowledge by applying a method I call collective strategy. In this book, I define collective knowledge as knowledge created as a result of adopting a collective strategy. Could there be room for further improvement in the area of knowledge creation at the group level, which is considered to be an expertise of Japanese enterprises? What kinds of methods are available that could stimulate interactions between tacit knowledge and explicit knowledge at a group level? Drawing on case studies, I will introduce some new ideas on how to bring about the rise of collective knowledge. The following chapters cover this subject in further detail, elaborating on relevant methods. How can we build organizations that can skilfully manage the creation of collective knowledge? Let us seek an answer to this question in the following chapters.[23]

NOTES

1. For example, Kogut and Zander (1993) investigate technology transfer in the internationalization process from the viewpoint of codifiability.
2. This passage is checked from Japanese translation, pp. 21–6.
3. This passage is checked from Japanese translation, p. 97.
4. The significance of internalization is mentioned in another context apart from the development of the automatic electric baking oven, namely a case study of shorter working hours and its possibility (pp. 118–20).
5. For example, Martin-de-Castro, Lopew-Saez, and Navas-Lopez (2008) conducted an empirical study using the Nonaka and Takeuchi (1995) model as an analytical framework.
6. Yamazaki (2004) introduces Snowden (2002).
7. According to Gourlay (2006), the only persuasive case example in Nonaka and Takeuchi's (1995) knowledge creation theory is the example of the automatic electric baking oven by Matsushita Electric (name changed to Panasonic in 2008).
8. What this point indicates is not necessarily persuasive. In Polanyi (1966a), there is the expression of tacit knowledge in addition to the expression of tacit knowing. As far as I was able to confirm, this expression of tacit knowledge appears on pages 9, 22, and 61 of the original work of Polanyi (1966a). Nonaka and Takeuchi (1995) do not use the expression of tacit knowing and explain the importance of behaviours oriented towards acquiring tacit knowledge with the oriental concept of mind–body oneness and the unity of the individual with others (Chapter 2, pp. 29–32). It is unreasonable to declare that the process-priority viewpoint is omitted just because this difference between the two expressions exists. Moreover, even Collins (1974), who carried out a sociological analysis of scientific discovery, adopts the expression of tacit knowledge, and in his 1975 work seeks authority for this expression from Polanyi (1966a).
9. Gourlay (2006, p. 1422) cites the phrase that "explicit knowledge must rely on being tacitly understood" in Polanyi (1966b, p. 7). The following is a quote from Polanyi (1966b, p. 7).
"We have seen tacit knowledge to comprise two kinds of awareness, subsidiary awareness and focal awareness. Now we see tacit knowledge opposed to explicit knowledge; but these two are not sharply divided. While tacit knowledge can be possessed by itself, explicit knowledge must rely on being tacitly understood and applied. Hence all knowledge is either tacit or rooted in tacit knowledge. A wholly explicit knowledge is unthinkable" (p. 7).
In this context, subsidiary awareness is for example when the muscles of your eyes contract in response to seeing a hand being waved in front of them. It is a manifestation of the coping mechanism of the ability to see. Focal awareness is the attempt to discover what is going on when you pay attention to the hand being waved in front of your eyes.
10. In the second chapter of Horaguchi's (2002) work, this model was used as the basis for a feasibility study of the Japanese multinational corporation.
11. Even when Nonaka and Takeuchi's (1995) clockwise spiral continues, there exists the possibility that knowledge won't help acquire gains. For example, let's say two juvenile delinquents smoke marijuana (socialization), then go on to verbally explain the sensations experienced to a friend (externalization), then place an order with a marijuana dealer (combination), and then a different friend smokes marijuana in the way it was verbally explained to him by another person (internalization). In such a case, the act of consuming a drug concludes in a picture of a spiral. However, the knowledge born in this process is at most the knowledge of how to purchase marijuana and how to smoke it. This is not valuable knowledge, but just mimicry of an existing criminal act. Even when a company commits a scandal, it may be depicting such a spiral. As another example showing that the clockwise spiral may not lead to the creation of knowledge that can acquire gains, one can cite a certain type of meeting that takes place in companies. In this type of meeting, there is a participant who is cognizant of the decorum

of paying respects to elders (socialization). For this reason, this participant makes long-winded remarks that are not productive at all (externalization), and in response to such remarks, another participant begins to express his own reminiscences (combination), and yet another participant, upon hearing such remarks, resolves to bail out from the company (internalization). In such a meeting, the knowledge created will not be valuable. Companies engaged in knowledge creation and companies that create knowledge that is not valuable both depict the spiral of knowledge conversion modes. This spiral then turns out not to be a requirement for the creation of "valuable" knowledge. If the concept of knowledge conversion modes explains the process of forming knowledge in general, management strategy would require a different guiding principle.

12. See Peirce (1868, p. 143) and Miyahara (2001).

13. Horaguchi (2002, p. 76) already warned of the corruption of tacit knowledge.

14. "Senba Kicho [a well-known Japanese restaurant company], Leftover Recycling Mandated by Ex-President, 'It's Wasteful,'" *Nihon Keizai Shimbun*, 3 May 2008, morning edition, p. 35. Additionally, a Nikkei report dated 29 October 2007 described Senba Kicho's involvement in manipulating expiry dates of pastry products. The morning edition dated 30 October 2008 reported on personal bankruptcy filings made by the ex-presidents of Senba Kicho.

15. While the differences of such concepts may be defined by experts of mathematics, as far as this author understands it, if it is an arithmetical operation, and if we include simplified symbols such as arithmetical ones or Σ and !, and trigonometric functions and operations of differential and integral calculus, then it can be thought of as calculation. In addition, if we include analyses and simulations that make use of proof problems and programming languages, then we can consider it as computation.

16. For example, the fact that you can explain why the matrix $\left[\begin{smallmatrix} \cos\theta & -\sin\theta \\ \sin\theta & \cos\theta \end{smallmatrix}\right]$ shows rotation apparently indicates that this is the minimum knowledge necessary (explicit knowledge) for a computer program to report the results of the factor-axis rotations it automatically carries out.

17. See Polanyi (1958) and Inoki (1985, 1987).

18. Such an intuition is necessary for mathematicians when attempting to create proofs. For example, consider the problem of proving that $\sqrt{2}$ is an irrational number. To prove this, you need to understand the concept of rational and irrational numbers and the method of presenting a proof through the refutation procedure. After doing so, you must recall them and then make associations. Unless you possess the ability to understand the definition of rational and irrational numbers, a piece of explicit knowledge, and the ability to make associations for the purpose of proving them, you will not be able to carry out the work of formulating a mathematical proof. Prior to writing down a proof, which is a verbal explanation, there is mathematical intuition, which is something that cannot be explained through words. Only a person who has the ability to feel this intuition is able to write a proof. This point is emphasized by Polanyi (1958).

19. The following is one kind of explanation about note 16. If you express the point in the two-dimensional plane with x–y axes to be converted on the unit circle with polar coordinates $\left[\begin{smallmatrix} \cos\alpha \\ \sin\alpha \end{smallmatrix}\right]$ and multiply from the back to the matrix $\left[\begin{smallmatrix} \cos\theta & -\sin\theta \\ \sin\theta & \cos\theta \end{smallmatrix}\right]$, you can see the formation of an addition theorem of a trigonometric function. One cannot develop problem-solving abilities by learning the above-mentioned prose as "knowledge". What is important is the process of answering problems through using knowledge related to basic mathematics such as matrix algebra and trigonometric functions, and this process cannot be understood through operating computer programs. See notes 8 and 9 of this chapter.

20. Horaguchi (1996) proposes a mathematical model to show the idea of restricting player behaviour on the assumption that a rise in the cost of processing information occurs to the extent that it becomes difficult to compare the ups and downs of payoffs. In addition, as reflected in relevant literature I introduced in Horaguchi (1996), there's also the idea of describing behaviour patterns with automatons and programming players to carry out only specific behaviours. In addition, Yamagishi (1998) showed, through the

application of experimental psychology, that cooperation can emerge if you motivate players to be concerned that their reputations will suffer if they betray.

21. As examples, the product developments of Honda's City and Nissan's Primera are cited. To make comfortable cars with roomy interiors, development teams set up training camps and tracked overseas market trends to create new-product concepts. After this work of socialization, design information was turned into data. Detailed data including car height and width, design, and window shapes were externalized and combined. Knowledge creation theory also accounts for subjectively including the uncertainty of the environment within the organization. In other words, this is the idea of intentionally and proactively including environmental uncertainty inside the organization, and in so doing, attempting to bring about new knowledge required by the organization.

22. The attitude to learn from one another and teach one another "what is not understood" is important. While this may seem obvious, it is a mindset essential for building collective knowledge. However, this is easy to say but difficult to do, and its difficulty may be attributed to humans' sense of pride and shame. A preliminary attempt at shedding some light on the problem of the formation of the human being is discussed in Horaguchi (2008d).

23. While Horaguchi (2008c, 2009a) presented ideas on the relationship between collective knowledge and collective strategy, this book develops this subject further, and explores the foundation of their argument.

2. Collective strategy and collective knowledge

1 INANITY OF CROWDS AND COLLECTIVISM

The thinking process of crowds has often been considered unwise rather than careful thought. Descriptions such as "mob psychology" or "group think" indicate a situation where many people gather and indulge in idle behaviour or foolish ideas.[1] Japanese proverbs such as "people crowding like crows" or "too many boatmen heading towards the mountain (too many cooks spoil the broth)" are used as often as "Three people together are better than *Monju*, Bodhisattva of intellect (Two heads are better than one)."

There are three major schools of thought insisting on the stupidity of "group think". One view is that of social psychologists, who discuss mob psychology. The second view is found in discussion by economists, who advocate methodological individualism. The third view is the explanation given by game theory.

Mob psychology explains the stupid behaviour of crowds. Le Bon (1895) asserts that it is psychologically incorrect to assume that "many people can make wiser and more spontaneous decisions on a certain problem than a few people" (p. 172).[2] He cites the parliamentary system as an example of the general behaviours of mobs. It has characteristics of "simple thought, easily excited, vulnerable to being swayed, exaggeration of emotions, and strong influence of leaders" (p. 172).[3] Le Bon (1895) also points out that anonymity leads to the emergence of mob psychology. People take irresponsible actions when it is not identified who they are. Le Bon observed stupid actions by crowds during the French Revolution.

One can notice a resemblance to Internet society in modern times. When people are anonymous they may harm people by irresponsible slander or crime. When people act anonymously, are emotionally agitated and allow irresponsible behaviour, one can see mob psychology emerge. If this is an undeniable fact, who will create collective intelligence? What kind of attributes can sustain intelligence in a group of people? I will answer these questions in the following chapters, and sum up in Chapter 7.

The second view is related to methodological individualism in economics.

It was Hayek (1946) who explored the view that knowledge possessed by individuals is superior to that of collectivized planning. It was he who criticized the planned economy under collectivism. In the paper "Individualism: True and False", Hayek (1946) says that true individualism considers "human affairs as the unforeseen result of individual actions", while false individualism "traces all discoverable order to deliberate design" (p. 8). Hayek also notes that under true individualism "men will often achieve more than individual human reason could design or foresee" (p. 11).

Hofstede (2001, p. 243) points out the fact that the word "collectivism" has a connotation of communism, mainly in the United States. This understanding may be attributable to Hayek's proposition. Hayek (1944) wrote *The Road to Serfdom*, in which he insisted that both socialism based on Marxism and state-socialism based on German Nazism have the same root of collectivism. He contrasts individualism in the United Kingdom and in the United States with collectivism in Germany and Russia.[4]

We share common ground with Hayek's understanding of knowledge when we discuss the nature of collective knowledge. We see this point by checking the original writings of Hayek (1945), "The Use of Knowledge in Society":[5]

> we must show how a solution is produced by the interactions of people each of whom possesses only partial knowledge. To assume all the knowledge to be given to a single mind in the same manner in which we assume it to be given to us as the explaining economists is to assume the problem away and to disregard everything that is important and significant in the real world.
> That an economist of Professor Schumpeter's standing should thus have fallen into a trap which the ambiguity of the term "datum" sets to the unwary can hardly be explained as a simple error. It suggests rather that there is something fundamentally wrong with an approach which habitually disregards an essential part of the phenomena with which we have to deal: the unavoidable imperfection of man's knowledge and the consequent need for a process by which knowledge is constantly communicated and acquired. Any approach, such as that of much of mathematical economics with its simultaneous equations, which in effect starts from an assumption that people's knowledge corresponds with the objective facts of the situation, systematically leaves out what is our main task to explain. (p. 530)

Hayek understands that human beings as individuals have only imperfect knowledge, and that constant communication can reinforce the accumulation of knowledge. Therefore it is impossible to have a planned economy organized by a single mind. Collectivism in this context is denied. Hayek appreciates the works of Carl Menger and points out the way in which methodological individualism and its combination are created.[6] Hayek admits that individuals belong to some form of combination of people. In other words, Hayek admits that there is some stable structural combination of people which act in micro-economics. This stable structure is a pattern of collectivized individuals. Even though Hayek proposes methodological individualism, one can see a proposition which says that individual behaviour is linked to some stable pattern of structure. Arrow (1994) clearly points out that methodological individualism is compatible with social knowledge. He suggests that externality in information or diffusion of technology help in accumulating social knowledge. We then need to verify the existence of such patterns.

What we would like to show in this book is that Hayek's proposition is a foundation for the theory of collective knowledge and its foundation shall be based on "methodological individualism". This conclusion may seem somewhat ironical or complex if one superficially understands the words individualism and collectivism. The key to linking methodological individualism and collective knowledge is a combination of self-organization and emergence, which will be discussed in Section 5 of this chapter.

Theories on collective behaviour have been developed since the age of Hayek and Menger. As I introduced the logic of the prisoner's dilemma in the previous chapter, game theory proposes models of herding behaviour. It assumes rational behaviour and leads some forms of inanity as if it corresponds to false individualism. Economic models show detailed research on herding behaviour as a typical example of collective inanity. It is far from a creation of knowledge. A market equilibrium price is merely derived from reservation prices which are ranked by individuals. Even though a market equilibrium price is attained by collective behaviour of individuals, attainment of equilibrium price in economics is not seen as a result of collective knowledge but a result of aggregated reservation prices.

Schelling (1978) scrutinizes the fact that collective behaviour of individuals leads to macro-economic phenomenon. This may be interpreted as a forerunner of collective knowledge creation, but Schelling emphasizes inanities rather than intelligence. For example, he notes an episode when he was asked to give a lecture. Schelling noticed that his audience did not sit in the front row of the auditorium. When he asked the organizer why people were not allowed to sit in the front row, there was no sitting rule in the auditorium, and the audience were spontaneously sitting away from the front row.

According to surveys by Namatame (2003) and Takayasu (2003), there are no simulation models of economic behaviour which suggest creation of collective intelligence. They conclude that those models of economic behaviour show at most something better than random.[7] This book does not scrutinize the game theoretic approach for human behaviour, but the reader can see how rules of the game are rewritten among players in

Chapters 3–6. From the non-cooperative game to the cooperative game, or from incomplete information to complete information, games are observed accordingly as the organization evolves over time.

Managing Knowledge in Business

There is no doubt that individuals create knowledge. The important task of management, however, is to create knowledge collectively. The reason why Japan had attained the second largest GDP until it was surpassed by China in 2012 is attributed to the practice of managing the collective knowledge creation process. If this is true, one can infer that competitiveness of Japanese firms might vanish if the mechanism of creating collective knowledge collapses. If Japanese tend to shirk an effort to create collective knowledge, they will be impoverished not only economically but also culturally. We need a systematic approach to a practical method of knowledge management.

I adopt the following premises. The first premise is that the pattern of collective knowledge depends on collective strategy. Depending on what collective strategy is chosen, the pattern of collective knowledge is formed. If an individual has a relationship with another individual and they make a commitment to an organization, there would be a situation that one can call an inter-organizational relationship. This situation has a decisive effect on collective knowledge creation. Take a pianist for example. He or she is an example of a one-man company with superior managerial resources. However, at the same time, for a commercially successful pianist, there will be a talent agency taking orders and managing the musician's schedule, an advertising agency, a music company carrying out CD production and sales operations, and a network of composers and musicians who play other musical instruments.

The second premise is the contrary to the first, that is, collective strategy must be deliberately chosen depending on what type of collective knowledge is to be created. A manager has to understand the collective strategy by which a certain type of collective knowledge shall be created. In "The Theory of the Growth of the Firm", Penrose (1959) discussed the process of how "resources" accumulate within a company. Examples include the sense of "trust" underlying business transactions, and in the act of procuring funds for a company, a work method disclosed and taught to each employee, technology accumulated in the form of a patent and/or knowhow, brand equity etched in the minds of customers, in-company management techniques, and networks using resources of external, specialized companies, such as design, advertisement and distribution. Resources are accumulated in the course of disclosing information from an individual to another who comprehends the information. Trust, work method, technology, knowhow, brand equity and management techniques all have this property of exchanging information. If managerial resources are accumulated in a firm as organization, the firm becomes able to handle harder tasks with intellectual rigor than one entrepreneur can realize.

A literature survey on this subject to build the theory of collective knowledge is presented in the following sections.

2   LITERATURE SURVEY ON COLLECTIVE STRATEGY: TYPOLOGY

While the inanity of collectivism was stressed by many researchers, a new type of corporate strategy was recognized in the 1980s, which focused on the collective power of people. The concept of collective strategy was presented by scholars who tried to link the academic findings in population ecology, or population biology, to organizational behaviour of human beings by analogy. In those literatures biological concepts were introduced ad hoc, that is, the corresponding relationships with competitive strategy were left untouched. The purpose of this literature survey is to clarify the correspondence between population ecology and competitive strategy which is based on industrial organization as one applied field of microeconomics. Rigid definition of concepts and a mathematical approach are the characteristics of research in industrial organization. So a bridge must be built in this literature survey among management strategy, population ecology and industrial organization in order to see their inter-relationships.

Collective strategy is one of the analytical frameworks for inter-organizational relations. Astley and Fombrun (1983) and Astley (1984) proposed the concept of collective strategy, which is based on an idea of population ecology. The idea assumes that symbiotic relations are applicable to corporate strategy. Such a biological relationship as a crocodile and an Egyptian plover is applicable to two corporate interactions. They classify collective strategy into four strategic forms, namely confederate, conjugate, agglomerate and organic. Their terminology has been applied to corporate strategies such as merger and acquisition, interlocking directorates and joint ventures. They took a view called "ecology of the organization" (see Table 2.1).

Astley and Fombrun (1983) call one of their collective strategies the confederate type when the mode of interdependence is commensalistic, and when direct association is made. If it has an indirect association and is commensalistic mode, it is called the agglomerate type. When the mode is symbiotic and association is direct, it is called the conjugate type. The

Table 2.1   Collective strategy by Astley and Fombrun (1983)

		Mode of interdependence	
		Commensalistic	Symbiotic
Type of association	Direct	Confederate	Conjugate
	Indirect	Agglomerate	Organic

Source: Astley and Fombrun (1983).

combination of symbiotic mode and indirect association is referred to as organic. It is explained that strategic partnerships differ in type depending on the limitations of the participants of the collective strategy.

Astley (1984) discusses that business strategy, corporate strategy, industrial strategy (competitive strategy) and collective strategy emerge accordingly as strategic application enhances its domain to be enlarged. The research by Astley and Fombrun (1983) has been followed by other research and has gradually been accepted among academics around the world. Bresser and Harl (1986) noticed that collective strategy operates anti-competitively, like a cartel. Oliver (1988) applied four types of collective strategy to test the degree of organizational isomorphism in voluntary social service organizations in Canada. Dollinger (1990) explains the generation of collective strategy, quoting an argument by Axelrod (1984), by which cooperation is born as a result of repeated games. In Japan, Yamakura (1993) surveyed the works of Astley and Fombrun (1983) in relation to inter-organizational behaviour, and Mitsuzawa (1996) stressed the negative side of collective strategy, which eventually requires anti-monopoly public policy.

In the 2000s, the concept of collective strategy received academic attention among European researchers, and was applied in empirical research. Yami (2006) edited a special issue on collective strategy in *Revue Française de Gestion* (*Review of French Business Administration*), and proposed his survey on collective strategies in France. Le Roy (2003), for example, interpreted the fishery cooperatives in France as an agglomerate strategy and analysed them as one form of collective strategy. Mione (2006) described the process of setting industrial standards as a collective strategy. Mione (2006) carried out a questionnaire survey among product development and marketing personnel in companies. As a result it was concluded that the personnel who are in charge of product development are more eager for collective standardization. A German scholar of management, Haak (2004) analysed a case of international joint venture in China as an example of collective strategy.

The Meaning of Commensalism as a Complement of Competition

As we have surveyed above, the theory of collective strategy and its concepts were proposed independently from the academic field of competition such as strategic management and corporate strategy.[8] The empirical studies and its application by the theory of collective strategy have been conducted with a unique position in academics. It had nothing to do with the mainstream in strategic management such as the positioning school or the resource-based view. Porter (1980) proposes generic forms of corporate strategy as cost leadership, differentiation and focus. This is classified as the positioning school to explain competitiveness of companies. The company can occupy a unique position as producing the same product more cheaply, adding additional attributes at the same cost, or creating new demand in a market.

Astley (1984) argues that collective strategy is one of the wider varieties of these strategic alternatives. It encompasses business strategy, corporate strategy, industrial strategy (competitive strategy) and collective strategy. Therefore, the distinction between "commensalistic" and "symbiotic" corresponds to the distinctions between whether a similar organization or a different organization, or between whether the same industry or a different industry is involved. In other words, a relationship is considered commensalistic when the organization belongs to the same industry. If the organization belongs to a different industry, it corresponds to the definition of symbiotic.

Astley and Fombrun (1983) explain that "commensalism is exhibited both in competitive interaction, as when chickens rival for food thrown into their pen, and in cooperative interaction, as when antelopes herd together to increase their immunity from attack by enemies" (p. 578). However, the adjective "commensalistic" adopted in the theory of collective strategy seems to have a deeper meaning in population ecology.

In biology, at least five patterns of symbiotic relationship between two kinds of creature have been classified. Table 2.2 summarizes these relationships. In the table, "+" means that the influence given by a partner is beneficial, and "−" means that the influence of the partner is harmful. "0" means that both influences are neutral. If both sides receive beneficial effects, it is called mutualism. Animals and plants profiting from one another belong to this category. If one party benefits from the other but does not give any negative effect, the relationship is called commensalism. If one receives benefit while it does harm to the other, it is called parasitism. If one does not benefit from the other, while the partner suffers a negative effect, it is called amensalism. When both sides harm the other it is called competition.

Table 2.2   Pattern of symbioses

	Player B		
Player A	+,+	+,0	+,−
	Mutualism	Commensalism	Parasitism
	0,+	0,0	0,−
	Commensalism		Amensalism
	−,−	−,+	−,0
	Parasitism	Amensalism	Competition

Notes: Sign shows the payoff of the players. The left-hand sign is the payoff for Player A and the right-hand sign is the payoff of Player B. "+" means positive payoff or benefit, "0" means neutral, and "−"means negative payoff, or harm.

Source: Based on Vandermeer and Goldberg (2003).

The theory of corporate strategy merely uses the broad classification of cooperation and competition. The situation in which two companies compete falls under "competition" in Table 2.2, and mutualism is the case in which two companies cooperate and create a win–win relationship. Yet from the perspective of population ecology the arguments about competitive strategy in business are not limited to these two patterns. Under the influence of game theory[9] the payoffs after the competition[10] are the single most important criteria in corporate strategy. Two major results are widely discussed. One is the prisoners dilemma, where two companies are worse off. The other is the win–win relationship with two collaborative firms.

In a company participating in a strategic partnership, there may be a case of "commensalism" by which the participants learn a core competence from the partner company to raise their own competence. On the other hand, there may be a case in which joint venture did not succeed because of "amensalism" caused by the partner company. In some cases merger and acquisition may result in "parasitism" in business relationships. This happens when a merged company has inadequate human resources and did not do sufficient due diligence before the M&A to discover hidden bad assets. When a large enterprise acquires a small firm through M&A, on the surface, the relationship between the two firms may seem to be near predation. However, if the merged small firm is mired in deficit and the large enterprise is bailing it out, the relationship is near parasitism. Whereas predation is a one-off act, parasitism appears to continue over a certain length of time.

Let us note here that Astley and Fombrun (1983) utilized the concepts of commensalism and symbiosis but not the ones of "parasitism" or "amensalism". Their understanding on commensalism was much simpler than the explanation in modern population ecology. Extension of such ideas into the theory of corporate strategy was left for the future. If we can find examples of business case studies corresponding to "parasitism"[11] or "amensalism" along with "commensalism", resulting from corporate strategy, we may be able to depict subtlety in business practices. Commensalism, for example, seems to be important as a strategy for a small company. A stationery shop nearby a school is a typical example of commensalism. Parasitism, together with amensalism, can explain how an organization becomes malfunctioned by a small number of incompetent people. This type of malfunctioning of organization can be termed as organizational necrosis, as a decayed cluster in the organization can be spread or be metastasized.

3 LITERATURE SURVEY ON COLLECTIVE INTELLIGENCE

The distinction between knowledge and intelligence is by all means arbitrary. The latter seems to have a connotation of higher relevancy to capability than the former but the concept of collective intelligence is discussed in wider context. Brown and Lauder (2000) define collective intelligence as "empowerment through the development and pooling of intelligence to attain common goals or resolve common problems" (p. 234). They emphasize that intelligence is created upon some relations with the society and each individual behaves differently when they take advantage of collective intelligence. People can connect knowledge at home, in school, in the workplace and in the community.[12] In this context the argument of Brown and Lauder (2000) is akin to the perspectives on social capital.[13] Avis (2002) connects social capital, collective intelligence and expansive learning to discuss that the knowledge-based society requires a new education method for the younger generation.

The Japan Academy of Artificial Intelligence featured "collective intelligence" in 2003, and several papers were proposed in the journal. Ikegami (2003) grasps collective intelligence as micro- and macro-feedback loops. Micro-behaviour can induce the emergence of behavioural patterns in which a self-organization process was observed. Then the emerged pattern acts as a macro-constraint for each actor. This constraint can be called an emergence, or the emergence of a behavioural pattern. For example, the pattern that the march of ants makes is an example of self-organization. On the contrary, the emerging pattern by the march of ants sets limits on the ways by which the ants can find food. Micro-influences can create collective intelligence, and then it gives knowledge to each individual. Collective intelligence is regarded here as macro-phenomena although there is an underlying micro-feedback.

Takadama (2003) defines collective intelligence as "intelligence held by many independent groups which interact with one another". Collective intelligence is created through the ability of problem-solving, adaptation and robustness. Problem-solving ability is used to solve difficult tasks by cooperation between various entities. Adaptation ability refers to the easiness of adding participants when a division of responsibility is made. Robustness is the capability of replacing a participant by some others so that the group itself can maintain its total functions. These characteristics are called fault-tolerance, robustness, stability and reliability. Factors affecting interaction are goal-setting, communication and information-sharing, while the group consists of interaction of individuals, group or organization.

Surowiecki (2005) describes "the wisdom of crowds" and summarizes its characteristics. Diversity, independence, decentralization and coordination are four characteristics of the collective activities. They are wiser than an individual expert in recognition, coordination and cooperation. In an "Afterword" in the paperback edition, he replies to the question as to why "a group of people off the street can know more about a complex question than an expert." The answer by Surowiecki is that "'crowds' will include experts as well as amateurs" (p. 277). He also adds that it is hard to identify true experts and even brilliant experts have biases and blind spots (p. 278). Surowiecki (2005) suggests that his "crowds" means an intellectual group of people who are experts with detailed knowledge yet their popularity is low.[14]

Liang (2004) attaches great importance to collective intelligence which is accumulated inside the organization and states that the "intelligent organization" expands when it exchanges knowledge resources. He points out that the organization is a complex system adapting itself to the higher intellectual dimension. Ohmukai (2006) proposes collective intelligence as contents of an Internet site such as "Wikipedia", or "Jinriki Kensaku Hatena" (a Japanese Human Power Search System), which acts as a community on the worldwide web. He points out that collective intelligence possesses characteristics of diversity, independence, decentralization and coordination. Boder (2006) takes an example of collective intelligence from a medical unit for diabetic patients in Geneva. The members of the medical staff such as medical doctors, nurses, assistant nurses, psychologists and nutritionists work together to take advantage of their expertise from mutual collaboration.

Some researchers are influenced by complex system[15] or network theory[16] when they discuss collective intelligence. Fukuda and Kurihara (2003) point out that collective intelligence is supported by the small world, which is linked by the network. According to their definition, collective intelligence emerges when participants interact to become intelligent even though each individual acts simply. Horaguchi (2008a) dealt with a model of networked interaction of competition, which leads to abrupt exponential increase of output. If we interpret this output as the amount expressed by information bids, we may be able to interpret the model as mutual stimulus in knowledge.[17]

Nakakoji (2001) defined "collective creation" as personal creative activity by using the expression which was already made for it. For example, a support system to write a thesis, a support system for conducting research by rearranging notes or memos, and a product development support system by the mapping of brand image or products. According to Nakakoji (2001) "collective creation" has the following characteristics. First, it is impossible to define the domain of the problem to be solved. Second, it is impossible to define the knowledge and information needed before the problem-solving starts. Third, there is an interdependence of understanding what the problem is and what the solution will be. This interaction also evolves progressively over time.

Collective Intelligence and Organization Theory

Although Takadama (2003) does not explicitly mention it himself, it is extremely interesting that the factors he points out concerning collective intelligence are similar to the definition of formal organization prescribed by Barnard (1938). The definition of the formal organization is the common goal, communication and cooperation. According to Takadama (2003), collective intelligence is enacted when a goal, communication and information-sharing exist. Ohmukai (2006) introduces websites as collective intelligence, which has a structure to overcome the "bounded rationality" that Simon (1945) described. The website satisfies the capability of overcoming bounded rationality because the existence of such a site as Wikipedia serves a common purpose to satisfy the intellectual desire to know some information. Information is accumulated as a result of collaboration by people with the desire to "explain what I know". Rewriting the information contributes to the upgrade of knowledge on the site, and explicit knowledge is a tool for communication on the site. These websites are considered as a field of "organization" as far as they suffice the definition of the formal organization of Barnard (1938). In order to understand this point we compare a database with a website functioning as collective intelligence. The database comprises numerical values and a pile of hoarded letters, which are stored for use. In the website, collective intelligence establishes a common purpose to exchange information, and the structure of the website sets the macro-structure for individual knowledge to get feedback. The individuals then renew the micro-structured knowledge base, which eventually leads to the agglomeration of data for further renewal.

The concepts of tacit knowledge and explicit knowledge are useful to clarify the difference between information and knowledge. When explicit knowledge is stored, it is in letters and does not differ from information. But there will be tacit knowledge from outside the website. Tacit knowledge supports the interpretation of information by which knowledge has a higher dimension than information itself.

Several concepts coexist in existing research on collective intelligence, collective knowledge and collective wisdom. As I noted, collective intelligence has been widely accepted as a way to describe a new wave of Internet society. There are, however, some studies using the concept of collective knowledge. Huang (1997) raises the examples of knowledge-sharing carried out by the IBM Consultancy Group and the supercomputer Deep Blue, which defeated the chess world champion. Through these examples, he points out that collectively assembled information and software programs can be superior to tacit knowledge. As an extensive database created by IBM consulting group won the chess match, collectively constructed information and programs were stronger than the human ability of calculus and tacit knowledge.

Antonelli (2007) discusses punctual change in technological development by describing changes in the production frontier, caused by the accumulation of collective knowledge and networking among firms. Antonelli (2007) argues the possibility of achieving discontinuous technological advances by changing the production possibility frontier. This is realized when companies form networks and consequently accumulate collective knowledge.

There are three expressions: collective intelligence, collective knowledge and collective wisdom. Henceforth, I discuss collective knowledge as a complement of collective intelligence. By doing so, I want to position collective knowledge as a theoretical concept of knowledge management, which gives a higher meta-dimension to the existing theory of explicit knowledge and tacit knowledge. This is to position collective knowledge in the family tree of knowledge management theory, giving a higher dimension to the dichotomy of explicit and tacit knowledge.

Collective knowledge is created as the combination of explicit and tacit knowledge. When collective knowledge is accumulated, collective intelligence would also be raised. The method of creating collective knowledge is not confined to the case of Wikipedia, to which information technology contributes. I will show that there exist various methods from the traditional way of Japanese management style to current trends. In section 5 of this chapter I show that collective knowledge follows collective strategy.

4 SOURCES OF NEW COMBINATIONS

Re-examining the Schumpeter System

Schumpeter (1926) assumes that entrepreneurs act to create "new combinations". The concept of "new combinations" is considered as a forerunner of collective knowledge, although Schumpeter (1926) discusses macro-economic developments at the level of the national economy. Furthermore, for Schumpeter, "entrepreneurs" function as a key dynamic element in achieving new combinations (Schumpeter 1926, English translation, p. 74).

If this interpretation of Schumpeter (1926) is correct, I can say that Schumpeter (1926) discusses the process by which knowledge is combined by a single person, namely the "business entrepreneur". Let us examine how he developed his logic of economic development. Why, in his logic, can an individual unit in the economy be an engine of growth? If that is the only case, we do not need to consider collective strategy to create collective knowledge.

Schumpeter (1926) explains economic development using the concepts found in the first chapter of his book, titled "The Circular Flow of Economic Life as Conditioned by Given Circumstances". Why did Schumpeter choose to begin discussing "The Theory of Economic Development" from the section titled "The Circular Flow of Economic Life" or "Static Economics" (p. 151)? The primary reason is probably

Table 2.3   Table of contents of "The Theory of Economic Development" by Schumpeter

Chapter 1	The Circular Flow of Economic Life as Conditioned by Given Circumstances
Chapter 2	The Fundamental Phenomenon of Economic Development
Chapter 3	Credit and Capital
Chapter 4	Entrepreneurial Profit
Chapter 5	Interest on Capital
Chapter 6	The Business Cycle

Source: Schumpeter (1926).

because he wished to distinguish the idea of extensive economic expansion from the idea of economic development. In more contemporary terminology, he discerned that economic development (growth) and internationalization (globalization) are qualitatively different. If extensive economic expansion were grasped as "development", economic development would accordingly mean the acquisition of colonies. The secondary reason follows the line of thought that sees technological advancement as a dynamic driving force accelerating economic development. Consequently, he seems to have taken the static economic situation as the starting point of the theory for a conceptual reference.

The economic circulation mentioned here is the circular structure of the economy, which led to the input–output table that was still incomplete at the time when Shumpeter (1926) developed his theory. Grasping economic activity as a circular, human activity began as early as Quesnay's "Tableau Economique". Marx (1890) proposed a schema of reproduction which also belongs to this tradition. Walras's system is understood as the foundation upon which Schumpeter's *The Theory of Economic Development* is based. The history of economic thought was intensively studied by Schumpeter himself.

Walras (1874/1926) begins his research topics in the "Elements of Pure Economics", from the exchange of commodities and proceeds to the principles of production, the principles of capitalization and credit, and the principles of distribution and money. Such a structure of chapters in Walras (1874/1926) resembles the one found in Schumpeter's *The Theory of Economic Development*. However, Walras (1874/1926) developed his argument by disregarding technological progress. This is the point Schumpeter (1926) devised in his work.

Walras (1874/1926) argues that infinite growth of products is made possible when narrowly defined capital services are applied to the use of land. In this case, a distinction arises between two cases. One is the case where a change in the value of the production coefficient is caused by a decline in land use and a rise in capital use. Walras names this economic progress. The other case is where a change in the production coefficient of productive services is made, and new production methods are adopted. In the discussion that follows, the topic of technological progress has been disregarded so as to solely concentrate on economic expansion (translation, p. 208). Walras is considered as the founder of general equilibrium theory, and if he had included technological progress into his own theoretical system, his system of equations may have had to be rewritten as simultaneous differential equations. The technological progress that Walras disregarded would have been seen by Schumpeter as a driving force that propelled "development".[18]

How is development possible, even while the quantity of factors of production remains the same in the economy? To answer this question, Schumpeter (1926) prepares a concept called "new combination" in Chapter 2 of *The Theory of Economic Development*. The so-called "new combination" consists of goods, production methods, market channels, crude materials/semi-finished products and organizations. Innovation through "new combination" is born, he argues, by putting together production factors in original ways.[19]

The person who succeeds in bringing about a new combination is the entrepreneur, and, Chapter 3, titled "Credit and Capital", is devoted entirely to discussing them. As entrepreneurial activity continues, Chapter 4 "Entrepreneurial Profit" follows, and a part of the profit flows to the entities that loaned capital, described in Chapter 5 "Interest on Capital". Because entrepreneurs have the feature of emerging by growing "in clusters"[20] during an economic boom, after such a period, a brief period of panic ensues, followed by a recession, as Chapter 6 "The Business Cycle" explains.[21]

Here, Schumpeter raises five factors explaining why entrepreneurs tend to grow in clusters. The first factor is that pioneering entrepreneurs remove obstacles in the course of pursuing a new combination. The second factor is that conditions arise to make it possible for even entrepreneurs with lesser talents to appear, thanks to the opportunities opened up by the first factor. The third factor is that innovation and imitation spill over from the one in which the pioneer or pioneers appeared to the other processing sectors of industries. The fourth factor lies in the fact that the leading role assumed by the pioneering entrepreneur becomes not imperative. The fifth factor is that, by this phenomenon of emerging large numbers of entrepreneurs, boom periods are brought about.

At this point, let us review the first question I posed regarding Schumpeter's system. Why, in his logic, can an individual unit such as an entrepreneur in the economy be an engine of growth? The answer is that Schumpeter prepared the feature of emerging by growing "in clusters". Then, can we say if Schumpeter satisfactorily answers the question of why entrepreneurs emerge by growing "in clusters"? I believe Schumpeter's answer to the question is inadequate. If the number of imitating companies rises through the spillover of knowledge, it will just turn out that competition will intensify among firms, and companies will fail to grow and become unsustainable over the long term. In effect, they share a certain level of demand to exploit.[22] With only the five explanations discussing the removal of obstacles by pioneers and imitation following the pioneers, it merely explains the existence of knowledge led by the first entrepreneur. It is collective knowledge added by emerging entrepreneurs "in clusters" who are envisaged in Schumpeter's system that may sufficiently explain why so much entrepreneurial activity is sustained through imitation and additional innovation by followers. I explain the types of collective behaviour in the next section of this chapter. I will revisit this point of why entrepreneurs emerge by growing "in clusters" in Chapters 5 and 7 of this book.

The Non-excludability and the Non-rivalry of Knowledge

When we consider the concept of "new combinations" among factors of production in Schumpeter's argument, the next question arises. This is an important, albeit simple, question. In other words, if certain factors of production are used for realizing a new combination, we should then see that the level of pre-existing production with such factors falls. Those factors of production would be transferred from the sector in which they were previously used. In order to increase production through a "new combination", the following condition needs to be fulfilled. If significant economic development is to be achieved, the decrease in the production level arising from the transfer of outdated production processes must be more than compensated by the gains from the production in the "new combination".

We know that later Schumpeter (1942) proposed a concept of "creative destruction", but one can answer this simple question by including knowledge in the discussion. Materials can be joined together to realize a new combination based on new knowledge. In order to make such a realization possible, a particular body of knowledge must be found. Even if the factors of production move from one product to another to create a new combination, the level of production does not necessarily fall as long as the new knowledge can sustain the production. This becomes possible if the new knowledge acts as a public good in a production site.

Knowledge acts as a public good as long as people have the ability to understand it. In economics textbooks, the utilization of radio waves is explicated as a typical example of a public good. Public goods possess the properties of non-excludability and non-rivalry. Non-excludability is a property that does not prevent usage by a specific individual. The property of non-rivalry means that the goods will not decrease even after the good's usage. A property of disclosed explicit knowledge must be reviewed here. In the case where explicit knowledge is disclosed, anyone is able to obtain this knowledge by understanding it. For this reason, explicit knowledge does not decrease.[23] A special feature of explicit knowledge is the characteristic that it changes before and after its disclosure. In effect, concealed information prior to the disclosure subsequently becomes disclosed information, as in the case of expertise or technical know-how. Specifically, such an instance occurs when a patent is sold, or expertise or technical knowhow becomes available for use due to the expiration of its patent protection. Therefore, the relationship between the giver and the receiver of explicit knowledge prior to disclosure is substantially changed after disclosure. To the giver who has disclosed some explicit knowledge, this knowledge is merely one piece of information out of many. To the giver, this knowledge is something that has already been understood and it does not add any new knowledge. On the other hand, from the perspective of the receiver, whether the information received becomes knowledge or not depends on the receiver's aptitude for understanding. In this sense, if certain factors of production or giver are used for realizing a new combination for the receiver, we see that the level of pre-existing production does not fall but sometimes increases. Understanding an incomprehensible document is a clear example between the giver and the receiver. Incomprehensible documents may include documents written in a foreign language, documents showing source codes or programming languages, documents showing phonetic symbols, and records of games such as chess, *Go* and *Shogi* (Japanese chess). So even if a particular form of explicit knowledge is disclosed, the transmission of its contents depends on the level of comprehending the receiver possesses.

As already mentioned, there exist two types of people: those who transmit information without comprehending it, and those who transmit information with sure understanding. The latter have a possibility of inventing applications. The following postulate is one example in which people can understand and verify the process behind it: "If we differentiate $e^{(\mu-x)^2}$ with respect to x, the solution becomes $-2(\mu - x)e^{(\mu-x)^2}$." There are, however, people who just write the equations without understanding the meaning behind them. In the terminology of Nonaka and Takeuchi (1995), transmission from tacit knowledge to tacit knowledge is known as socialization and from explicit knowledge to explicit knowledge is called combination. However, whether this transmission is actually carried out or not is a difficult question to answer. In fact, it is fairly difficult to confirm whether a form of explicit knowledge has been understood or not. Furthermore, the transmission of explicit knowledge, that is to say combination in terms of Nonaka and Takeuchi's terminology (1995), will also be more difficult the more complex the knowledge becomes, because it requires a considerable investment of time. In such a case, the giver being physically present at a site offers an important opportunity to raise the receiver's capability of learning.

When we take such attributes into account, we can postulate the internal structure of the concept of "new combination" which Schumpeter described. "A new combination" is brought about by combining knowledge. Just as there are protons and neutrons found in the nucleus, it has been claimed that there are forms of tacit knowledge and explicit knowledge found in knowledge overall. However, the patterns of the ways in which they are combined are not necessarily clear. The term "patterns" refers here to what Hayek (1973) calls "certain type of stable structure" (p. 103). If knowledge is a factor of production and functions as a public good within an organization, no production level will decrease even if factors of production were to be newly recombined.[24]

Walras (1874/1926) disregarded technological advancement, and Schumpeter (1926) then superseded this with the concept of new combination. I attempt to explain the combination of certain bodies of knowledge underlying technological advancement at a number of specific levels. To this end, I would like to refer to studies on collective knowledge and show its various roles. Schumpeter (1926) started his discussion as a cycle for a static-state economy. As a logical consequence, he attached much importance to the aspect of newly recombining extant production factors. However, there is also another source of innovation, other than the "new combination", which Schumpeter exemplified. I will explain later that this source of innovation arises through the creation of collective knowledge among collaborations of firms, universities and local companies, which in turn can lead to the phenomenon known as entrepreneurs emerging by growing in clusters.[25]

Surprisingly, with regard to the static-state economy, Schumpeter had overlooked the activity of research and development. When you carefully read *The Theory of Economic Development*, you will notice that the phrase, "research and development" rarely appears. Why is this so? The first reason may be that the process of research and development is latently embedded in the phrase "new combination". The second reason can be said to be the fact that what Schumpeter was describing was the development of the "economy" rather than the development of technology or individual firms. The third reason is that while the expression "new discovery" can be seen to be implied within the expression "new production methods", the idea that invention and discovery are sporadic are also connoted at the same time. Alternatively, it could be because the year 1926, the year that saw Schumpeter publish *The Theory of Economic Development*, was prior to the onset of the Great Depression. So the attempt to carry out organized research and development was not yet triggered by the sharp rise of the chemical and medical industries during the era of the Great Depression. The emphasis Schumpeter placed on the importance of research and development carried out by large enterprises is characteristic of his later writings as a Harvard professor in the United States.[26]

Economic Characteristics of Research and Development

Research and development (R&D) is a kind of investment, of which the risk is remarkably high. The return on R&D investment is made only over the course of a long period of time. Foreseeing what results can be attained from the activity of R&D is more challenging than foreseeing economic repercussion effects gained from public investments such as public construction made for the purpose of building roads. Even if funds for research and development were spent by a talented researcher, more often than not, the results achieved may remain at just a technical level, and nothing more. Let us assume that the funds for research and development were spent by an incompetent researcher. In such a case, the funds would merely turn out to have the same effect as funds that provide relief to the unemployed.

If the concept of R&D was embedded in the model of the "static-state economy", which Schumpeter assumed as a theoretical starting point, then from this point onward, the economy can change to be in a "dynamic state". In an economy where the role of the entrepreneur and executive is to make decisions on how extensive financial investments in R&D projects should be, the economy cannot be "static". Nelson and Winter (1982) describe the state when the economic success of an R&D project would follow a certain probability distribution and would lead to various states depending on parameters. When R&D activities succeed, a new technology element is born. In other words, even if you do not assume extensive economic expansion, factors of production that exist within an entire national economy will change its quality. This will increase the possibilities of new combinations among existing factors of production. If combinations of existing factors of production are being considered, you will see that the "number of combinations" will increase in geometric progression.

Let me summarize some questionable aspects of Schumpeter's discussions on economic development. In effect, this system might be based on the premise that there is a body of knowledge that underlies the realization of new combinations among factors of production that can be combined together. It is a body of knowledge that makes such combinations possible. However, what types of knowledge patterns are there to be found during the creation of the new combinations? By establishing a hypothesis that accounts for the patterns of knowledge combinations, what types of analytical insights can we attain? I elaborate on this point in Chapters 3–6 of this book. In each chapter, by introducing principles that give rise to combination patterns and by introducing examples, I summarize implications that could guide a future corporate strategy.

5 CIRCULATION OF COLLECTIVE KNOWLEDGE

Self-organization and Emergence

A survey on the literature of collective intelligence and collective knowledge helps us understand the dynamic process of its formation. In effect, the self-organization must take place in an interactive process, nurturing the emergence of collective knowledge. Once self-organization is established to form a "certain type of stable structure", emergence occurs. Emergence is a state in which self-organized entities integrate with an existing body of knowledge. The interaction between self-organization and emergence can be understood in relation to the concept of collective knowledge.

Figure 2.1 shows the association between self-organization and emergence as defined by the process of forming collective knowledge. Micro-entities, such as individuals or firms, submit knowledge and self-organization then occurs through their aggregation, such as in organization or in industry. Self-organized knowledge turns out to be a macro-system, which then puts constraints on micro-subjects. Self-organization with "stable structures" can be defined as the act of reproducing constant patterns of collective knowledge. As one can see that self-organization results in fractals in the field of geometry, a routine process occurs through the iteration of numerous similar patterns to create an entire picture, the process of certain simple patterns of thoughts repeating themselves can be frequently observed, as is depicted in Nelson and Winter (1982). The states of such examples of emergence and routine are discussed again in each of the following chapters (Chapters 3–6).

Emergence is a term which indicates that a new type emerges among various mutations having undergone in the process of evolving, and thereby exerting an influence on future generations. If we transpose this concept

Circulation of Collective Knowledge

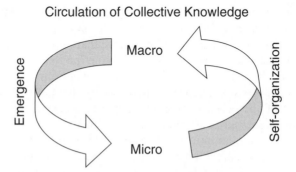

Figure 2.1   Circulation of collective knowledge

of emergence to the context of managing an enterprise, we can define emergence as the act of new management having an influence over future management. Emergence should therefore be contrasted with the idea of strategy. Whereas strategy arises from a human aim, emergence results without any conscious intention causing it. This is the same as saying that the aims or intent of life itself are not reflected in the process of evolution.[27]

Types of Collective Intelligence

As surveyed above, the theory of collective strategy and the theory of collective knowledge were considered independently from each other, and also developed as empirical studies in separate domains of application. In this book, I propose that combination patterns of collective knowledge vary in collective strategy, on which it depends. In Astley and Fombrun's (1983) work on collective strategies, the following four types were discussed: confederate, agglomerate, conjugate and organic. I discuss four types of collective knowledge corresponding to the four types of strategies: shared, symbiotic, local and common knowledge. The collective knowledge that corresponds to the confederate strategy, I refer to as shared knowledge; the collective knowledge that corresponds to conjugate strategy as symbiotic knowledge; the corresponding patterns arising from agglomerate strategy as local knowledge; and the collective knowledge corresponding to organic strategy as common knowledge (see Table 2.4). I explain below the logic behind these allocations and give definitions.

Shared Knowledge

The knowledge associated with the confederate strategy is referred to as "shared knowledge". Shared knowledge can be defined as knowledge born

Table 2.4   Types of collective strategy and collective intelligence

		Interdependent forms	
		Commensalistic (related segment)	Symbiotic (unrelated segments)
Types of association	Direct	Confederate strategy Shared knowledge	Conjugate strategy Symbiotic knowledge
	Indirect	Agglomerate strategy Local knowledge	Organic strategy Common knowledge

Source: Based on Astley and Fombrun (1983).

from the mutual contacts in a particular segment of business. A typical example of confederate strategy is found in mutual contacts between the rank-and-file in a firm. They possess specialized knowledge at their workplace.

As an example of knowledge-sharing among members of an organization, I suggest the case of the Toyota Production System. The remarkable feature of Toyota's collective knowledge is that a specific language developed with the successful application of the confederate type of collective strategy, which involves collaboration among production engineers and operating personnel. I discuss such a case in Chapter 3. Furthermore, examples of collective knowledge being applied from outside a company can be seen in information systems built for alliances between international airline service companies, and in the use of wire reports from Reuters by the major newspaper companies of Japan.[28]

Shared knowledge is a form of knowledge that arises when members of an organization, under the guidance of a confederate type of collective strategy, share concrete information with each other, engaging in a process of continually creating anew. Therefore, when a confederate strategy is adopted as a collective strategy by members of the same industry, the product types are narrowly targeted by applying specialized knowledge in the place of production. For this reason, we often see that continuous innovation is based upon improvements and reforms that entail adding new functions to be accumulated. Chapter 3 of this book traces this type of knowledge creation.[29]

Symbiotic Knowledge

A conjugate collective strategy involves direct work collaboration between individuals belonging to different industries and/or dissimilar organizations, and symbiotic knowledge is the collective knowledge born from such collaboration. In other words, symbiotic knowledge can be defined as collective knowledge created through the joining of disparate bodies of knowledge by participants from dissimilar fields whose purposes intersect. By creating symbiotic knowledge, participants obtain a higher level of economic welfare, or ensure their survival. I discuss symbiotic knowledge in Chapter 4 with a typical example of a university–business–government alliance.

Local Knowledge

Local knowledge is intelligence formed by an agglomerate strategy, and is defined as collective knowledge. The concept of local knowledge, which falls in the domain of agglomerate collective strategy, is highly compatible with arguments concerning social capital and industrial clusters.[30] The fact that a specific industrial collective is often formed within a certain local community has been pointed out by many researchers since Marshall (1920). The general idea of externalities explains such collective phenomena and is also commensalistic. Unlike the confederate model, the agglomerate model sees the condition of local knowledge being formed in a situation where the parties involved are not bound by any direct contract or are not engaged in any partnership relations. Agglomerate strategy is born from the process of achieving a common goal by habitants who show mutually interactive behavioural patterns with one another. These habitants share a specific local place, but are not bound by any contractual obligations. I elaborate on these points in Chapter 5 with case studies on industrial clusters.

Common Knowledge

Common knowledge can be defined as knowledge whose specific organizational associations are tenuous. Common knowledge develops as a result of endogenous knowledge accumulation within society. Collective intelligence that arises from the application of an organic collective strategy is common knowledge, and is translated into Japanese as *Jyoshiki* (common sense).

When I say common knowledge is created endogenously, you can imagine the table of input–output analysis, which consists of human knowledge number 1 to number n. Knowledge output from a sector number 1 is accepted by a sector i, and sector number i amplifies knowledge received. This process circulates among whole sectors in the economy. Such as in the case of people using cellular phones, organic collective strategies entail the condition of growing common knowledge endogenously. When unrelated industries are linked through investment and/or production relations in the overall economy, or when the supply and demand engendered by a certain industry are linked, we see emergence of new common knowledge. A straightforward example of this type of knowledge is found in the form of information accumulated at Wikipedia through the medium of the Internet.

Furthermore, one can see that knowledge of such cultural aspects that have been handed down over generations is considered as common knowledge. Common knowledge thus covers myths, traditions, festivals, cuisines, customs and observances. Considering them as one form of collective knowledge, one can apply the principles of collective knowledge to other disciplines in liberal arts. I cover these issues in Chapter 6.

The Need for Relativity

If we define the four terms shared knowledge, symbiotic knowledge, local knowledge and common knowledge, then at the level of definition we can immediately understand characteristics that correspond to characteristics of collective knowledge. I mention them here so that the reader will understand the premises I am taking in the following chapters.

The first characteristic is that there are differences in the cohesiveness of participants. Cohesiveness indicates an opportunity cost being large when a participant of a specific collective strategy attempts to leave the group. Employees in companies, for example, can be viewed as people with high opportunity costs who are acquiring shared knowledge. If they leave the company, however, they confront a huge opportunity cost of losing the means to earn a livelihood. In order to acquire local knowledge the choice of a company's location can be made for the purpose of securing a certain level of cohesiveness. If the choice is made to locate adjacent to a client's company, or to locate within an offshore production area, free trade zone, industrial complex, or a research park in response to a government-led industrial promotion policy, moving to the new location will incur a huge opportunity cost due to the lock-in effect (or irreversible sunk cost). On the contrary, in the event of participating in an inter-organizational project for the purpose of gaining symbiotic knowledge, and when attempting to determine whether to post remarks on the Internet for the purpose of acquiring common knowledge, the opportunity cost of abandoning a specific collective strategy decreases.

The second characteristic is that the communication methods between participants vary among these four types of collective strategies. Tarde (1901) describes a community as an observable gathering of people within physical proximity to each other, and refers to the public as people influenced by newspapers and public opinion. One can see a sharp contrast to the fact that face-to-face exchanges of opinion are vital in the sphere of shared knowledge and symbiotic knowledge, whereas business relations are generated through economic activity in the case of local knowledge, and information exchange being mediated via the Internet become key in the case of common knowledge.

Thirdly, the criterion for discerning between shared knowledge and symbiotic knowledge is only a relative matter. In terms of a specialty's level of sophistication, the criteria for discriminating between shared knowledge and symbiotic knowledge are not clear-cut. For example, the production of engines and seats in car production comprise shared knowledge in the sense that they both belong to the same automotive industry. They own properties without any attribute of substitutability; however, they comprise symbiotic knowledge. What distinguishes symbiotic knowledge is the diversified areas of expertise in engine production and in car-seat production.

Another example is the difference between the work a movie director performs and the work a movie producer performs, which corresponds to the difference between shared knowledge and symbiotic knowledge. The movie director gathers people who specialize in making movies, and has command over the entire production process. The director brings shared knowledge along with the people required for the particular task of movie production. A producer is entrusted with the serious task of raising funds and, in this sense, requires a specialty that is of a different nature from the one required for making movies.

Fourthly, collective knowledge exists in the real world as well as the virtual world. If we note that the illustration of tacit knowledge by Polanyi (1966a) was the recognition of "faces", a plurality of people can look at images and share knowledge that eludes expression through words. Tacit knowledge can be shared through virtual experience on the Internet. The sharing of tacit knowledge is also possible from moving images uploaded on Internet sites or communicating through Skype. In addition, in the event that it is possible to read explicit knowledge expressed in words written on an Internet-based website, collective knowledge is shared by a plurality of people. If we see it in this way, we can understand that the concept of collective knowledge has a dimension that differs from the explicit knowledge *vis-à-vis* tacit knowledge dichotomy.

In Chapters 3–6 that follow, I offer accounts of four collective strategies and their corresponding types of collective knowledge. I point out principles[31] that account for the patterns of each body of collective knowledge and give examples. Taking these points into account, I summarize management methods for generating a stream of collective knowledge. In Chapter 7, I revisit the arguments on collective knowledge laid out in the introduction and in this chapter, and offer answers to questions while summarizing this book's particular discoveries.

NOTES

1. See Ohashi and Sasaki (1989, Chapter 14) and Le Bon (1895).
2. This English quotation was translated by the author referring to a Japanese version of a translation from French. Le Bon (1895) originally wrote "Il traduit cette idée, psychologiquement erronée mais généralement admise, que beaucoup d'hommes réunis sont bien plus capables qu'un petit nombre de prendre une décision sage et indépendante sur un sujet donné" (p. 172).
3. This English quotation was translated by the author referring to a Japanese version

of translation from French. Le Bon (1895) originally wrote "le simplisme des idées, l'irritabilité, la suggestibilité, l'exagération des sentiments, l'influence prépondérante des meneurs" (p. 172).

4. See Hayek (1945, Chapter 12, "The Socialist Roots of Nazism").

5. Hayek (1945, p. 530) discusses "how a solution is produced by the interactions of people each of whom possesses only partial knowledge". This is the same logic as Simon's (1945) bounded rationality, by which he implies the limits of human cognition and its conquest by the organization.

6. In Hayek's 1973 work, titled "The Place of the Menger's Grundsätze in the History of Economic Thought", the following statement is found. He says, "The fact is, of course, that if we were to derive from our knowledge of individual behavior specific prediction about changes of the complex structures into which the individual actions combine, we should need full information about the conduct of every single individual who takes part. Menger and his followers certainly believed that we could never obtain all this information. But they evidently believed that common observation did supply us with a sufficiently complete catalogue of the various types of individual conduct that were likely to occur, and even with adequate knowledge of the probability that certain typical situations would occur" (p. 9). According to Hayek's understanding, Menger and his supporters were certainly aware that we could not obtain all this information on the individual actions. However, they clearly offered us a sufficiently complete list of various types of personal acts in which normal observations seemed likely to occur, and even believed these acts to be contributing appropriate knowledge regarding the probability of the emergence of certain typical situations. Hayek continues, "What they tried to show was that, starting from these known elements, it could be shown that they could be combined only into certain types of stable structures but not into others. In this sense such a theory would indeed lead to predictions, of the kind of structures that would occur, that are capable of falsification" (p. 9). If a "certain type of stable structure" exists, Hayek thinks that micro-economic theory is confined by "pattern predictions" or "organized complexity" (p. 9). In essence, if one admits the existence of a certain type of stable structure in economy, this structure corresponds to a collective body of individuals.

7. Of course one needs to be aware of the distincton between intelligence and inanity. Stand-up comedians know the ambiguity of the distinction between intelligence and inanity so that they can induce people to laugh.

8. In addition to a standard textbook such as Barney (1997), Mishina (2004) gives a standard account regarding management strategy in Japan. He advances the concept known as "emergence strategy". Chapter 6 of Mishina (2004) contains a survey of the genealogy of corporate-strategy theories. Accompanied by commentaries, the theories are named as follows: planning strategy, organizational strategy, conceptual strategy, structural strategy, architectural strategy and compositional strategy.

9. For more on game theory, see Gibbons (1992) and Fudenberg and Tirole (1991), and for more on micro-economics and industrial organization, see Kreps (1990), Tirole (1988), Vives (1999), Greenhut et al. (1987) and Waterson (1984).

10. For more on types of economic competition, see Scherer and Ross (1990).

11. According to Miyashita and Noda (2003), in population ecology, when an association becomes positive for one and negative for the other, besides parasitism, there emerge predation and herbivory. Miyashita and Noda (2003) express a symbiotic model with a differential equation by Lotka-Volterra. In this book, for simplicity's sake, I would like to represent associations that become + or – with the term parasitism.

12. For an account that attaches great importance to the formation of the character of an individual being dependent on the society to which the individual belongs, there is Riesman (1960).

13. Coleman (1988) talks about social capital by pointing out that goals become easier to achieve when people mutually influence each other. To illustrate, he raises case examples such as the behaviour of diamond wholesale traders mutually checking bags that have

diamonds in them, or the act of a woman being influenced by a friend when she chooses fashion items. Putnam (1993) states that Italian districts tend to be affluent so long as they contain civic communities. Localities that do not contain them, however, lack the spirit of civic duty, and tend to have fallen into a vicious spiral of increasing crime. Putnam refers to social capital as interdependent relationships that assure that the network supporting a community of citizens facilitates mutual rewarding. The concept of social capital was applied in explaining Silicon Valley's networks of entrepreneurs and investors.

14. "Afterword to the Anchor Books Edition" is the official title of the chapter in the book (pp. 273–84).

15. In the work by Axelrod and Cohen (1999), there is an explanation of the theory of complex organizational review systems and a review of discussions on diversity, inter-activity and selection. While I was unable to touch upon the topic of selection in this book, let me point out here that the formation of an organization involves selection, and in the event an organization is dismantled, even shared knowledge may not survive. See Horaguchi (1997b).

16. As for network theory, see Horaguchi (2008a).

17. Horaguchi (2008a) combines network theory by Barabasi and Albert (1999), Barabasi (2002), Watts (2003), graph theory by Harary (1969), the economic application for network theory by Bara and Goyal (2000), Goyal and Moraga-Gonzalez (2001), Hendricks et al. (1995), Horaguchi (2007b), Jackson and Watts (2002), Jackson and Wolinsky (1996) and computing oligopolistic models such as Kolstad and Mathiesen (1991), Murphy et al. (1982) and Sherali and Leleno (1988).

18. What Schumpeter (1939) takes pains to explain in the starting point of the argument is the treatment of oligopoly theory, which underwent development since it first appeared in his 1926 work. This is because the modelling of a general equilibrium economy as presented by Walras in his 1874 work fails to hold true when economic features of an oligopoly exist, such as economies of scale.

19. Tarde (1895) argues that in a critical society, a large amount of inventions will occur, such as combinations of stone mills and waterwheels, seal types and books, and cars and steam pistons (translation p. 222). In the English translation published in 1934, a note found for Schumpeter (1926). It is written: "Add successively as many mail coaches as you please, you will never get a railway thereby" (English translated version, p. 64). I discuss this matter further in Chapter 5.

20. Schumpeter (1926) originally wrote in German: "Warum treten die Unternehmer nicht kontinuierlich, in jedem Augenblick also vereinzelt, sondern scharenweise auf? Ausschließlich deshalb, weil das Auftreten eines oder einiger Unternehmer das Auftreten anderer und dieses das Auftreten weiterer und immer zahlreicherer erleichtert und eben dadurch bewirkt" (p. 339, 1997 version). This passage was translated into English by Redvers Opie while Schumpeter was alive in 1934: "Why do entrepreneurs appear, not continuously, that is singly in every appropriately chosen interval, but in clusters? Exclusively because the appearance of one or a few entrepreneurs facilitates the appear-ance of others, and these the appearance of more, in ever-increasing numbers" (p. 228, 1981 version).

21. Schumpeter (1939) advocates Fourier analysis in Chapter 5, which combines the Kondratiev cycle, the Juglar cycle, and the Kitchin cycle. In Schumpeter's 1950 work, the emphasis shifts from the topic of business cycles to systemic transformations.

22. Schumpeter's explanations resemble the logic of the concept of extra surplus-value production found in Marx's *Das Kapital* (1890, chap. 10, p. 336). For the production of absolute surplus-value (absoluten Mehrwerts), which increases the number of working hours within the limitation of the 24-hour period, Marx offered the explanation of extra surplus-value (Extramehrwert), while the growth of capital is achieved through the logic of producing relative surplus-value (relativen Mehrwerts).

23. For example, a product displayed in a store conveys information and knowledge to potential customers. The display satisfies the conditions of non-excludability and

non-rivalry. With these conditions met, it is possible for you to see the product while somebody else is also looking at it. Additionally, while someone else is looking at the product, the product value of the display will not diminish. The cost of "the need to compare" depends on travelling time. The electric town of Akihabara and the entertainment district of Kabuki-cho found in Shinjuku, Tokyo, can be explained by this "need to compare". By virtue of having an agglomeration of similar stores in a small area, the cost of carrying out a price search falls. You can obtain information, including those on the quality and performance of electronic products, and the contents and prices of meals and drinks. If knowledge remains undisclosed or if it cannot be disclosed due to the fact that it is in the form of tacit knowledge, the properties of non-excludability and non-rivalry will not exist. A person with knowledge can exclude a person without knowledge, and if this knowledge leaks from the one who has it, its value decreases. I elaborate on this point in Chapter 5.

24. In the annals of industry, we find that technological elements such as the quartz clock and the liquid crystal have been incorporated into the displays of clocks and computers. Studies by Shintaku (1994) and Numagami (1999) discuss the former and the latter, respectively. This is an example of adopting knowledge, of taking advantage of it.

25. Amidst the innovation of the Internet, the examples of Google and Yahoo, which developed a new search engine, are recalled.

26. This point is based on Kiyonari (1998).

27. A model of evolutionary process is proposed in Horaguchi (2013a).

28. These are the kinds of example taken into consideration in the model of Horaguchi (2008a).

29. Essentially this type of knowledge creation process in chapter 3 is not different from what Nonaka and Takeuchi (1995) depicted.

30. For example, what Kenney (2000) observed in Silicon Valley is that in an agglomerated industry, having a common index helps to clarify in what ways the companies are competing.

31. The meaning of the term "principle" used here is the same as the phrase "principles of marketing" as expressed by Kotler and Armstrong (1996). A large number of principles related to the business practices of marketing appear in each chapter of Kotler and Armstrong (1996), and are aggregates of local knowledge classified under specific circumstances. The term "principle" in this sense should be understood as is closer to idioms and expressions in language, skills and standard practices, established tactics in the games of *Go* and *Shogi* (Japanese chess), "theories" in high school baseball, formulas in mathematics, and equations in chemistry. This differs from basic recognitions, such as grammar in language, game rules in *Go*, *Shogi* or baseball, rules of operation and numerical concepts in mathematics, and the periodic table and atomic weight in chemistry. I use the term "principle" to signify the existence of a method that improves effectiveness *vis-á-vis* an aim within a certain determinate situation. I do not wish to emphasize in each chapter that some sort of a principle is absolute or that it is the only one of its kind.

3. Shared knowledge

1 PRINCIPLES OF MANAGING SHARED KNOWLEDGE

Problem-solving through Organizing Activities

Shared knowledge arises after an organization is formed. Shared knowledge is derived from intellectual activity in an organization. The organization offers a place where participating individuals mutually react for intellectual stimulation. Shared knowledge is formed when an individual provides intellectual stimuli to another individual who gives an intellectual response as a consequence. Cognizant of such a context, multiple participants cooperate with each other to solve specific problems so that new knowledge is created to the level that an individual alone cannot attain.

Specific problem-solving is a task within a business organization. Organization members conceive future visions as higher-ranked goals to set the task. Future visions posed by chief executive officers (CEOs) influence issues that need a solution by a group of people in the workplace. Examples of such issues are: problems in business that require new solutions, discoveries for needed improvements during business processes, new products that need to be elaborately planned, and development objectives with imaginations supported by feasible new systems.

Intellectual stimulus motivates people. Participation in a business organization is no exception. Problem-solving processes can induce talented people. For example, cost-reduction and product-development objectives function as intellectual stimulus, given a future vision as a higher-ranked goal. Once intellectual stimulus is given, intellectual responses can be understood in terms of an internal sense of fulfilment and observable incentives. The former, internal sense of fulfilment, includes feelings of gratification that come from applying personal knowledge and from being thanked for a contribution made to an organization. A sense of belonging consequently arises from communication that makes use of one's knowledge. It often induces the sense of responsibility (*noblesse oblige*) commensurate with one's official post and rank. The latter, observable incentives, includes such incentives as expectation of receiving a promotion, reward money, commendations, and other such honours.

Who actually becomes the one providing intellectual stimuli is by no means definite. A corporation's top executive may propose aims for the tasks, while on-site workers may submit proposals regarding business processes. The reason why middle management plays an important role is because they are entrusted to make decisions on whether to ignore problems detected by line workers, or take them up as issues to be considered through the entire organization. If middle management always ignores these line-related problems, the line worker who discovered them may lose motivation and leave the workplace, only to be replaced by another worker who does not find any problem. Conversely, the motivation of the worker who detected problems will rise if these problems are taken up as important issues to be resolved for the organization as a whole. The challenge for middle management is to decide whether or not the problem posed by the line worker is too small to be taken up as an issue for organizational consideration.

Middle management can ignore corporate visions expressed by the top executives. The middle management as a subordinate may not comply with the order from the superior. Conversely, middle managers may spare some private time for the purpose of supporting a vision. Barnard (1938) explicated this attitude by a concept of the zone of indifference. Middle management plays a key role in systematizing organizations, and is responsible for determining the strength of a strategy based on a confederate collective strategy. Intellectual response in confederate strategy contributes to the creation of shared knowledge. Intellectual response to create shared knowledge depends on the sense of gratification attained from applying one's knowledge in problem-solving. People even spend money to attain this sense of gratification through, for example, participating in an international volunteer programme. Let me put this in another way: people are willing to incur monetary expenditures just to experience the pleasure of solving problems. Shared knowledge emerges where the problem-solving is pursued by a group of people. Shared knowledge has a high degree of cohesiveness and specialization, and is created within the sphere of face-to-face communications.

Organization and Shared Knowledge

Shared knowledge arises while an organization is formed. Individuals who participate in the organization begin to mutually provide intellectual contribution. The organization is built to sort out knowledge proposed by various participants. It was Marshall (1920) who stated that "Organization aids knowledge; it has many forms, e.g. that of a single business, that of various businesses in the same trade, that of various trades relatively to one another, and that of the State providing security for all and help for many" (pp. 138–9 in Book IV, chapter I; p. 115 in eighth edition). A series of studies concerned with organizational learning has focused on the question of how the organization, a collectivity of individuals, can demonstrate superior learning capabilities as a group.[1] Barnard (1938) defined the organization as "a system of consciously coordinated personal activities or forces" (p. 72) of more than two people. He stated that a formal organization is defined by three conditions: common goal, willingness to cooperate and communication. In this situation where the formal organization is formed to fulfil a common goal, knowledge is not shared among its members. Knowledge does not exist "a priori" to sort out intellectual tasks. It is through the process of pursuing the common goal, communicating and working together that both tacit and explicit knowledge arise in accordance with the course of communication adopted. Explicit knowledge arises via communications using words. Tacit knowledge arises via communications rooted in common experiences. Shared knowledge arises in this way.

However, it is not always self-evident whether shared knowledge is better than knowledge conceived by an individual in terms of quality. We need to take manpower into account when we compare an activity carried out through collaboration to an activity carried out by an individual. It is necessary to compare the output of work performed by a single unit of, for example, three individuals collaborating with each other and the sum total of the output of work performed individually by three people. When considering emergence, we must qualitatively compare the results of intellectual work. Emergence may be attained through the collaboration of three individuals. This work must be compared qualitatively with the results of work carried out by three individuals who independently perform intellectual work.

Researchers of cognitive science have been attempting to create such preconditions through preparing experimental spaces. Ueda and Okada (2000) compiled multiple studies that compared groups performing actual collaborative work with groups performing only mechanical aggregations. These studies showed that the former did not necessarily exceed the latter. According to Miwa (2000), "generally speaking, if the only thing shared was an experimental space, no matter what types of combinations of strategies you may have, not only would emergence fail to arise, but you will rather come to see that stand-alone work conditions will show better performance than cooperative work conditions" (p. 99, translated from Japanese). However, he also suggests that emergence becomes possible when the number of experiments sees a rise (p. 99). What you should ascertain here is that collaboration will not necessarily produce shared knowledge.

Organizational Goal

Shared knowledge arises from activities driven by a sense of purpose. The foundation for producing shared knowledge is formed when management leaders purposefully adopt those activities that engender the emergence of knowledge within the organization. However, as experts of cognitive science point out, shared knowledge brought about with only such a foundation may not necessarily be one of high calibre in the end.

Three factors contribute towards elevating the higher quality of shared knowledge within the corporate organization. The first factor is that companies can absorb superior talent through the selection of recruits. When superior talent is attracted to a specific company due to various aspects such as job content, wage, rank in official post, and the popularity of the company, these "best and brightest" talent will carry out new technological developments. New talent equipped with problem-solving abilities will add innovative potential to the company. Innovations may be nurtured by technological developments in such companies.

The second factor is that companies are subject to competition where only the fittest survive. Businesses that fail to produce adequate shared knowledge are weeded out. If you drive alongside a national highway of a local city in Japan, you can spot closed restaurants with a big signboard, such as "Japanese noodle shop". Conversely, you can also spot restaurants or noodle shops where people stand in line to enter them. This indicates that the form of organization known as the corporation is not permitted to permanently transmit shared knowledge of a low standard.

The third route is to invite outside experts for specific purposes. Through such routes as business-to-business transactions, patent acquisition contracts and consultants with expertise, it is possible to set up partnerships from outside the organization for the purpose of generating shared knowledge. When such activities spread out into different areas of expertise, shared knowledge is transformed to symbiotic knowledge. I will discuss this transformation in further detail in Chapter 4.

The Reintegration of Knowledge under Division of Labour

Productivity is raised when a large number of people are allocated to different production processes. This allocation is called division of labour. A famous case was the production of pins as cited by Smith (1776). Shared knowledge could be created through the people working under the division of labour. In the production of pins, the division of labour involves workers who cut wires, who quench them, who sharpen the tips and who open pinholes. Workers repeat their assigned tasks during work hours.

If you only take into account this short span of production time, you could say that there is no room for any intellectual activity to be introduced into the workplace. In other words, if you regard this situation from a static viewpoint, shared knowledge may not be found in the workshop. You will believe that the management, such as supervisors, handles the jobs of production engineering, production management and of operational processes. With such a one-way determination of tasks, it would not be possible to incorporate suggestions from workers into the agenda of organizational goals, nor would it be possible to promote spontaneity in workers where determining tasks is concerned. In this scenario, labour is stressed, and motivation to participate is solely dependent on monetary reward.

The emergence of shared knowledge arises when division of labour is dynamically managed. Shared knowledge emerges when division of labour is performed with the collaboration of the workers. As Hayek (1945) pointed out, when an individual worker is in charge of his own "job site", this worker will acquire discrete knowledge. If all work is performed alone, just as a craftsman carries out his work, there will be no room for the exercise of shared knowledge. You will find only personal knowledge there. For a confederate strategy involving multiple workers to work in a work area, tasks need to be allotted to the workers in order to work effectively.

If division of labour is dynamically managed, it becomes possible to train multi-skilled workers. When cultivating a multi-skilled worker with the ability to be in charge of multiple production processes, the worker's range of duties expands through such versatility. This worker will then begin to have ideas on how to improve work methods used by other workers. If versatilization is realized in the production of pins, the person who drills holes will be able to efficiently cut wires and quench as well. Then it becomes possible to judge whether there is room for improving ways of cutting wires and carrying out quenching.

The creation of shared knowledge under division of labour comes about in accordance with how much improvement can be realized once the allocation of tasks is determined. As for the length of the pin, its thickness and the size of its hole, these are determined prior to carrying out the division of labour, and it is thought that workers are unable to change these specifications. However, in reality, the worker deals with the issue of avoiding defective units through realizing more precision in their work, while also having the incentive to raise productivity. If productivity sees a rise in line with the experience curve, the worker can use free time afforded at their own discretion. In addition, there are cases where self-esteem is satisfied through demonstrating competitive superiority over other workers. The self-esteem may be realized as receiving a promotion or a wage bonus.

When a worker is in charge of multiple duties, it becomes possible for this worker to point out whether another worker's modus operandi is extraneous and time-consuming or simply incorrect. In addition to being able to acquire tacit knowledge specific to those duties, the worker receives the opportunity to improve the ways of other workers. This becomes possible when a worker is promoted and acquires authority to carry out job improvement. However, it also becomes possible via the improvement suggestion (*Kaizen Teian*) scheme typically found in Japanese companies. I explain this point in detail in section 2 of this chapter.

The initial stages of division of labour require job allocation. In collaborative situations where shared knowledge emerges, however, it becomes possible for each participant to bring their respective knowledge to bear and improve productivity.

2   CASE EXAMPLES

Determining Factors of Competitiveness

Painters, novelists and musicians who carry out their activities solo can be found in various countries around the world. Regardless of nationality, the artist's sphere of activity is global. Even when you look at athletes of individual sports such as track and field participating in the Olympics, you can see that the nationalities represented are diverse. By comparison to such individual activities, advanced industrial development is not so diverse, and shows a much larger country bias. Why is it that countries that can produce cars for worldwide use are limited to only several countries in the world? Nations considered to be leaders in the design and development of automobiles are the USA, Germany, Japan, France, Italy and Sweden, and automobiles of such assembly-maker countries are imported into various countries of the world. Not to mention there are also countries that allow multinational companies from leading car-producing nations to come and form joint ventures with local companies for joint production. Protected by high tariff rates, the local manufacturer then carries out production for the home market.[2] However, companies that enjoy a global market share while also possessing the capability to carry out automobile design and development in foreign countries are limited.

Manufacturing industry depends on the collaboration of many people. The collaboration is carried out for the purpose of securing the collective knowledge necessary for a manufacturing industry. Then the competitiveness of each company is determined by the way it uses collective knowledge. The skill in creating shared knowledge establishes the competitiveness of the company. Specialists who get together for a single purpose create new knowledge in the company. Examples of shared knowledge can be witnessed in collaborative relationships in confined spaces. Factories, university laboratories, research institutes of companies, kitchens of restaurants, offices and music studios are all cases in point.

There are also cases where we see knowledge being accumulated even when the sites of collaboration are spatially remote from each other. Such accumulation occurs through the exchange of information via radio and Internet. Examples of this include the dispatching of radio-taxi vehicles, air traffic control knowhow, sales of goods over an Internet site, and information-sharing and data entry via an intra-company intranet. While there are instances of sharing tacit knowledge, as in the cases of group work that takes place among mountain-climbing parties or on automobile assembly lines, there are other instances where explicit knowledge is shared, as in the course of carrying out such work as editing the content of a manual.

Production System

Japanese companies are skilful at creating shared knowledge in manufacturing industries. Shinobu (2003) studied "cell production systems" in the area of electrical equipment manufacturing, and pointed out that their defining characteristics are self-organization and coordination (p. 220). Fujimoto (1997) makes much of the coupling technique of the knowledge known as "Suriawase". "Suriawase" literally means "to join by rubbing together", a concept related to practices found in the product or production process. This word of "Suriawase" is used to emphasize emergence in his analysis of Toyota Motor Corporation's product development organization. Fujimoto (1997) attaches great importance to emergence in the evolutionary process of Toyota's production system, and suggests that unique knowledge has been shared within Toyota's factories.

Mishina (2006, p. 79), who discusses Toyota's production system, refers to the connection between the part and whole. Having evaluated Toyota's Kentucky plant over the long term, Mishina emphasizes that even if you disassemble the whole Toyota production system into its parts, you will not arrive at an "understanding" of Toyota's production system.[3] One can interpret this phenomenon as follows: what was created with the Toyota production system can be seen as a state of emergence that saw this self-organizing system at the macro-workshop-level. As is shown in Figure 3.1,

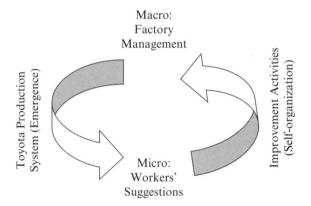

Figure 3.1   Circulation of shared knowledge: Toyota production system

work activities at the micro-worker-level evolve into macro-workshop-level production engineering through suggestions of improvement coming from the micro-level organization of operators.

The evolution of the production system brings about shared knowledge. The process of creating shared knowledge is specifically observable in small group activities and the suggestion system.[4] In the automobile production in Japan, we see the achievement of such small group activities. If you observe a car assembly plant, you will find a board installed at a corner of the work area, showing pre-improvement and post-improvement pictures, emphasizing that the results were devised through an employee group effort. For example, on the assembly line, a components rack was introduced which moved in accordance with the speed of the moving assembly line. It was produced after a suggestion was made by operating personnel. And in the welding line, jigs were improved to raise the level of production efficiency of welding robots.[5]

The interview by Matsushima and Odaka (2007) records the oral history of Yuzo Kumamoto, who had worked in Toyota Motor Corporation from 1956 through 1991. According to this account, the total quality control (TQC) in Toyota began in 1961, and there was a strong influence from the Union of Japanese Scientists and Engineers. Kumamoto testified, "it began as the company's management policy, and was adopted into all activities of the company's organizations; into research and development, production engineering, production, finance, quality, operations, and personnel" (pp. 55–6, translated from Japanese). Small group activities that take place in the production workplace are placed in the low rank of the TQC. The suggestion system is a component that ranks even lower than small group activities.

The hallmark of the shared knowledge of Toyota's production system is the fact that a distinctive language was developed, one that was peculiar to a workplace where a confederate strategy exists between operating personnel and production engineers. Through the emergence of a vocabulary peculiar to the Toyota production system, such as *kanban* (a sheet of paper for ordering parts), *pokayoke* (failsafe for preventing defects), *andon* (a sign board to show production procedures), *gouguchi* (regular production with high volume), *soto dandori* (external setup) and *uchi dandori* (internal setup), you can understand that effort of creating vocabulary had been expended towards converting tacit knowledge into the explicit knowledge. The vocabulary in Toyota helps operating personnel to share the explicit knowledge. Understanding through the explicit knowledge of Toyota vocabulary, operating personnel are then immersed by experience to understand the tacit knowledge which is shared inside Toyota's plants. As it turned out, the conversion from tacit knowledge to explicit knowledge was performed collectively there.

Suggestion System

The suggestion system in Japan acts as a method for creating shared knowledge in the manufacturing industry. The suggestion system is a system by which groups within the work organization seek solutions for improvements regarding the work area based on suggestions proposed by individual workers. Depending on the level of importance of the suggestion for improvement, a medal of honour is given along with a small amount of pecuniary reward as incentive payment. The suggestion system is often understood in terms of a type of small group activity or its component.

The Japan HR Association (Nihon HR Kyōkai) carried out a sustained investigation into the suggestion system. The number of business establishments that responded to the 2007 survey was 593. According to the survey carried out by this association, the sum total of suggestions made for all business establishments over a one-year period was over 11 million (11 568 489). Based on the survey carried out by the Japan HR Association and Akashi (1996), which analysed historical data of small group activities and the suggestion system, Table 3.1 shows the top ten companies with the highest number of suggestions up to 2007. Akashi (1996) compiles the tabulated data of the Japan HR Association, showing that this number fluctuates every year. According to Akashi (1996), this number showed a declining trend in the 1990s after having shown a rising trend in the latter half of the 1980s. As is evident in Table 3.1, the total number of suggestions made in 1985 for just the top ten companies was more than 23 million, and in 1994, the number recorded was over 12.8 million, exceeding

Table 3.1 *The Japan HR Association survey of top ten companies by number of improvement suggestions*

(Unit: 10 000)

Ranking	1970		1985	
1	Matsushita Electric Industrial	65.6	Matsushita Electric Industrial	664
2	Sumitomo Metal Industries	27.9	Hitachi	433
3	Kobelco	17.7	Mazda	295
4	Fuji Electric	12.0	Toyota Motor Corporation	245
5	JVC	5.8	Fuji Electric	139
6	Toyota Motor Corporation	4.9	Nissan Motor	129
7	Hitachi Zosen	2.5	Nippondenso	120
8	Toray	2.3	Aisin Seiki	118
9	Nippon Gakki	2.2	Bridgestone	92
10	Omron Tateisi Electronics	2	Canon	89
	Sum total of top ten companies	142.9	Sum total of top ten companies	2324
Ranking	1994		2007	
1	Toshiba	257	Matsushita Electric Industrial	91.6
2	Matsushita Electric Industrial	237	Toyota Motor Corporation	74.5
3	Mazda	152	Idemitsu Kosan	69.1
4	Cyubu	118	Yazaki Corporation	62.7
5	Ohtsu Tire & Rubber	117	Gunze	46.6
6	Idemitsu Kosan	94	Denso	41.8
7	Toyota Motor Corporation	89	Central Japan Railway Company	40.8
8	Yazaki Corporation	81	Yamaha Motor	34.5
9	Sanyo Electric	76	Fuji Heavy Industries/ Gunma Works	29.3
10	Kubota	62	Koito Manufacturing	24.7
	Sum total of top ten companies	1283	Sum total of top ten companies	515.6

Notes:
1. Regarding the data for 1970 and 2007, they show up to the first decimal place.
2. Nippondenso is the former name of Denso. Matsushita Electric Industrial was renamed Panasonic in 2008.

Table 3.1   (continued)

Sources: For 1970, 1985 and 1994 data: Table 4, Akashi (1996). The source documents are from Japan HR Association and they are "Hito to Keiei (People and Management)", "Soui to Kufuu (Originality and Ideas)" and versions of various years of "Kaizen Teian Katsudou Jisseki Chosa Report (the Report on the Performance of Improvement/Suggestion Activities)". The 2007 data was cited from Japan HR Association's "2007 nendo Kaizen Katsudou Jisseki Chosa Report (2007 Report on the Performance of Kaizen Activities)", available at http://www.hr-kaizen.com/jisseki.html.

not only the sum total of the 2007 survey for the top ten companies, which was 5.1 million, but also the total number registered for the 593 business establishments (factories) mentioned above, which was 11.5 million.

What should be noted here is that at all four times shown in Table 3.1, Matsushita Electric Industrial Corporation (which changed its name to Panasonic in 2008) and Toyota Motor Corporation appear in the top ten lists. In 1985, Matsushita Electric Industrial recorded the top number of suggestions with 6640000, and in 2007, it recorded 916000. Toyota Motor Corporation was in fourth place in 1985 with 2450000, but came in second place in 2007 with 745000.[6] The fact that the number of suggestions made was high in Panasonic and Toyota, which are companies that are representative of Japanese manufacturing industry, indicates that the suggestion system was functioning as a classic method for creating shared knowledge. This means that shared knowledge was being created at manufacturing industry sites in Japan long before Surowiecki (2005) discussed the concept of the "wisdom of the crowd" as a mode of creating collective intelligence in the society of the Internet. The figure of about 11.5 million, which is the sum total of the number of suggestions made in 593 business establishments in one year, shows a level comparable to the levels of accessing highly popular Internet sites.

The following factors are thought to contribute to the decline in the number of suggestions made. The biggest may be the phenomenon known as de-industrialization, causing most of the manufacturing companies to operate factories abroad and close down ones in Japan. There is a possibility that the total number of suggestions is seeing a decline because the number of employees making suggestions has been decreasing. Another factor is the prevalence of the use of dispatched workers in business establishments in Japan and the outsourcing of work processes labelled as in-plant subcontracting. For the dispatch worker anxious about future employment prospects, it is difficult to understand the significance of the suggestion system. The limited contract period possibly lowers the level of their motivation to participate in making improvements. Typically, in the event that a period of employment ends within the short term of around three months, the worker's contract, as it turns out, expires right after they fully understand the operational process. A further possibility explaining why the number of suggestions declines over time is that middle management may not be given enough leeway in terms of time. Although they aim to work out concrete measures for improvement, they may not have ample time to examine the importance of improvement suggestions. After the bubble economy reached its pinnacle in 1989, Japanese companies streamlined their human resources amid sluggish economic conditions. This may have created a substantial burden for middle management.[7] Under such a situation, they cannot afford to coach people to narrow down the number of suggestions from the line, and thereby it may be impossible to work out solutions through coaching small group activities.

The 2007 survey carried out by the Japan HR Association states the figure showing "the per-capita economic effect" (in Japanese yen). The total amounts of "economic effect" are listed in Table 3.2. There are no survey responses regarding Toyota and Matsushita, and there is no detailed mention of even how the figure of economic effects was estimated. The data is problematic in many ways, but if you were to assess that the respondent companies had arrived at the "economic effect" by carrying out estimations in a uniform way, you know the size of the effect in each company. In Figure 3.2, you will find a summary of the findings.

In the case of Aisin Keikinzoku Co. Ltd, which ranked in first place, there were 147 428 suggestions made by 759 employees, and the economic effect per capita was estimated to be 6 392 503 yen. "The incentive sum" for that purpose is 30 026 yen, according to the response. In second place was Daido Steel, and the per-capita economic effect was 5 348 653 yen and the incentive sum was 10 107 yen. In the case of the third place company, JAL Engine Technology, the figures were 4 629 630 yen and 3472 yen respectively.

When arriving at the sum total of all companies in this way by multiplying "the number of subjects" (people) by "the per-capita economic effect" (in Japanese yen) the figure turned out to be 162.9 billion yen. Similarly, the total figure for companies arrived at by multiplying the "incentive sum per person" (in Japanese yen) by "the number of subjects" (people) "was 3 billion yen". A straightforward calculation tells us that this yielded for incentive sums a cost-effectiveness of 54 times. The economic effect of about 160 billion yen is a quasi-rent (or, margin) for the shared knowledge that improved existing technologies possessed by companies.

The quasi-rent of shared knowledge is born from employees who make suggestions[8] and the work team and managers who understand the significance of those suggestions and go on to realize them. For example, a large workload involves accepting more than 100 suggestions from every

Table 3.2   Top 30 companies of suggestion scheme based on a survey by the Japan HR Association

(Units: Case, Person, Yen)

Company name	No. of cases of kaizen & proposals	No. of persons involved	No. of kaizen & proposal cases per person	Economic effects in yen per person (Yen)	Incentives per person (Yen)
1 Aisin Keikinzoku	147 428	759	194.2	6 392 503	30 026
2 Daido Steel	29 465	2524	11.7	5 348 653	10 107
3 JAL Engine Technologies	575	648	0.9	4 629 630	3472
4 Koito Manufacturing	246 574	3784	65.2	4 571 786	11 636
5 Stanley Iwaki Manufacturing	4652	272	17.1	4 332 831	7537
6 Kanto Chemical Soka Plant	5933	288	20.6	2 821 007	83 090
7 Idemitsu Kosan	691 126	5292	130.6	2 738 284	–
8 Sankyo Oilless Industry	4196	333	12.6	2 234 985	8168
9 H&F	21 320	335	63.6	2 227 463	14 149
10 Toyotomi Kiko	10 436	953	11	2 227 377	3778
11 Fujitsu General Ichinoseki & Shinjo Plants	11 162	373	29.9	2 002 091	9062
12 TCM Shiga Plant	5299	382	13.9	1 831 099	2906
13 Suyama Construction	2300	255	9	1 593 490	7020
14 Aisin Takaoka	40 993	1714	23.9	1 581 593	8057
15 Nittan Valve	61 313	668	91.8	1 525 539	13 159
16 Aisin Seiki	141 615	8850	16	1 494 473	7608
17 Nagano Electronics Ind.	27 832	459	60.6	1 486 819	25 664
18 Topy Industries Toyohashi Factory	15 162	613	24.7	1 386 444	56 117

Table 3.2 (continued)

(Units: Case, Person, Yen)

Company name	No. of cases of kaizen & proposals	No. of persons involved	No. of kaizen & proposal cases per person	Economic effects in yen per person (Yen)	Incentives per person (Yen)
19 Fujine Group Main Office Plant	903	80	11.3	1375000	375
20 Aisin Sinwa	7296	362	20.2	1265193	4972
21 Prano	253	49	5.2	1264898	12653
22 Aisin AW	103383	9004	11.5	1220878	5342
23 Banyu Pharmaceutical Menuma Plant	2776	214	13	1213692	12850
24 Xomox Japan	420	25	16.8	1200000	122000
25 Sanden	50031	1951	25.6	1167319	6750
26 Osaka Organic Chemical Osaka Plant	1396	99	14.1	1141616	12525
27 Omron Sanyo	2292	134	17.1	1137910	11269
28 Aisin AW Industries	21141	1380	15.3	1051826	5761
29 Oji Specialty Paper Ebetsu Plant	2750	234	11.8	1028120	14402
30 Aisin Kiko	13466	962	14	996611	10717

Source: Japan HR Association "2007 Performance Report Based on Kaizen Activities Performance Survey." Table based on data available at http://www.hr-kaizen.com/jisseki.html.

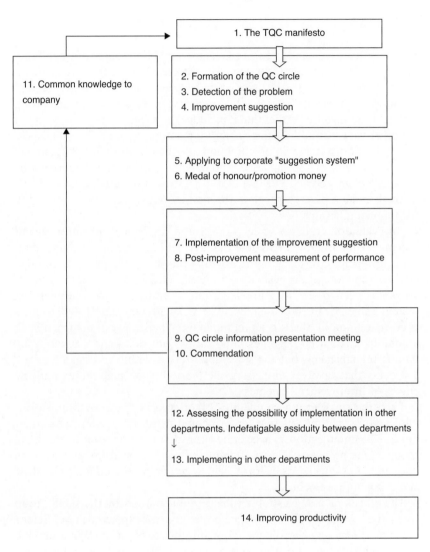

Figure 3.2 Improvement suggestion process by small group activity

employee, prioritizing those suggestions, and then issuing instructions to have employees deal with concrete measures for improvement. The suggestion system does not seem sustainable without the minding of such a load by people engaged in the administration of shared knowledge, such as the team leader, group leader, chief clerk, chief manager and factory superintendent. However, this matter of heavy workload is solved as follows.

Suggestion System Embedded in Small Group Activity

Japanese firms typically attempt to create shared knowledge through functionalizing the confederate strategy for collective knowledge management. It is important to clarify the association between small group activities and the suggestion system.[9] Plainly speaking, the relationship of a small group activity is defined by the fact that it includes the suggestion system, and not the other way around.[10] If the small group activity is not fully established, the suggestion system will not function adequately. In Figure 3.2 you will find a summary of the suggestion process for improvement facilitated by the small group activity. The fact that suggestions function more effectively through small groups rather than through individuals can be attributed to the following reasons.

An evaluator needs to screen, assess and implement an improvement scheme. While the role of middle management as evaluator is important, prior to reaching this stage, it is essential that the small group is empowered to function as an evaluator by itself. This is, so to speak, what is known as peer review; it is, in effect, mutual evaluation by colleagues. As seen in Table 3.1, in 2007, there were between 247 000 and 916 000 suggestions made among the top ten companies. When suggestions reach such a copious level, what becomes important is not the direct evaluation by middle management, but the screening process within the small group – a process that involves discussing the feasibility of suggestions and the effects of improvement schemes.

Then the small group contributes by offering a space for brainstorming, creating an atmosphere whereby people are encouraged to speak their minds. Communication is accelerated through the organization of small groups, making it possible to attempt the conversion from solo work to "organization", which is in turn held together by the common goal of achieving improvement.[11]

The effects of a suggestion system are understood by the small group when they witness how senior personnel of a workplace behave. Senior personnel then act as a role model within the small group. When the role model, who in effect functions as a proposer, is promoted within the workplace, a new proposer follows this role model. They will be stimulated in the course of communicating with experienced proposers who had realized their suggestions through the small group activities.

A Case of the Development of Technology Elements, MEMS

The second example regarding shared knowledge can be found in the domain of product development. It is possible to point out the MEMS (micro electro mechanical system) as an example of new product development realized by multiple researchers and developers. Since the level of specialization sought in the development of technology elements is high, the sharing of knowledge within the organization becomes a key foundation. MEMS is a semiconductor with a mechanical movement. The market size in 2003 was 700 billion yen with annual growth rate estimated to be 20 per cent.[12] Among the MEMS technologies that have already found application are: (1) ink jet head, (2) pressure sensor, (3) acceleration sensor, (4) angular velocity sensor (gyro sensor), (5) light MEMS, (6) biochip and (7) small-size fuel cell.[13]

(1) The ink jet head is a device necessary for printers to make printouts. From 2001 through 2002, companies including Ricoh, Seiko Epson and Kyocera applied for many related patents.[14] The function of the ink jet head is to form a minute pump using a metal that changes shape with the application of an electrical voltage, and then applying ink to paper from there.[15]

(2) The pressure sensor, (3) the acceleration sensor and (4) the angular velocity sensor (gyro sensor) fall under the expertise of analogue devices. These sensors, in addition to being used for airbags in automobiles, are used for image stabilizing devices found in digital cameras and mobile phones. The largest company in the business is Analog Devices. Our research team visited the company's branch office in Silicon Valley on 7 September 2004. There, the company emphasized that their business performance was satisfactory, even though the dot-com bubble had burst and the business climate in the Silicon Valley was in a slump.[16]

(5) A representative product of light MEMS, as already mentioned above, is the digital micromirror device (DMD) from Texas Instruments in America. Here we see a prominent American manufacturing company which Japanese companies follow. The digital micromirror device (DMD), which is an example of a MEMS technology, is a technology element used in projectors, and is known as a product that was developed over more than 20 years by a team led by Larry J. Hornbeck in the central laboratory of Texas Instruments Inc. (TI) in America.[17] It is a chip used in video projectors. The video projector that incorporates this DMD is sold under the name DLP (digital light processing).[18] In Japan, we find OMRON producing in its Mizuguchi factory in Koga-gun, Shiga, an array of microlenses used in micro-machines and liquid crystal projectors, in addition to semiconductors such as the bipolar IC.[19]

As for examples showing the development of (6) the biochip and (7) the small fuel cell, I introduce a case by Japanese firms in Chapter 4. Shared knowledge is embedded in a product through the effort that various international firms try to improve the characteristics of the product. This effort includes widening the applicability of the product and improving the technological quality.

Alliance

The third example regarding shared knowledge can be seen in the sharing of explicit knowledge among several companies. You can see that the print media, such as newspapers, are also the product of a vast repository of shared knowledge. The four major Japanese newspaper companies make use of wire reports from Reuters. One article is completed only when it passes through a workflow, starting from a reporter writing the article, an editor editing it, a photographer shooting pictures, and an expert ranging from carrying out trimmings on those pictures, to proofreading of the article, and then finally the printing of the article. Articles from contract news agencies such as Reuters are also edited at the same time. Such elements comprise the whole of what is called the newspaper. The same thing is true of magazines as well.

The information system built for serving the alliance of international airlines is another example of shared knowledge *vis-à-vis* explicit knowledge. As a case of collaboratively launching a brand, there is the successful precedent of the Star Alliance, in which All Nippon Airways takes part. On 14 May 1997, the five companies – Air Canada, Lufthansa, Scandinavian Airlines System, Thai Airways International and United Air Lines – established the Star Alliance, and thereafter, All Nippon Airways joined as an official member. As of 2013, the alliance had the participation of 28 airlines. Depending on the international airline and beyond rights, it used to be difficult for a particular airline to offer its own transit flights to domestic destinations. However, thanks to the alliance, various cities of the world became connected. There are also merits, such as the common utilization of the mileage programme, and the securing of customer convenience through offering joint services.

In the management strategy known as "strategic alliance", there are business alliances forged on a project-by-project basis, technology grants that are not tied to any capital contribution and, furthermore, joint research developments without any licensing agreements in place between two companies. In such examples, the formation of networks determines the state of knowledge.[20] The integrated system for inventory management, marketing performance and financial management of corporate businesses is called the enterprise resource planning (ERP) system. The ERP system works as a means for connecting information among individual stores of a franchise business, such as convenient stores running multiple stores. Shelving allocation of a product in retail outlets are determined by the headquarters based on the sales information they gather from retail outlets.

3 HOW TO MANAGE SHARED KNOWLEDGE

The Role of the Manager

Shared knowledge with which a manager can be in contact is knowledge that is based on up-to-the-minute information available within the company. From the moment they launch a company, people start thinking collectively. Managing this interaction is one of the roles played by managers. At this point, the authority of the manager comes into play. In effect, the manager is able to interpret the newest information, give meaning to it, and deliver it throughout the company while saving it as their own newly acquired knowledge.

Knowledge management performed by managers is one of the traditional ways among various methods to induce collective knowledge. What requirements must be met when a manager tries to engender knowledge from an organization? The manager has the role of gathering people with certain abilities. The manager assigns required tasks for an employee only during the initial period after the employee is hired. In many cases, employees are requested to think for themselves. The results of their thinking performance are evaluated regularly by the manager and, in the meantime, employees acquire much tacit knowledge and explicit knowledge in the workplace.

An individual employee alone will not suffice to create shared knowledge in the workplace. Somebody must play the role of rejecting suggestions for improvement made in the company. Alternatively, it will be necessary for someone to fulfil the role of recommending improvement suggestions that are superior. In a situation where multiple suggestions are submitted at random, there is a challenge in recognizing what kinds of suggestions should be adopted. In fact, some Japanese companies have abolished the suggestion system because their workers tend to make too many suggestions for the purpose of winning prizes. A group of people ought to sort out suggestions from a large number of workers and then carry them out. In other words, it is the role of the manager to control the procedure of how shared knowledge will arise.[21] Companies such as Toyota and Panasonic have been successfully continuing the suggestion system. The manager has to make decisions based on assumptions which lead to a "better" type of shared knowledge, as far as they believe.[22]

Personnel System

It is necessary to motivate employees to have them participate in the creation of shared knowledge. To that end, there are some particular motivating factors that need to be met in an organization. The first is to carry out a careful recruitment process. It is necessary to gather employees who understand that contributing useful knowledge to their workplace has a good repercussion effect. This explains why Japanese companies attach great importance to hiring new graduates from universities and high schools. If there are employees who focus only on absorbing knowledge provided by the training programme in the organization for the purpose of raising their individual aptitude, and if all the employees only ever seek knowledge from the organization without contributing any of their own, then in terms of knowledge, the organization will not become rich, but instead, it will lose its wealth of knowledge and become poor.

The company will end up being a stepping-stone for its employees if the employees acquire knowledge for the purpose of changing jobs. In that case, there is no incentive for a person with long-term experience in the company to teach their own particular knowledge of the business to newly recruited employees. Conversely, if there are many employees who recognize that the growth of the company depends on its tradition of passing on knowledge, senior employees will teach their knowledge of the business to their younger counterparts, and the latter will in turn spread this knowledge throughout the company in the future.

The in-house job opening system for promotions is an effective method for sorting out employees who have the motivation to participate in a designated area of business in the company. An employee with such motivation can be considered as someone who seeks "a mentor" within the company in an attempt to acquire knowledge they find to be lacking in themselves. The in-house job opening system for staff promotions brings together motivated employees for new projects and aggregates the knowledge they possess.

Secondly, mutual trust between workers and management must be in place to assure the proper functioning of the suggestion system built into small group activities – one that dispels any fears of layoffs in the workplace as a consequence of making suggestions. In fact, it is necessary to show that suggestions are tied to promotions, and that they are not directly related to layoffs even if the suggestions are related to labour-saving working methods. To this end, it is necessary to introduce prize management systems for small group activities and the suggestion system, and, as proof of concept, employees who received promotions. It is desirable to plant the awareness that the results of a suggested improvement will be evaluated on an equal basis, regardless of educational background or professional career.

The third point is that the path to tenured, regular employment is open for temporary employees and contracted employees. Drawing the line between regular employees and temporary/contracted employees entails a large demerit. In such a case, the knowledge possessed by temporary and contracted employees will not be available for use. For example, even if a temporary employee realizes how to make an improvement in the work-place, the temporary employees tend to remain silent. They might assume that a regular employee would lose face if they use some suggestions made from a temporary worker's side. Inducements to draw out what temporary employees notice may not be sufficient. Managers should allow them to regularly submit improvement suggestions, and promote them into regular employees when they actively submit superior improvement suggestions. Compared with the manufacturing shop floor, small group activities and improvement suggestions are not so popular in Japanese offices. This may be a clue to improve productivity in office work for knowledge-creating businesses.

Sustaining Innovation

Shared knowledge brings about new combinations of knowledge. Regarding such combinations, Schumpeter (1926) emphasized that they occur in the following five areas: goods, production process, new market, raw materials and intermediate goods, and organization. Shared knowl-edge can even be created in these five areas. Here, the following points need to be noted.

First of all, development of technology elements can take place before new combinations are made. Let us look at "new combinations" in "pro-duction process" and "intermediate goods", which are among the five factors stated by Schumpeter (1926). When new combinations develop production procedures and half-finished goods, technology elements are propagated into the next production process. When tracing back a tech-nology element to its origins, we often arrive at the development of a raw material. In Japan, during the early part of the twenty-first century, the technique of "recombination" at the level of raw materials often saw the realization of new products. A case in point is the products made pos-sible by lithium: the secondary battery, the liquid crystal and the blue light-emitting diode. In this sense, the producers are able to pursue "new discoveries" and "create something for the first time", paving the way to easy patent acquisition. Then the patent acts as authentication of novelty.

Secondly, Schumpeter (1926) emphasizes the existence of things that cannot be described as the newness of the combination. He develops his argument by including new discoveries and new inventions, which are based on science and technology, but what Schumpeter emphasizes with respect to "half-manufactured goods" (p. 64 in English version) is not a new method of manufacturing them, but rather "the conquest of a new source of supply" (p. 64 in English version).

Thirdly, according to Schumpeter (1926), it is the entrepreneur who promotes "new combinations". The one who promotes the development of technology elements, rather than the entrepreneur, is the company's technician or a research worker in the central research laboratory of the company. In this sense, distinguishing an engineer from an entrepreneur is dependent on the behavioural characteristics of whether one seeks to make new combinations for the market or whether one devotes oneself to the development of new technology elements.

Fourthly, development of technology elements independently works on the five factors pointed out by Schumpeter (1926). For example, the "new production process" such as laser welding, which is detailed in Chapter 6 of this book, is not something that renews the attributes of the automobile, a finished good. However, it may raise the resilience of the automobile and thereby raise its level of safety. Another example is sought in the case of the pressure sensor. The pressure sensor is an intermediate good that uses MEMS, and from the perspective of a consumer using a commodity that makes use of this, it may even not be considered to be a "new good". However, the pressure sensor is necessary in air bags installed in cars, and it is very likely that the consumer is unaware that "a pressure sensor" is even being used.

Fifthly, as for the dichotomy between "sustaining innovation" and "disruptive innovation" as proposed by Christensen (1997), the distinction is made after the innovation process. In other words, this is an *ex post facto* concept. No one knows how a new product development acquires new customers and erodes the existing product area share *ex ante*, or how it could have been developed without meeting certain technical standards. Whether this turns out to be "sustaining" or "disruptive" depends on where customers end up shifting, and is therefore not in any way premeditated. Schumpeter (1949) called the latter process "creative destruction"[23] and both disruptive innovation and creative destruction have the same characteristics in common. They are only determined as *ex post facto*.

Sustaining innovation shows areas of product development that are apt to accumulate excessive quality. In consequence, if you only continue to solely focus your attempts to innovate in the area of technology elements, you may end up missing new opportunities for product development. Innovation of technology elements unmistakably functions as sustaining innovation. For example, developments of printers for the paper medium, such as ink-jet printers and laser printers, can themselves be categorized as sustaining innovation. Disruptive innovation, on the other hand, may be derived from technology elements that differ from the norm. The development of capacitive-type touch panel and resistive-type touch panel are classified in this category. Consequent development of the electronic book is another example to remove paper as a medium. "Innovation of technology elements" is a necessary precondition for realizing the diffusion of disruptive innovation, which is shown in the case of the electronic book in relation to the paper medium. The diffusion of electronic books will eventually eliminate the need for ink-jet printers and laser printers.

The Limitations of Shared Knowledge

The management of shared knowledge has certain kinds of limitations. Poor vision in management limits the creation of shared knowledge. The manager has the role of expressing the organization's goals that go beyond the level of self-organization. If a self-organized organization goes in a wrong direction, the organization will not survive in the market, even if it was formed on the basis of shared knowledge.[24]

Shared knowledge sometimes fosters narrow-mindedness, or creates tunnel vision. Putting priority on outdated practices in a company, defending the claims of flaws in products, and carrying out product development without improving technological standards of the developers – all these phenomena result from the inability of rank-and-file members who protect their status quo. However, some regular employees cannot contribute to the creation of shared knowledge and some temporary staff members display great intellectual creativity. It is inadvisable to subject them to job cutbacks based merely on their position as temporary staff without considering their contribution to the organization. A narrow-minded management will deteriorate the standard of shared knowledge.

As we reviewed in the discussion on tacit knowledge, there is no system of external inspection when corruption in shared knowledge occurs in corporate practice. This is similar to the mechanism that enables the cover-up of corporate wrongdoing over an extensive period of time. If shared knowledge is retained as tacit knowledge among rank-and-file members of the organization, the timing of disclosure for external inspection will be delayed when it is out of date.

While going public and airing TV commercials are a means to recruit superior employees, it is difficult for many companies to employ a sufficient number of talented employees who have superior expertise. Publicly listed companies number only several thousand in Japan. If quality employees cannot be assembled, the president of the company becomes the ceiling of corporate knowledge. If such a company is unable to recruit employees whose knowledge exceeds this ceiling, creation of shared knowledge in the company is limited. In such a case, external collaboration should be attempted, leading to the new challenge of creating symbiotic knowledge within the framework of a conjugate strategy.

The Tragedy of Shared Knowledge

Even if the management of shared knowledge turns out to be successful, honing it will still involve some problems. Creation of shared knowledge is often misunderstood as a mere reduction in costs. A subsequent problem is that quantitative comparisons will tend to be prioritized. For instance, in automotive manufacturing, the extent of quantitative reductions, such as the extent of reductions in the inventory of parts and in the number of defects, will guide the process of shared knowledge. Managers must assess the creativity embedded in these qualitative reductions but often it is forgotten.

Shared knowledge tends to be confined within specific areas of specialization so the ones that can be described as "interdisciplinary areas" may become scarce. The term "interdisciplinary areas" means researchers interact with other researchers beyond their own disciplinary fields. However, subjects that are rarely exchanged between different fields, but that need to be pursued in a cooperative fashion nevertheless, tend to be ignored. The automobile industry in Japan is a typical example. While American and European researchers in sociology in particular have pointed out, among other things, the scarcity of female employees found in the manufacturing sites of Japanese automobile makers, Japanese researchers focus on the competitiveness of automobile makers through product development and improvement activities. It cannot be said that these makers in Japan have taken the critique to heart to engender female product development managers and set a target to make improvements in this regard.[25]

The honing of shared knowledge cannot respond to complex problems that a particular field of expertise is unable to resolve, even when they are about to become an immediate social issue. In the case of automobiles, there are the issues of traffic jams, acid rain and CO_2 emissions. Long-term issues, such as the impending ageing society, the aim to break away from dependence on fossil fuels, and the aim to reduce CO_2 emissions, persist in Japan. These are accompanied by economic problems, including the accumulation of government debt and the maintenance of the social insurance system. Although the latter two problems mentioned are economy-related, no one believes that economists are the ones who would resolve them, since the problem itself is not due to only economic factors. Consequently, an approach to creating new knowledge that crosses over borders of specialties, namely a method for creating symbiotic knowledge, is in demand. Creation of symbiotic knowledge will be discussed in the next chapter.

4 IMPLICATIONS OF SHARED KNOWLEDGE MANAGEMENT

Allied Strategy as an International Management Strategy

The creation of shared knowledge is an expertise of Japanese manufacturers.[26] Many companies have actively grappled with small group activities and suggestion systems. These companies include world-leading giants as well as small-to-medium companies, which are almost unknown, but nevertheless have a sincere attitude toward exploring "*Monozukuri* (manufacturing)". Big-name enterprises build plants abroad and introduce small group activities and suggestion systems in their operation as a multinational company, contributing to technology transfer to the local economies. Japanese companies must continuously expand their strengths as "thinking organizations" in the future. I would like to summarize in the following the method to achieve that end.

The first step is to build a system in which managers can continually learn from the members of the organization. If managers assign tasks to members, the flow of knowledge would stay unidirectional. A manager is by no means versatile in terms of specialized knowledge, and besides, knowhow in the field evolves on a day-to-day basis. Managers can continue learning through small group activities and having a dialogue with those at the work front. On-site dialogues tend to lapse into becoming a means for communicating complaints on everyday activities, instead of serving as a means for building productive knowledge. While it is not meaningless to facilitate smooth communication by listening to the complaints of employees, it does not serve the objective of knowledge creation. To develop shared knowledge from the work front, organizing a taskforce for individual issues is effective. Employees must also take part in a system in which they can continue learning from their fellow workers.

The second step is to build an information feedback system. The flow of information must be designed so that feedback from clients to sales representatives, feedback from sales representatives to developers, feedback from production sites to development and design sections, and feedback from accounting to budget outlays can take place. The scheme must allow for complaints from clients to be conveyed to product development managers as feedback.

The third step is to set a place for presentations that convey problems discovered by a group of employees and the solutions they intend to attempt. Many manufacturers have already introduced quality circle presentation sessions, but only a few similar attempts have been made in industries that deal with service and knowledge. Even if it is the case that the problems are not difficult to quantify, it is also possible that managers may not be recognizing the importance of motivating group-based problem-solving. Management should employ those who are adept at making discoveries, rather than those who are adept at remembering things. The ability to set problems and resolve them is what is needed in the creation of shared knowledge. Individuals who excel in handling mass-produced information by providing fill-in-the-blank type solutions through memorization may not be enthusiastic about discovering problems and resolving them. Exercises for improving the ability to discover problems should be incorporated into in-company training programmes. Furthermore, individuals talented in such activities should be provided with a place where they can speak freely.

The fourth step is that there are fewer people who can solve problems than those who can discover them. The employee should be promoted to a managerial position if they have proved themselves as having the ability to solve discovered problems and specifically acted on them. A manager is, fundamentally, a person who rejuvenates the organization to ensure such activities be carried out. There are those employees who, despite having discovered a problem and despite potentially possessing the power to resolve it, choose not to do so because the level of their commitment to the organization is low. The presence of such people suggests that personnel treatment within the organization has been affected by inertia from the past.

The fifth and last step is that a manager of shared knowledge should be able to clearly prioritize among numerous problems. Long-term issues such as R&D, personnel development, earning credibility from clients, employees and shareholders must be balanced with issues concerning personnel development, R&D and short-term issues that concern regular operations. Even though everyday routine operations consist of inconspicuous tasks and low-key operations, they comprise the essential base of forming an organization for the creation of shared knowledge.

In summary, to create a "thinking organization" you need to develop "acting people". As a manager, you need to treat them appropriately with backup from the other managers. The examples in this chapter focused on cases involving "production", but the importance of a "thinking organization" and "acting people" in service management should also be recognized. Not very many would oppose the idea that service industries, such as finance, insurance, securities, retail and wholesale, logistics and public affairs could improve convenience for clients by enhancing quality and by improving productivity. This could be done when managers in service industries emulate an internationally competitive manufacturing industry endowed with shared knowledge.

NOTES

1. See Lee and Roth (2007). They also quote Engelstrom (2001) in the context of pointing out the magnitude of "learning by expanding". I referred to the study in Horaguchi (2008d), which discusses learning solutions for seminars held by departments of the university the author serves. As written in this book, what I gained together with students through these seminars may have been one form of shared knowledge.
2. China, Thailand and Indonesia fall into this category. Regarding the influence of the ASEAN Free Trade Zone, see Horaguchi and Shimokawa (2002).
3. The subtitle of Chapter 10 of Clark and Fujimoto's work (1991), which compared car product developments that took place in Japan, the United States and Europe, is also "Parts and the Whole". It may be that certain perceptions come to be shared in common among researchers who make close observations of the Toyota manufacturing system.
4. The author visited and observed car assembling plants located in Japan, Korea, Taiwan, China, the Philippines, Thailand, Indonesia, Malaysia, Australia, the USA, Germany and Sweden. In south-east Asia, the plants were those of Japanese makers, such as Toyota, Nissan and Mitsubishi Motors, but elsewhere, the author observed plants of local manufacturers. In Korea, the plants were those of Daewoo, in China, Changchun Train, in the USA, Pontiac, in Germany, Volkswagen, Daimler, BMW, Porsche and Audi, and in Sweden, Volvo. In Japanese car companies, kaizen (improvement activities) were carried out more or less without exception. Regarding findings on the auto industries of the Philippines, Thailand, the USA, France, the Netherlands and Sweden, refer to Horaguchi (1991, 2000, 2003).
5. This fact is based on the plant tours on 28 September 2007 and on 6 February 2008 to Central Motor of the Toyota group. Visits to Toyota Motor Corporation's Motomachi plant were made on 28 June 2005, 8 March 2006 and 16 March 2007.
6. There is something to note here regarding the research methods applied by the Japan HR Association. Since the format of their survey was designed to obtain answers on a voluntary basis, it is thought that there are cases of corporations or other business establishments (factories) with a large number of suggestions who did not respond.
7. Clark and Fujimoto (1991) point out that the quality circle (QC) is normally effective for carrying out continual improvements, but it proves to be problematic in that it turns out to be a slow way of decision-making for realizing ramp-ups, which is the production of new products at times of emergencies, such as during war time. In the case of Japan, when dealing with problems, we see the product line's foreman mobilizing workers, technicians and engineers. In contrast, in the case of Europe and America, it is said that the engineer plays a key role in dealing with the implementation of a ramp-up (pp. 202–3).
8. The word "suggestion" can be construed as another way to contribute to "an activity of managing an enterprise". If the marketplace accepts the suggestion of a company, the company can then sell the commodity or service it has suggested. In terms of such an understanding, the marketplace on the whole determines the course of action collective knowledge takes. The market system dictates the standard of collective knowledge within the range of a certain cultural association, or in other words, typically within

the domain of a certain country. In the course of action collective knowledge takes, there are two aspects that co-exist with each other. One is the aspect similar to self-organization, which determines the characteristics of the market system, and the other is the aspect of emergence, which sees the course of action that self-organized institutional knowledge takes being determined by a pre-existing market system. Financial markets and their new products are seen as examples of this. These aspects of common knowledge are to be discussed in Chapter 6.

9. In history lessons taught to Japanese primary schoolchildren, there is an account of the "Meyasubako", or complaints box, installed in the Edo era by Yoshimune Tokugawa, the eighth general of the Tokugawa Shogunate in the eighteenth century. The creation of the five-person system as a method of rural-community governance also took place in the Edo era. It is tempting to conclude that small group activities and suggestion systems seen in the production fields of manufacturing industry have been applied as methods that are deeply etched in the Japanese psyche. However, the two may have absolutely nothing to do with each other. The complaints box in the Edo era may have been a ruler's technique to encourage the disclosure of information, while the five-person system may have been a mutual monitoring system designed to prevent desertion. We cannot yet conclude historical roots on small group activities at this stage.

10. Takekawa (2001) is a case study that investigates the association between small group activity and the suggestion system. For example, she categorizes the cash rewards for suggestions of auto maker, Company C, made in 2000 from the best suggestion (300 000 yen), to the 9th grade (1500 yen), and the 10th grade (0 yen), and writes that the QC circle activity and the achievement of a suggestion become subject to merit rating.

11. The small group activity has not become the de facto standard for manufacturing industries around the world. To learn about the results of observing Malaysian companies in the manufacturing industry, see Horaguchi (2001b).

12. Nikkei Microdevices/Nikkei Electronics (2005), pp. 12–13.

13. It is based on Figure 3 which was found in Nikkei Microdevices/Nikkei Electronics (2005), p. 28.

14. The Department of Patent Distribution Promotions (http://www.ryutu.ncipi.go.jp/about/index.html) in the Kenshukan of the Independent Administrative Agency of Industrial Property Information (http://www.ncipi.go.jp/) creates "patent distribution support charts". Regarding MEMS, two "patent distribution support charts" are made: one in 2002 (Heisei year 14) and the other in 2004 (Heisei year 16). See http://www.ryutu.ncipi.go.jp/chart/H16/kikai07/frame.htm.

15. In September 2005, NGK Insulators Ltd in Japan developed the piezoelectric micro-actuator, a device that raises the level of the positioning accuracy of the magnetic head of the hard disk drive (HDD). It succeeded as the world's first wooden slider drive model put into practical use. This product was mass-produced for and shipped to magnetic head manufacturers and is said to be slated for installation in HDDs that major American HDD makers are planning to release. These HDDs would have a 500GB capacity, which was the maximum capacity in the industry. This was based on interviews conducted on 27 July 2004 with the head and chief scientists of the central laboratory of the research and development head office of the headquarters of NGK Insulators. Along with the records of the NGK Insulators interviews, the research records were compiled in the works of Horaguchi, Yaginuma, Matsushima, Kim, Konno, Amano, Yukimoto and Lee (2007).

16. Based on interviews conducted on 7 September 2004 with the vice president and the manager of design engineering of Analog Devices. Details are compiled in Horaguchi, Amano, Kim, Konno, and Yaginuma (2005b).

17. Nikkei Microdevices/Nikkei Electronics (2005), pp. 147–69.

18. Based on Nikkei Microdevices/Nikkei Electronics (2005), pp. 196–7.

19. Based on interviews conducted on 17 June 2005 with members of the Micromachining Group of the Vanguard Device Institute of the Technology Headquarters of OMRON.

20. I explained in detail the theory of knowledge collaboration in Horaguchi (2008a). This

article explored that some companies achieve a prominent output even though they carry out activities under homogenous conditions. By allowing joint use of knowledge, some companies emerge so that they are able to show prominent output levels.

21. In Mintzberg (1973), the view on knowledge management is not explicit.

22. It is said that the managers of a German automobile manufacturer downplayed the development by Toyota of the hybrid engine. Rather than due to technical difficulty, it is said to have been due to their thinking on development and in-house power politics. More importance was attached to the criterion of mileage efficiency gained from the engine itself than the mileage gained by hybrid technology, or combining the engine with the battery. In particular, this criterion means savings in fuel costs gained by the use of a diesel engine. Such a decision made in companies is sometimes labeled as a "political decision". This is because when the correct answer is unforeseeable while speculating about the future, the decision is adopted as an opinion supported by a majority of in-house managers.

23. Such a terminology is called an oxymoron. "Open secrets" also indicates such usage, and it is a literary expression rather than a scientific one.

24. There is an anecdote of a large swarm of ants in the African continent. These ants continued to circle around a gigantic anthill for one week and consequently starved to death. If the direction the executive shows is wrong, a big business can also collapse. The American investment bank, Lehman Brothers, failed in September 2008 and I wonder if the management policy to continue searching for opportunities to invest in speculative money was a sustainable vision. The responsibility for the failure of the investment bank may lie with the management who did not uphold the managerial goal of supporting the continuous development of companies that became targets for investment.

25. The practice of having a preponderance of female tellers in Japanese banks is also bizarre, but these facts are seldom pointed out.

26. This author was not able to obtain data on the actual situation of small group activities and on the number of suggestion systems found in the American manufacturing industry. If you take a survey on Japanese-affiliated companies that entered the USA, you might be able to confirm that they have introduced, to a considerable degree, small group activities. However, to contrast with the data found in this chapter, it would be necessary to acquire data related to joint venture companies operating with American capital.

4.   Symbiotic knowledge

1   PRINCIPLES

The Need to Add New Dimensions

Symbiotic knowledge is knowledge derived from the attempt to solve problems by combining knowledge of different dimensions. Knowledge dimension is defined by limitations specialists have in understanding theories. While knowledge of varying fields varies in degree, I would like to refer to their variation as dimensions of knowledge. There are cases where new products are created while possessing a high level of specialty, and by synthesizing knowledge of completely different types. In some instances, problems which are considered impossible may be resolved. Conjugate strategy is a domain to connect different dimensions of knowledge in collective strategies.[1]

New creation becomes possible by combining knowledge of varying dimensions. For instance, it is difficult for a medical expert to understand mechanical engineering, and it is difficult for a literary expert to organize a molecular-biological experiment. This is because each area of specialized talent has invested the length of time to establish the level of specialty. No matter how superior the general ability of the person in question may be, in order to gain a high level of specialty, they require a long time to tackle specific problems.

The need to connect knowledge of different dimensions to one another arises from the fact that a problem to be solved often arises from complex factors, and what should be a solution remains too broad for application. Symbiotic knowledge is created in the process of dealing with problems whose solutions are difficult for particular problem-solvers to identify at the outset. For example, new product development may be achieved by juxtaposing medicine with engineering, and a copywriter or a literary expert may come up with a slogan for marketing that reflects a cosmetic product making use of the technology of molecular biology. Knowledge that arises in such a way is what I refer to in this chapter as symbiotic knowledge.

Responding to Uncertainty

In the discipline of economics, uncertainty is defined as "a problem whose solution is difficult to identify ahead of time". Uncertainty is a concept that differs from risk, in which the probability distribution is known. For example, like casualty insurance for automobiles, you can calculate the probability of the occurrence of a specific event, which in this case is a car accident. This is what is called a risk. However, uncertainty is like "a dish using three eggs and seasonings": there is a problem in defining what specifically is going to be made. There are cases when you will make not only dishes that have names such as scrambled egg, boiled egg or fried egg, but also new, unnamed dishes. In Japanese cuisine you can find *Chawanmushi* (hot egg pudding with salty ingredient) and *Datemaki* (baked egg roll) as examples of egg dishes. To discover solutions that are impossible to define beforehand, you need to take steps to respond to uncertainty.

Knight (1921) advocated that the role of the entrepreneur was to respond to uncertainty. However, entrepreneurs are not the only people who deal with uncertainty. There are people who deal with it as a group. What is furthermore important is the fact that there are also people who create such groups. You can refer to this activity as "producing". For example, consider a case to newly create "a dish that uses three eggs and some seasoning". If there is a person who creates a chance where a cook of Japanese cuisine and a chef of Italian cuisine can cooperate with each other, then that person is a producer of an opportunity to give rise to symbiotic knowledge.

The Domain Connection

A corporation has its own particular strategy domain. Entrepreneurs define their domain of operation in their mission statement of what the company was established to do. For them, it is self-evident to identify the types of activities from which they obtain their profit. The companies will not be allowed to continue if there are no executives who are thoroughly informed about these activities. This fact is equivalent to the fact that experts of the medical and literary professions have their own domains of research.

Just as shared knowledge stands on the basis of the division of labour within a company, symbiotic knowledge stands on the basis of the division of labour found within a society. The company uses the societal division of labour, and continues to exist as an organization through its specialization within this division of labour. Assuming that society has achieved sophistication of specialized knowledge, symbiotic knowledge can be created by its reintegration. In some cases, companies with a profit motive become the centre of reintegration and exert a centrifugal force, while again in other cases, government or local autonomous bodies may play such a role. In the latter case, there are cases where the purpose concerns the sustainability of the human environment. This purpose is to respond to appropriate global environmental problems by creating employment through the promotion of technological developments and corporate activities.

2   CASE EXAMPLE

The Character of "The Knowledge Cluster Initiative"

"The Knowledge Cluster Initiative" run by the Ministry of Education, Culture, Sports, Science and Technology (MEXT) was carried out in 12 local communities in 2002.[2] In 2003, it was carried out in three more communities, and in 2004 in another three. Each area carried out the project under a five-year plan. Specifically, the policy aimed to give rise to intelligent clusters, which were agglomerations of organizations for harnessing internationally competitive technological innovation. To that end, the policy assisted by providing an annual sum of around 500 million yen per local community, or about 2500 million yen for a five-year period. The total amount of subsidies of 18 local communities became about 45 billion yen. The policy, in effect, accomplished the following tasks: (1) installation of the headquarters of an intelligent cluster, (2) placement of science and technology coordinators, employment of advisors such as patent attorneys, (3) conducting industry–academia–government joint research, (4) acquisition of patents through industry–university research collaborations, (5) establishment of forums for the presentation of research results.[3] From 2007, phase 2 began, and saw the designation of six local communities. In 2008, three more local communities were designated, raising the total to nine. The annual budget allocated for them was 7500 million yen.

   This policy differs from an industrial policy, which protects or supports and fosters specific industries. The policy for generating intelligent clusters is twofold – one is the science and technology policy and the other is the regional promotional policy.[4] Since the university plays a pivotal role in providing subsidies, the Knowledge Cluster Initiative can be regarded as part of a science and technology policy. On the other hand, since existing agglomerated localities such as university towns found in Tokyo and Tsukuba have not been included among the designated 18 localities, the policy has an aspect of being a local city-led promotion of regional localities. So, in effect, what is being pursued is a science and technology promotion that excludes the Tokyo metropolitan area.[5]

The phrase the Knowledge Cluster Initiative includes the word "cluster". While I shall examine in detail in Chapter 5 the significance of the cluster, for now, it will suffice to say that the relevance of "cluster" to the Knowledge Cluster Initiative is unclear. Because it is uncertain whether a cluster will be formed by carrying out the Knowledge Cluster Initiative, there has been no substantial assessment of this matter. It is also not clear whether the method adopted in the Knowledge Cluster Initiative is effective in light of the objective of generating clusters. The reasons for this are summarized as follows.

Figure 4.1 is the schematization of the policy scheme of the Knowledge Cluster Initiative. By comparing this with Figure 4.2, which shows a schematization of the process of an industrial-cluster formation, the difference between centripetal force and centrifugal force becomes clear. The method

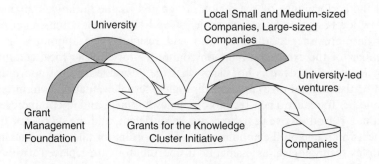

Figure 4.1   Structural outline of the attraction of "The Knowledge Cluster Initiative"

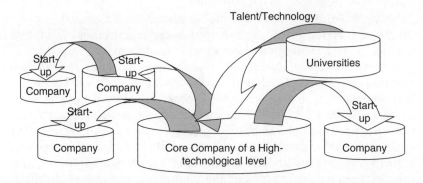

Figure 4.2   Structural outline of spinoffs in a cluster

adopted for promoting the Knowledge Cluster Initiative is driven by a centripetal force realized through providing subsidies. Without an annual subsidy of 500 million yen per year, it would be impossible to gather participants. As a condition for providing subsidies, the government demands collaboration between an industrial firm and a university. If you examine the configuration of an assigned project, it appears that support from the MEXT is biased in favour of corporate bodies and government-run universities of Japan.

Cluster formations in America's Silicon Valley have a centrifugal force. In other words, there are core companies such as Fairchild and Hewlett-Packard generating many entrepreneurs, and spinoffs were realized on the basis of the high level of knowledge such companies produced in their employees. The social system supporting this process characterizes the formation of industrial clusters.[6]

In the case of the Knowledge Cluster Initiative in its five-year plan, the coordinator in the Kyoto region, for example, resigned in the second year, and the performance of the region designated by the initiative remained at low levels, with its research projects rarely becoming commercialized. Furthermore, the coordinator who had resigned was appointed as a member for the external evaluation committee for another local community. In other words, it is not clear what the desirable form of coordination or the method of evaluation through external evaluation committees should be. To realize a new technological development and its commercialization, a period of five years may not be sufficient, and the success of the project will hinge on the appointment of a coordinator talented in making complex technological assessments. If coordinators are replaced within a span of only a few years, the research and development expenses incurred may merely be spent on purchasing machines and equipment used to run tests and to carry out measurements. Such spending will not easily lead to new, creative technological developments.

From 2003 through 2009, the author visited the designated area for the phase 1 period of the Knowledge Cluster Initiative and conducted research by interviewing in corporations (foundations and business corporations), university laboratories, university-led ventures and start-up venture projects considered as the main candidates for receiving grants. The summary of these interviews appears in Appendix Table 1 of Horaguchi (2009b). In terms of social science, these business communities are precious samples to be observed. While they vary in terms of the initial conditions, such as the scale of cities and the number of universities participating, they are key case examples that help us monitor the relationships between innovation policies and innovation management. In effect, monitoring them is tantamount to observing 18 eggs in an incubator, and in a sense they offer the opportunity to witness a certain type of social experiment set in motion.

The general description of the questionnaire survey appears in Horaguchi (2007a). A statistical analysis of a questionnaire survey given to the first-phase coordinators appears in Horaguchi (2008b). In the course of compiling the data for this chapter, I became aware of a few issues shared in common among the respondents, such as the execution of the annual budget, the selection and evaluation of the project, the difficulty of research and development that foresees a product development referred to as "exit" and the paucity of talented staff who could undertake university-led ventures. Among the cases observed, the Toyama/Takaoka district appeared to have brought about results that were the most in line with the policy objectives of the Knowledge Cluster Initiative.

The Biochip Development Process in the Toyama District[7]

When the Toyama Biomedical Cluster of the Toyama and Takaoka district was planned, Professor Muraguchi, who was at the time lecturing at the Toyama Medical Pharmaceutical University, had a discussion with Mr Yasuo Nannichi, who was to become the deputy general manager and head of business integration of the local Knowledge Cluster Initiative. They discussed what types of seeds were available.[8] With Mr Nannichi as a coordinator, Professor Eiichi Tamiya, who was teaching a graduate course at the time at the Japan Advanced Institute of Science and Technology in Ishikawa prefecture, joined the fold, and in 2002, they discussed ideas of new businesses that could start in Toyama.[9]

While the Knowledge Cluster Initiative was started with 12 local communities in 2002, within one year the programme had additionally designated six local communities as preliminary starting projects, and Toyama was one of these. Therefore, there was a period when Toyama was designated for a test run of the Knowledge Cluster Initiative, and in that year, a budget of 100 million yen was expended. Since the three communities, Toyama, Nagoya and Tokushima, started as trial areas after a one-year delay in 2003, the project period of the first phase finished in these places in 2007. Three other areas among six were Gifu, Ishikawa and Ube, which became operational in 2004 under the policy.

In the Knowledge Cluster Initiative, each cluster is named. The cluster in the Toyama and Takaoka district is named "The Toyama Biomedical Cluster". As of 2006, the following research projects were set in motion: (1) the development of cell chips, (2) the creation of a database via the analysis of the protein, proteome, to retain data related to people on whom the Chinese medicine, *Keishiburyougan*, works and on people on whom the same medicine does not work,[10] (3) the development of a kit for testing the presence of urinary diseases, including phenylketonuria,[11] and (4) the realization of the high performance of tea catechin through oxidizing enzymes.[12]

What (2), (3) and (4) research projects share in common is their adoption of a search-and-quest approach. In other words, although the aims of their research – namely the detection of proteins that become diabetic markers, the artificial generation of enzymes that become markers of urinary diseases, and the synthesis of catechin – are clear, the way they arrive at their aim is through a search approach, which requires the execution of trial and error procedures. It may be said that this is a project that adds substantial weight to the term "science" found in the expression "science and technology".

Among such multiple projects, in this chapter, I focus on project number (1), the cell-chip development project. There are three reasons for doing so. Firstly, this development was the most enthusiastically talked-about topic among the people interviewed at the Toyama Biomedical Cluster. Secondly, this project was driven by collaboration between university laboratories and multiple centres of expertise, such as the public technology centre, and corporations. Finally, the project had given rise to university-led ventures. In other words, this is a typical case example that lived up to the expectations of the expression "the Knowledge Cluster Initiative" by indeed seeing the union of "science and technology" take place.

The Toyama Biomedical Cluster, which served as the cornerstone for the Knowledge Cluster Initiative, began by having the governor of Toyama as its headquarters chief. This is an example that saw the establishment of a university-led venture (under the company name SC World) through the collaboration between the Research Department of Medicine and Pharmaceutical Studies of the Graduate School of Toyama University, the Research Department of Science and Technology Studies of the Graduate School of Toyama University, the Technology Centre of Toyama prefecture, the local companies, Sugino Machine and Richell, and coordinators (see Figure 4.3). The scale of the budget for the Knowledge Cluster Initiative is 2500 million yen for a five-year period, and in the Toyama Biomedical Cluster, there are three science and technology coordinators.

University of Toyama and Toyama Industrial Technology Centre

The Muraguchi Laboratory, to which the research teams of Professor Atsushi Muraguchi and Associate Professor Hiroyuki Kishi of the University of Toyama Graduate School of Medicine and Pharmaceutical

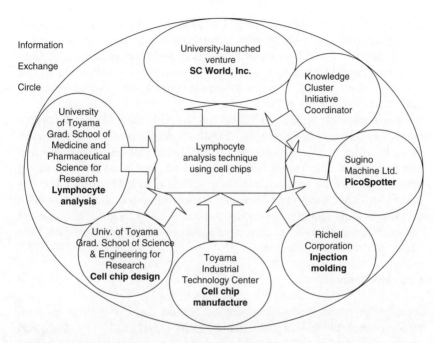

Figure 4.3   Creation of university-launched venture

Science belong, consists of ten members and conducts research on anti-body gene analysis and lymphocyte analysis.[13] The laboratory's research results are published in the academic journals *Journal of Immunology* and *Blood*, and the university has applied for patents concerning analysis methods. Previously, as analysis involved the use of single cells it was per-formed by microscopy. However, the use of cell chips makes it possible to obtain data from hundreds of thousands of cells at a time. Cell chips have 250 000 micro-wells (apertures) per square centimetre and contain one cell per micro-well. Lymphocyte analysis involves the tracking of phosphate in the cells using calcium to show a signal. As it is possible to observe cell propagation and antibody secretion using the same method, the expression of new proteins on cell surfaces can also be observed. Research on protein expression and secretion and the function of cytokines in the brain using today's chips has also begun.

In the screening of cells that react specifically with antigens associ-ated with infectious diseases, B lymphocytes are placed in cell chips and stimulated with antibodies, and cells that have reacted are removed. Only a few cells that can produce antibodies occur among the 250 000 cells on a cell chip, and it is difficult to locate cells that occur in such a small ratio using conventional methods. The detection of antigen-specific cells can be applied in diagnosis and, if software development progresses, it can be used in the diagnosis of illnesses including tuberculosis, hepatitis, influenza and rheumatism. As of 2006, antibodies obtained in this way have been cloned, injected into mice bearing human liver cells and evaluated.

Coordinator Mr Kihachiro Tohbo was formerly the director of Toyama Industrial Technology Centre. Dr Satoshi Fujiki[14] was at the time of interview the chief of the institute in Toyama Industrial Technology Centre, Mechanics and Electronics Research Institute, and joint research in the cell-chip project advanced due to his association with Mr Tohbo. For this reason, both Mr Tohbo and Dr Fujiki assumed that cell-chip development was successfully completed in a few months.[15] Chip research had reached the third generation of the chip development when the author visited the site in 2006.

Cell-chip Hardware

At his laboratory, Professor Masayasu Suzuki had carried out research into biosensors.[16] It is a field that combines the areas of biology and engineering, and in these past 20 years, he has been covering the micro-miniaturization and integration of biosensors. Professor Suzuki moved to Toyama University in 2000, and at that time participated in a research project involving cell chips, prior to taking part in the Knowledge Cluster Initiative. He began the research based on his experience in the micro-miniaturization and integration of biosensors.

In the Toyama Biomedical Cluster project, Professor Suzuki was in charge of work related to immune cell chips and devices. It was possible to create simple chips in the labs of Suzuki Laboratory. The actual silicon processing was entrusted to the technology centre of Toyama prefecture. As for the design, Professor Suzuki and his research group made a well (a hole) large enough to accommodate the size of a single cell, placing considerable weight on incorporating measurement functions. They had lined up these resins called PDMS (polydimethylsiloxane), or in other words, these 10 micron holes made of a type of silicone rubber, and they inserted cells in there. At the bottom of a hole, they attached a sensor.

Richell contributed by making superior chips through its technology of injection moulding. The material for which a patent was acquired was a resin that had an additive to polypropylene. At Richell, they had been manufacturing tableware, buckets, garden supplies and casings for mobile phones, all out of polypropylene. Creating minute chips with resins had been a technological theme over the past several years. Professor Suzuki and his research group did not succeed in making the superior chip because they carried out the research using acrylic-based resins. Richell succeeded with soft resins, however. In the technology centre of Toyama prefecture, there are people who are familiar with materials, and the patent was applied prior to the beginning of the Knowledge Cluster Initiative. A total of three patents were acquired by the Toyama Biomedical Cluster project.

When examining a protein with a biosensor, Professor Suzuki and his research group coupled a protein molecule for measurement on the surface of a metallic thin film that coupled an antibody molecule via a chemical reagent at the bottom, and observed using a two-dimensional surface plasmon resonance (SPR) sensor. In the case of sensor boards for measuring cellular activity, they put cells in and measured the changes in fluorescence intensity. There was no need to add anything to the sensors. The placing of each cell, one by one, was prescribed by the size of the holes. The size approached the size of a cell as much as possible, and since they also had a ceiling for the depth of the wells on the chip, those cells that were too big fell out of the wells. The sizes of the cells were spread apart. In the case of B-lymphocytes, the size was on average 7 micron. Professor Suzuki has seen a large number of cells and noticed that B-lymphocytes had a tidy form and their sizes did not vary that much. Each of them was nearly the same.

The practice of placing a single cell in a well and then taking it out has not yet reached a level whereby anyone can do it easily. Such a practice involves the act of pouring. Depending on how you combine with the structure of a chip, though, the technologies of inserting cells vary. If the quantity of cells is large, it is managed by pouring. Since the sample quantity becomes limited when extracting cells out of a person's blood, one cannot insert cells by pouring. So this was a technical problem to be solved. While electrophoresis was suggested, a microarray of 10 micron made it difficult. Second-generation cell chips adopted a method that draws cells out by force.

The recollection of cells from the cell chip went unexpectedly well.[17] It was accomplished by using a device for absorption. Specifically, this device was one that applied and remodelled the DNA spot machine developed by Sugino Machine Ltd, a machine tool manufacturer based in Toyama prefecture. Although the cells could have been absorbed by applying capillary action, it became necessary to draw with a weak force when the viscosity of the solution rises. While it was a challenge to precisely position them, Sugino Machine succeeded. It adopted the method of absorbing with a nozzle made of artificial ruby. The development supervisor at Sugino Machine went to great lengths. The postgrad in charge at the Suzuki

Laboratory was in charge for three years, and this person was finally able to succeed in the final year. To take over this task was hard, and it seemed as though one good result was obtained for every two attempts made by two different people in charge.

Sugino Machine Ltd and Precision Positioning Technology

Sugino Machine Ltd[18] manufactures drilling tools, high-pressure pumps, high-pressure cleaning equipment, automated drilling units, small machining centres and nuclear power plant maintenance equipment. The company is capitalized at about 230 million yen, has annual sales of 18 900 million yen, and employs 673 people as of March 2006.[19] The company employs more than 40 development personnel: the Research and Development Division has a staff of 14, and each of the six business divisions has an applied development team consisting of 5 members. The company was founded in 1936 in Osaka City as a specialty production shop for pneumatic and hydraulic tube cleaners.

Sugino Machine has been carrying out research on materials, and has been developing a device called the starburst system, a super wet-process atomizing unit. Applying high-pressure techniques, this is a mechanism that makes crude materials (ultra-fine particles) collide with each other and break up into smaller pieces. The fields of application include fuel batteries, capacitors and cosmetics. In addition, the technology is also applied for materials, such as electron-element condensers. Even major domestic cosmetics makers are showing interest and are considering potential applications in the area of cosmetics manufacturing. While powder production at the nano level is carried out through another method, the fine particles immediately congeal and end up becoming large particles. While the aim is to loosen highly coherent materials, this is considerably difficult to accomplish. The technology is also used for the minimization of material used in capacitors. Until around 2006, processing was achieved with a roller mill. While the roller mill technology has been carried out in Europe and the USA for a long time, there have been no companies that have applied the high-pressure technique.

Sugino Machine had previously engaged in a regional project regarding the Medical Bio-cluster Project jointly with Toyama prefecture, and due to that relationship, it received a request to participate in the Knowledge Cluster Initiative. In accordance with the request, the company has developed a machine called "PicoSpotter" for biochip analysis apparatus, which is to check a reaction of lymphocyte in the micro-well and some other types of analysis apparatus for PCR (polymerase chain reaction).

Around 30 patent applications are filed on average every year. While cluster operations involve joint patents, basically many of them are Sugino Machine's own ones. It produces spa-roll related items, drilling units, tapping machines, water jets and high-pressure washers. Sugino Machine manages research and development relevant to products of operating divisions. It received commendation from the Toyama Invention Society in 2006 with regard to the invention of the drilling unit. This is a mere example of proving its technology level.

The company received a request from Professor Eiichi Tamiya of the Japan Advanced Institute of Science and Technology of Ishikawa prefecture and developed the "PicoSpotter" and micro-well reaction apparatus jointly with Professor Tamiya. The PicoSpotter was also used by Professor Masayasu Suzuki of the University of Toyama. Although the exact development cost was unknown to the author, it was mentioned that two engineers spent two years developing the apparatuses: one was in charge of software development and the other was a mechanical engineer. The materials cost of the PicoSpotter was about 10 million yen. If the cost of parts discarded at the trial-and-error stage is included, the amount would be rather substantial.

With respect to the connection between the apparatuses and Sugino Machine's technologies, nozzle technologies account for half of the development effort. As the PicoSpotter requires accurate positioning, it is closely connected with technologies relating to small machining centres. The company has conducted research in fluid technologies for many years. The PicoSpotter mechanism involves suction using capillary action by artificial ruby nozzles. The narrower the capillary tube, the greater the suction. Control is exercised to prevent excessive suction due to pressure and to ensure that an appropriate quantity of liquid can be dripped. Nozzles are cleaned using ultrasonic waves. The company has adopted a similar structure for "Cellporter", an automated cell recovery apparatus. The mechanism for dropping cells one by one uses the same principle as that used in coin-counting machines. One issue was improving the dispensing injection rate of lymphocyte: it proved difficult to exceed 50 per cent. There are also issues with the surface condition of the chips themselves, and the company has devised a surface treatment method. Currently, injection rates of about 60–70 per cent have been achieved.

The Cellporter was developed in 2005. Although the technologies were nearly perfected in 2005, work to complete the product and to respond to new needs has extended into 2006. It has not yet reached the level of commercialization or the generation of profits. Prior to the Knowledge Cluster Initiative project, the company had nearly no exchanges with professors at universities in Toyama prefecture. However, it has developed networks since participating in the project.

Richell Corporation and Development of Resin Cell Chip[20]

Richell Corporation was founded in 1956 as a manufacturer of children's eating utensils from urea resin. The moulding technique at the time was not injection moulding, but compression moulding. Richell acquired from NHK (Nihon Housou Kyoukai, Japan Broadcasting Corporation) the copyright to the popular TV program BOO-FOO-WOO, a puppet show in the 1960s, and enjoyed a hit product by printing images from the programme on children's rice bowls. The company succeeded in expanding its sales channels nationwide and subsequently came to sell nursing care products, pet products and other products through home centres and garden centres. Although sales of housewares previously exceeded 15 billion yen during the 1990s, they have fallen to about 8 billion yen in the 2000s. The company also manufactures mobile phone casings and has sales of about 4 billion yen from this business. Total sales in fiscal 2006 were about 12 billion yen.

In 2006, Richell manufactures housewares at three factories – the headquarters factory (Mizuhashi Factory), the Ohsawano Factory in Toyama, Japan, and the Dongguan Factory in China – and also uses OEM manufacturing overseas. The company manufactures about 1000 items and has a domestic manufacturing rate of 55 per cent. It operates Richell USA Inc., in Dallas, Texas, as a distributor of home and pet products. Richell manufactures mobile telephone casings at the Kamiichi Factory in Toyama prefecture. The company built the factory as a mould manufacturing plant in 1993 and produces nearly all the moulds used for casing manufacture in-house. The company sources nearly all the moulds from external suppliers. These moulds are used for manufacturing housewares.

On the basis of microchip production technology proven through participation in the Knowledge Cluster Initiative project, the company aims to establish a microchip business involving precision moulding. The company has the technology to manufacturer precision moulds (precision of 1/100 of a millimetre or less) to support the business and has machine tools that make possible high-precision processing.

Despatch of Researchers to the Industrial Technology Centre

What prompted Richell's involvement in Toyama Medical Bio-cluster was the despatch of researchers to Toyama prefecture's Industrial Technology Centre. The company had not participated at all in "the Regional Concentration Project" prior to the Knowledge Cluster Initiative project or other projects. It had nearly no ties with universities, and lacked even the experience of involvement with the Ministry of Economy, Trade and Industry (METI) or MEXT-subsidized projects.

Richell was then trying to develop new food containers similar to Tupperware that were suitable for refrigeration, freezing and microwave warming. The company engaged in research and development of materials that offer high transparency and heat resistance (130°C or higher). As part of that effort, the company at first despatched one engineer to Toyama prefecture's Industrial Technology Centre and began joint research with centre engineers.

The materials research for new household products failed. The reason was that although Richell achieved the transparency and heat resistance it sought, the surface of the resulting material had numerous minute blemishes that made commercialization difficult. The cause of the blemishes was minute irregular blemishes on the surface of the moulds that were imprinted on the products during moulding. However, this experience of failure was turned to advantage in the Toyama Medical Bio-cluster project. Although the project had been developing a silicon microchip for cell arrangement, the use of silicon entailed several problems, including high cost due to breakability of the expensive needles used for cell collection when they came into contact with the silicon chips, the fact that separated blood does not flow readily, and difficulty in collecting lymphocytes. Consequently, Mr Tohbo, former chairman of Toyama Industrial Technology Centre, who was serving as a coordinator of the Knowledge Cluster Initiative, offered guidance to the researcher despatched from Richell: "Is precision moulding using resin possible?" It occurred to the researcher that it might be possible to take advantage of the characteristic minute irregularities on the surface of resin material, and the researcher conducted a successful experiment. Using resin, which offers high transparency and heat resistance, Richell was able to create micron-sized apertures on the surface of chips and inject cells into the apertures comparatively smoothly. Richell and other companies participate in the Knowledge Cluster Initiative projects at their own expense. Richell installed a clean room with a level of less than 3000 in the Kamiichi Factory. As the Kamiichi Factory manufactures mobile phone casings, the entire factory is a clean room. Nevertheless, the company invested about 30 million yen to install a higher-level clean room. A patent was obtained for a resin composition that has excellent transfer properties.

Richell, Toyama prefecture and University of Toyama jointly own the patent, with respective ownership ratios of 65 per cent, 30 per cent and 5 per cent. Richell has entered into a licence agreement with the prefecture and the university and manufactures and sells the resin composition. Under the agreement, the company pays dividends to the prefecture and the university at fixed allocation ratios in accordance with annual sales. In 2005 Richell paid the prefecture a dividend of merely 344 yen for its sales on the patented resin composition. As the University of Toyama holds a patent concerning the injection of cells to the chip and cell collection, Richell cannot sell the cell chip to customers other than the University of Toyama. As of 2006, the patent has been transferred to SC World, which is described below.

The micro fuel cell field is mentioned as a promising area of application for resin microchips. Richell knows that fuel cell efficiency can be further improved by arranging narrow flow channels to ensure the natural flow of liquid (methanol) and layering the flow channels. The layering technology has already been patented by Richell. Among two types of fuel cells (PEFC, which use hydrogen, and DMFC, which use methanol), the resin microchip can be applied to the latter type. A request has already been received from another university-launched venture, and Richell has manufactured a chip that has six layers of flow channels glued together.

Venture Business Launched from the Cluster

Mr Munehiro Sueoka,[21] President and CEO of SC World, Inc., was formerly General Manager of the Corporate Planning Department of INTEC Inc. He has about 20 years' sales experience and has also engaged in product planning and systems development. Mr Sueoka also has experience in the listing of INTEC Web and Genome Informatics Corporation (hereinafter "IW&G"), the first bio-venture to be listed on the Mothers section of the Tokyo Stock Exchange. Mr Sueoka, who hails from Toyama prefecture, was requested by the chairman of INTEC Inc. and the governor of Toyama prefecture to support the venture, which was an "offer he couldn't refuse". In 2005, he and a group of involved professors voluntarily started SC World, Inc. The company has obtained three basic patents concerning cell chips and has obtained the rights to a series of systems. Professor Muraguchi of the University of Toyama, who initiated the Knowledge Cluster Initiative in Toyama, serves as the company's chairman, and Mr Sueoka, who had been president of IW&G, was named president of SC World.

In July 2005, SC World, Inc. was able to recruit its first clinical trial leader. The company received a METI start-up subsidy of about 45 million yen, rented a room at Toyama Medical and Pharmaceutical University, and in October 2005 opened a laboratory. The company was able to begin experiments at the laboratory around December 2005. It engaged in work to create direct antibodies using cell chips. A prototype of an integrated cell screening system was completed in March 2006. As of July 2007, the company was working to collect antibodies. The company hired a sales representative in April 2006, displayed a panel at the BIO 2006 event in the USA, and exchanged information with companies from about 20 countries. In May 2006, SC World exhibited at the International Bio Expo in Japan. The company's exhibition was so crowded that a large audience was standing in the presentation room. Many companies left their business cards trying to make a contact with SC World. Mr Sueoka had an impression that in the USA, SC World is viewed as a company that can avoid existing patents in the antibody business. Its business and equipment would help obtain new patents concerning antibodies. It would lead to success even for a late entrant in the antibody business in the USA.

SC World, Inc. had not yet recorded sales from the antibody business. The market reaction was that the equipment price of 15 million yen was too high. Mr Sueoka felt that his company must reduce the price to less than 10 million yen. The company has two sales representatives, three including Mr Sueoka himself. The company's activities are system sales, development of the antigen and clinical trial businesses, and antibody acquisition. In June 2005, the company increased its share capital by 150 million yen after a capital injection from a partner. Further, in December 2005, the company obtained a capital injection of 200 million yen from multiple venture capital investors. The company receives OEM supply from Hitachi Software Engineering Co., Ltd, which it has commissioned to produce equipment software. So SC World is an exclusive agent for the software produced by Hitachi Software Engineering Co. SC World, Inc. moved into the University of Toyama's incubation facilities in April 2007.

Summary of the Case

In the business–university–government (BUG) collaboration presented in this chapter, a coordinator played important roles. Mr Tohbo, positioned between a company and a university, conjugated varied sets of expertise and technological capabilities together, and carried out new product developments. This can be considered as a case example in which a conjugate collective strategy was adopted. Due to different sets of expertise and technological capabilities, various dimensions for research and development came to be offered for the integrated cell screening system by SC World.

Under the conjugate collective strategy, the knowledge that supported the developments of the lymphatic analyser and the cell chip can be considered as symbiotic knowledge created by participants. The symbiotic knowledge in this case example was created by combining explicit knowledge of making the lymphatic analyser with the tacit knowledge of the knowhow for producing precision moulding using the resin composition.

Different expertise realized this synthesis through transmission of specifications for the equipment. The specification of fabricating cell chips with 250 000 holes in a 1-centimetre corner was given as explicit knowledge, and a search was conducted for the tacit knowledge that would allow the carrying out of a surface treatment that aimed at a higher dispensation rate, while meeting the said specification.

The case example in this chapter also suggests that it would prove effective to increase participants endowed with various technical competencies for the purpose of creating symbiotic knowledge. To this end, there are two methods. The first is the solicitation and sorting out of participants, and the second is the selection of which participants should continue. This resembles the process of the survival of the fittest seen in population ecology. Symbiotic knowledge is created by participants who continue the conjugate collective strategy in such a survival-of-the-fittest process. The adoption of the conjugate collective strategy by university researchers and companies with varying areas of expertise helped advance the development of the technique of lymphatic analysis. If the coordinator had not considered Richell as a participant in the conjugate collective strategy, Richell would have simply recorded the failed development process of a transparent, heat-resistant Tupperware.

Richell developed the precision-mould technique. It led to not only the narrow application in lymphatic analysis, but also in fuel-cell development. The latter was an application that went beyond expectations of the original purpose. This characteristic of the probability of being applied to a usage beyond the framework of the original purpose is due to the fact that

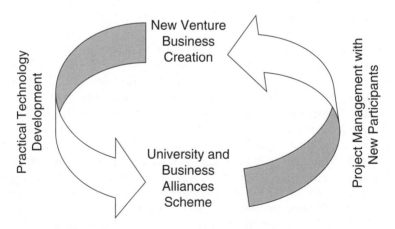

Figure 4.4   Circulation of symbiotic knowledge: case example of industry–
university collaboration

symbiotic knowledge is created through the connection of experts engaged in varying businesses and research fields. Technological development comprising a diverse range of potential applications has the possibility of triggering the emergence of innovation. In this sense, the search for the process of creating symbiotic knowledge may turn out to explain theoretically how innovation emerges: symbiotic knowledge is the closest concept to the new combination.

3   METHODS OF SYMBIOTIC KNOWLEDGE

The Role of the Coordinator

As I will describe in detail in Chapter 5, a cluster is formed when a management style sprouts out like the spring of a fountain. Its source consists of major companies that come to comprise the centre of technological advancement. The structure of the cluster is premised on the grounds of its power of major companies to spread with a centrifugal force applied from its core. An apt analogy would be a modern-day Mecca. We may be able to call a cluster the Mecca of a technological field.

In the case of BUG collaborations, a centripetal force applied from the coordinator is essential. It is necessary to shape company sentiments that prompt such thoughts as "I would like to participate in the collaboration" or "it looks likely that we can benefit from participating in the collaboration." The logic behind clustering has a totally opposite organizational principle working.

The special feature of the conjugate strategy, or BUG alliances in this chapter's case, is found in the facilitation of collective strategy taken by organizations of varied businesses. So what are the factors that lead to link-ups between companies, universities and third-sector firms participating in the Knowledge Cluster Initiative?

Conjugate strategy is realized if the following factors are considered to be important by the participants: (1) maintenance of up-to-dateness of scientific research by subsidy expenditures, (2) high societal regard associated with having acquired a subsidy, (3) acquisition of information concerning new technology, (4) creation of patent and knowhow related to new product production and/or new technologies, (5) contribution to the local community and region, and (6) acquisition and maintenance of organizational goals and budgets.

In order to receive external research funds, you will need a backward-looking, inductive idea in assuming the final stage of evaluation. Companies that are not confident about their performance in the final evaluative stage cannot sustain their deployment of the conjugate strategy. The same can be said of university researchers. Researchers such as professors and associate professors who are not confident about publishing research results will not attempt to acquire an external research fund. In the engineering field of research they will be required to present a prototype based on their research after a fixed period of time. Additionally, even if a researcher applies for receiving an external research fund, if their research performance of the past is found to be insignificant, they will be eliminated in the screening stage.

The central interest supporting industry–university collaborations is the intellectual interest in technology. Since payouts are granted from the government, it appears on the surface that collaborations are carried out for the sole purpose of allocating subsidies. However, the ability to acquire subsidies itself lies in the accumulation of expertise in a specific technology. If there were no accumulation of proven technological expertise in the university laboratory, it will not be possible to pass the screening process for acquiring subsidies.

The collaboration between universities and companies is formed when the two parties share a common interest related to a specific technology. When there is a new technology in which university researchers, executives and technical experts of companies show an interest, collaboration can be formed without the presence of a coordinator. If we seek examples in the annals of Japanese business history, we see well-known historical cases that saw entrepreneurs rely on the knowledge of university professors out of their own will. Such cases include the story of Kokichi Mikimoto's pearl, the story of Saburosuke Suzuki's Ajinomoto, and the story of Soichiro Honda's relationship with Hamamatsu Koutou Kougyō (currently Shizuoka University's Faculty of Engineering).

Symbiotic Knowledge and Innovation

Symbiotic knowledge is thought to form the basis of innovation. One of the major reasons is that the course of action taken by symbiotic knowledge brought about multiple specialties. A conjugate strategy secures the diverse specialties while being largely dependent upon the mode of connection. The number of nodes that can be connected is dependent on three hubs or, in other words, the activities of university researchers, companies and the government linked together by coordinators. When "a new combination" is made, the range of elements that can be associated broadens. When it becomes possible for Schumpeter's so-called "new combination" (1926) to be made, the range of selectable production factors that could be associated broadens. In the example of the Toyama Cluster, machining manufacturers do not have the technology to make resinous injection mouldings, and makers of resinous mouldings do not have the technology to measure lymphocytes. The state of symbiotic knowledge brought about by a conjugate strategy secures diversity.

When succeeding in connecting diverse subjects with each other, a high level of diversity is brought about in the mix of symbiotic knowledge, along with a range of options to choose from. The ability of the participants clearly defines the frontier of the technological development possible. You can expand the frontier of technological development if a newly invited person has high ability, or if this person is equipped with varied abilities. Since the group consists of determinant participants, you cannot expect anonymous experts to spontaneously participate, as in the case of common knowledge or Wikipedia. However, when certain ability is found to be deficient within a group, it may be possible to procure such experts from outside. Subsequently, the influence a new participant wields over other participants may be substantial.

Problems with the Conjugate Collective Strategy

There are problems with conjugate collective strategy, which define the limits to create symbiotic knowledge. Firstly, as it involves interaction among different organizations, objectives vary from participant to participant. Because participant benefits are multi-layered, free-riders tend to occur. In BUG collaboration, objectives co-exist: for instance, the allocation of research funds, research results, glory, social status and monetary income from new product development. Because benefits are multi-layered, slack within the organization may arise and participants who merely feed off subsidy money may appear.

Secondly, regarding tacit knowledge, each player possesses such knowledge, but they have to communicate with clearly defined language and data. When you need to make physical validations, the need arises to conjugate by being in proximity. If the heterogeneity is not fully utilized, the conjugate strategy becomes a poor version of a confederate or agglomerate collective strategy. With the development of the Internet, if the aim was to simply exchange information, there will be no need to be nearby. A net loss may also be incurred when a coordinator fails to choose the right constituent members for the conjugate strategy. If a participant, who is expected to add a new dimension to the project, does not have the ability to do so, then despite an increase in the number of participants, nothing truly new will be added.

Thirdly, distribution of results is ambiguous under the conjugate collective strategy. Yet the imposition of burdens is prone to occur. Until clear results are obtained all participants share the burden equally, and when results are obtained it becomes difficult to decide the rules for sharing them among the participants. The objective is likely to become obscured because participants come from different kinds of organizations. Each participant has a different purpose, so the time horizon tends to be shorter than other collective strategies. Collaboration for a project is typically preferred, and the project is dissolved when it attains the set purpose.

Fourthly, a free-rider may also join the conjugate strategic organization. It is not because of participants' ill intentions but because of ambiguity of the main objective. No one may suggest what to do, but the participant has to find what is to be done by oneself. For example, the objective of BUG collaboration is sometimes broad and has a long time horizon to function. As a consequence, the burden to sustain the collaboration is not shared evenly.

The leader of a conjugate strategy can choose participants comparatively freely, but a certain period of time is needed to judge whether the contribution of a new participant is superior or not. As long as the research fund is provided for a certain defined period of time, there will be cases when a university laboratory will release a prototype at the end of the designated research period. Then there would be no time to gain user feedback for the purpose of making improvements. This is a hit-and-run strategy, assuring that researchers and collaborators receive the research funds with less effort. Even if the prototype is not sufficiently completed by the end of the research period, they can consume research funds for the prototype in a way that cannot be improved.

4 IMPLICATIONS FOR SYMBIOTIC KNOWLEDGE MANAGEMENT

Conjugate Strategy as an International Business Strategy

When creating symbiotic knowledge, the most important factor is the tolerance to diversity of participants. I found this in science and technology-based case examples in this chapter. In several cases, however, a project is being carried out by not only the merging between parties such as universities, businesses and industrial technology centres, but also by the channelling of viewpoints from a diverse range of people. For example, by reflecting requests from parents with children, the disabled, the elderly and foreigners into managerial guidelines, it becomes possible to discover problems that could not have been recognized by company personnel alone prior to having such participants.

The second factor in promoting the creation of symbiotic knowledge rests in understanding the significance and value of coordination. While coordination has aspects in common with the management of in-house company affairs as an organizational activity, it contrasts directly with management of a company. In the activity of coordination that appears in the case example of this chapter, there is no prospect of gaining an appraisal, such as seeing a rise in salary or receiving a promotion. Whether the coordinator contributes in a superior way, or whether this person spends ordinary days without making such a contribution, there is no difference in how this person is treated. In addition, unlike the management of a company, the quality of coordination cannot be judged with the yardstick of sales or profitability. While assessing performance of R&D activities is possible, assessing its profitability is a matter for the more distant future, a time after the fulfilment of the objectives of coordination.

Coordination as a professional activity has nothing to do with promotions or salary increases for the coordinators. In this context coordinators are motivated by ideas such as loyalty and respect. To get diverse participants involved, and to have them contribute to R&D activities, it is necessary for the coordinators themselves to be devoted to the project. What motivates loyalty *per se* may be affection for the local community or pride as the director of the project. However, to motivate the project participants, you have to get them to recognize that a voluntary contribution for the future is being made.

From an organizational point of view, it is essential to appreciate the specialized nature of the job of a coordinator. The coordinator has to redefine the role of the expert, and foster the growth of such talent. To the extent that it is important to have a human network, this is one type of work where older people can contribute with one's advantage. The coordinator who fosters symbiotic knowledge is a person who steps outside of the company, seeks connections with a variety of people and demonstrates a good eye for selecting individuals with a high level of expertise.

Policy Implications

The many realistic problems became clear from the interviews that I summarized in this chapter. The interview records have some implications for innovation policies of science and technology. These implications are as follows.

Firstly, the Knowledge Cluster Initiative was showing a satisfactory performance and became active in a wide range of areas. In other words, it is very likely that the performance of intellectual products will improve if, from the project drafting stage of the innovation policy, the responsibility for budgeting was set to be realized through cooperation over a wide-ranging area. A local city's science and technology promotion policies and national innovation policy differ in terms of purpose and approach.[22] A characteristic of innovation is that "you cannot determine beforehand at just what point innovation emerges." Each local community designated in the Knowledge Cluster Initiative, including Toyama, is engaged in the development of technology elements. However, how the technology elements are applied and how their fields of application will be developed is not self-evident. For example, the speed of diffusion of the technology will be determined depending on the field of application used for the technology of analysing cell chips, which was transferred to SC World. At times, such applications may generate business opportunities and have broad social influence, while at other times they end by just meeting the needs of a narrow niche comprising experts. In addition, advanced technology may drift from one local community towards different local communities. Therefore, in order to create innovation, it will be necessary to incorporate advanced technologies into different local communities. Cooperation among communities designated within the domain of the Knowledge Cluster Initiative, or cooperation with those communities not designated within this domain, need to be recognized.

Secondly, a proactive effort needs to be made to use the results obtained from the Knowledge Cluster Initiative for a wide range of applications. To realize application developments, it is necessary to link information with the marketing department, and bear the risk involved in carrying out commercialization. For example, if we look at the existing situation in the Toyama District, this problem is handled as a risk borne by SC World, which serves as a "single outlet". However, it will probably be necessary to break through the regional limitation in a broader fashion, and make an attempt to proactively involve many other businesses. In this sense, the specific challenge faced is the issue of wide-area cooperation *vis-à-vis* the Knowledge Cluster Initiative as the future development of innovation policy.

Thirdly, innovation policy and the one-year budget principle are incompatible. The amount of 500 million yen earmarked for a designated area is largely arbitrary. To put it differently, it is difficult to conceive that a connection exists between the ordinary annual spending of 500 million yen and the spread of innovation. The foundation which manages the research funds with discretion must be established to tie the one-year budget principle to the indeterminate emergence of innovation arising from the Knowledge Cluster Initiative.

Problems with Industry–University Collaborations

In this chapter, I have considered BUG collaborations in Japan as exemplars of a conjugate strategy. However, some problems remain regarding this subject.

The first is that the level of decentralization is low. BUG collaborations in Japan have an aspect of being driven by government. The case example of this chapter was, in fact, a science and technology policy led by the MEXT. It would be preferable to see foundations planning BUG collaborations that enjoy a neutral relationship with the government and involve more diverse parties, but such foundations are few. Some Japanese private foundations function to allocate funds as grants in aid, but they rarely carry out the task of coordination. Securing decentralization for adopting a conjugate strategy is equivalent to the act of breaking away from the framework of industry–university–government collaboration.

The second problem is that external evaluations for BUG collaborations are not sufficient. In BUG collaborations, with the presence of the government, the contents of collaborative research are made public, and the mechanism for receiving assessments is arranged in the process. However, it is not even clear to members of an external evaluation committee what actually should be evaluated. For a researcher who has a certain level of ability, increasing the number of patents and of published papers is not difficult but most important. Rather, realizing successful product development is the most difficult part of the BUG project. Aims vary since the participants comprise a heterogeneous body of people, and if these participants with different aims fail to cooperate successfully, the grant will not be put to effective use.

NOTES

1. Examples of conjugate strategy are various. One is plans for activating shopping centres, where stores of different business lines are concentrated. This plan must encourage participation through collaborations of individual stores of shopping centres. Another is to solve environmental problems, such as global warming. Not only politicians but also specialists in varying fields exchange opinions and take joint actions to solve. These are case examples of conjugate strategies, and the knowledge born from such joint exercises is symbiotic knowledge. Business–university–government collaborations made up by coordinators are also collaborations between varying areas of expertise. Each subject contributes in their own field, facilitating new inventions and discoveries in the process. In the case of conjugate strategy and the symbiotic knowledge emerging from them, applications for the products are diverse, and there are even cases of discovering unexpected usages for them. They hold the possibility of triggering the emergence of new innovations.
2. In Japanese calendar it is dated *Heisei 14*.

3. See p. 3 of the pamphlet, "Knowledge Cluster Initiative, 2006" published by and available from the Regional Science and Technology Promotions Division of the Arts and Sciences Policy Bureau of the MEXT.

4. For information on technology policies, refer to Goto and Odagiri (2003) and Odagiri and Goto (1996). A wider range of perspectives is covered in the regional promotional policy, ranging from tourism through to agriculture, where regional industrial policies are concerned, see Kiyonari (1986, 1990) and Kiyonari and Hashimoto (1997).

5. In April 2004, the national university became a corporate body, a form of independent administrative agency, transforming the institutional foundation on which business–university collaborations are based. For more information on the system and patents of intellectual property, Goto and Nagaoka (2003) give a detailed and comprehensive account. The essential problem in business–university collaborations lies in what is called the "conflict of interests" among university instructors, meaning that the assets of the university are being utilized to pursue profit, in the event of launching a venture business based on their own research findings. This is the criticism. In addition, this is also referred to as reciprocity of duty, alluding to how the duty of education, research and management of operations that should be carried out at the university may be neglected because of launching a venture business. However, this is a study prior to the incorporation of the national university. Ijichi (2000) conducts international comparisons regarding this point.

6. Regarding historical development, see Lécuyer (2000). I elaborate on this point again in Chapter 5.

7. The contents that follow in this chapter are sourced from Horaguchi, Yukimoto and Li (2007). These authors carried out a field research on the Knowledge Cluster Initiative in 2006 to record the process of developing biochips for lymphatic analysis in Toyama.

8. This is according to the explanations offered on 28 July 2006 by Professor Atsushi Muraguchi, the vice president of the University of Toyama and a research director of the Cluster Headquarters at the Graduate School of Medicine and Pharmaceutical Science. The Toyama Medical and Pharmaceutical University was integrated into Toyama University in October 2005. In addition, on 27 and 28 July 2006, I received explanations from science and technology coordinator Mr Kihachiro Tohho.

9. The author interviewed Professor Tamiya on 22 December 2006. The author confirmed that the participants for the Knowledge Cluster Initiative were decided with Mr Yasuo Nannichi's coordination.

10. This is research advanced by Professor Ikuo Saiki, the Director of the Research Institute of Japanese and Chinese Pharmaceutical Studies of Toyama University (formerly the Toyama Medical and Pharmaceutical University). The interview was conducted on 28 July 2006. In the database creation made possible through the proteome analysis of proteins, transformative proteins were being searched for prior to the development of an anomaly in the diabetic blood sugar level. With this knowledge, markers can be identified, upon which prognoses could be made, facilitating the decision on diabetic risk.

11. This is a study advanced by Professor Yasuhisa Asano. Playing a key role in the programme, he helms the Life Studies Section of the Department of Engineering of the Toyama Prefectural College Bionics Research Centre, where he also serves as its director. On the day the interview was held, Professor Asano was absent, but we were briefed by Mr Hidenobu Yoneda, a lecturer at Toyama Prefectural College, and Mr Shinjiro Tachibana, a post-doctoral fellow of Toyama Prefectural College and dispatch researcher at the foundation, Toyama New Industry Organization (28 July 2006). They said they looked for nearby amino acid sequences from a modelled, three-dimensional structure of a protein, changed the combinations of about 20 extracted amino acids, and mechanically reconfigured the sequences, using a robot. While only about 400 samples could be screened per day manually, with the adoption of the robot, a screening rate of 1000 to 2000 samples became possible. The robot was purchased with funds made available from the budget allocated for "the Knowledge Cluster Initiative".

12. This is a study carried out by Professor Shinya Ito, who lectures at the Bionics Research Centre of the Bionics Division of the Department of Engineering of Toyama Prefectural College. I interviewed him on 28 July 2006. Professor Ito joined the Knowledge Cluster Initiative project in 2004. Added as a sub-theme of Toyama Medical and Pharmaceutical University's "Tailor-Made Chinese Medicine Prescription Project", led by Professor Ikuo Saiki, the project team carried out the construction and development of a system for analysing new functional compounds derived from plant foods. The adoption of this theme is attributed to the large presence of medium to small-sized pharmaceutical manufacturers in Toyama, the fact that they were unable to develop new medicines in-house, and on the other hand, the fact that they were placing considerable emphasis on functional foods. Professor Ito himself is an expert of the bioconversion process, using enzymes. Its application was mainly adopted in the chemical industry, but he is considering extending the technique to the food sector as well. Having entered into the field from polyphenolic analysis, he is currently carrying out research related to functional foods that raises the functionality of polyphenol, using enzymes. The contents of the interview was checked by Professor Ito in December 2006.

13. An interview was conducted on 28 July 2006 with Professor Atsushi Muraguchi and Associate Professor Hiroyuki Kishi, Graduate School of Medicine and Pharmaceutical Science at the University of Toyama and a Research Director of the Cluster Headquarters. The content of the interview summary was checked by Associate Professor Kishi in December 2006.

14. The interview was conducted on 27 July 2006 with the chief of the Institute, Dr Satoshi Fujiki of Toyama Industrial Technology Centre, Mechanics and Electronics Research Institute and Dr Masahiro Kadozaki of the Mechanics and Electronics Research Institute in Toyama Industrial Technology Centre.

15. This assessment is based on information from an interview conducted on 27 July 2006 with Mr Kihachiro Tohbo, the Science and Technology Coordinator of Toyama Medical Bio-Cluster, Toyama New Industry Organization. The content of the interview summary was checked in November and December 2006.

16. This part is based on the interview carried out on 28 July 2006 with Professor Masayasu Suzuki, who belongs to the Science and Technology Research Department of the Postgraduate Research Institute of Toyama University. As for the draft upon which this report is based, I had Professor Suzuki verify its contents in December 2006.

17. In the case of Toyama, the reason why such a situation did not arise is conjectured to be due to the fact that the main research workers were in the medical department, and were in a position to express their demands as users to the product developers. The user innovation that von Hippel (2005) talks about has the characteristic of being in a constant hurry, while denying the manufacturers of finished goods the right to have control of time management under their grasp. In contrast, if the main researcher were only a professor of the department of engineering, and if this person received the subsidy in accordance with their line of interest, the optimum allocation for spending the subsidy would be to make full use of the research period and allocate time for the preparation of papers and reports of research findings, and then, finally, create a single prototype. If we compare the act of creating a single prototype that has no practical use with the act of continuing to make improvements for the purpose of developing a product with a practical use, the latter has a degree of difficulty that is far higher.

18. The interview was conducted at the Sugino Machine Ltd Hayatsuki Plant on 27 July 2006 with General Manager and Operating Officer of Research and Development Division, Mr Ryoji Muratsubaki. The description of the interview content was checked in December 2006 by Sugino Machine Ltd.

19. This information was obtained in November 2006 from the following Sugino Machine Ltd website: http://www.sugino.com/menu/menu_index/profile/idx_profile.html.

20. The interview was conducted on October 26, 2006, with Mr. Mitsuru Miyamoto, General Manager, Microchip Business Development Office, Richell Corporation. The interview content was checked in December 2006 by Richell Corporation.

21. The interview was conducted on 27 July 2006 with Mr Sueoka. The interview content was checked in December 2006 by Mr Sueoka.

22. Porter (1998) has shown one of the indices of the geographic limit of a cluster; the condition of the distances between business footholds being below 200 miles (Japanese translation p. 114). Judging from a Japanese perspective, 200 miles, in other words, 320 kilometres, may appear to be a wide area. The distance covered by the Shinkansen bullet train from Nagoya to Tokyo is approximately 366 kilometres, and the distance covered from Nagoya to Toyama is approximately 316 kilometres. Herein lies the latent limitation that makes the application of Porter's theory and the working out of a policy based on this theory unworkable in Japan. Japanese clusters are defined in a much narrower sense and are far more coherent geographically. The cause of this is rooted in the administrative divisions of Japan, which comprise metropolises and districts (its enactment dates back to the Meiji era). Therefore, the qualification of "the Knowledge Cluster Initiative", which has as its unit the administrative divisions, is very likely too small in geographical scope. This point has already been made in the 2006 work by Amano, Kim, Konno, Horaguchi and Matsushima.

5. Local knowledge

1 THEORY

Sharing and Dispersal of Objectives

The key to differentiating between shared knowledge, symbiotic knowledge and local knowledge is found in seeing whether they possess the attribute of "purposefulness". In the case of shared knowledge, the number of participants is limited. The ones who participate in the suggestion system at Toyota's factory are limited to the employees of Toyota. In this sense, it is purposeful. Even in the case of symbiotic knowledge, we see people gathering, who were invited or urged by a coordinator to participate for a specific purpose. In the case of symbiotic knowledge what emerges is not as clear as in the case of shared knowledge, but there is a common recognition as to what it attempts to produce. In such a way, creating symbiotic knowledge is also a "purposeful" activity.

Local knowledge is knowledge that is rooted in a local area, but is supported by people who do not necessarily gather for a specific purpose. Therefore, even though local knowledge is endorsed by local people, there is no coercion to create it.[1] In this sense, local knowledge is not purposeful.[2]

As mentioned in Chapter 2 of this book, local knowledge is conveyed by agglomerate strategy. Accordingly, local knowledge is a process of knowledge that emerges from industrial agglomeration. The local knowledge emerging from specific local communities form processes of knowledge that support next-generation industrial clusters. Industrial agglomerations and clusters emerge because they offer the advantage of allowing you to be physically present at a particular place and thereby enable you to obtain knowledge that could be understood with the aid of visual observations and hands-on experiences. The creation of industrial agglomerations and clusters depends on the decision on where to locate the activities of firms. For this reason, it largely differs from the mechanism of the alliance strategy, which sees participation in contractual agreements by independent companies found in the case of Star Alliance in Chapter 3.

Industrial Agglomerations

It was Marshall (1920, Book II, Chapter 10, and Book III, Chapter 11) who had pointed out that industry develops by being geographically concentrated. He indicated that when an industry is located in one area, one could see the effect of the spread of technology and the increase in demand for parts and half-finished parts. He called this effect "external economies", which, in the discipline of economics, is also referred to as the Marshallian externality. According to Marshall, what produces positive externality is the diffusion of information caused by employees changing jobs. Furthermore, due to the situation of being adjacent to one other, competitors are able to observe each other's practices.

Regarding the inquiry into "industrial agglomerations", which Marshall (1920) is said to have initiated, it is difficult to find an originator just by tracing the history of the economic theory. For example, even in Adam Smith's *Wealth of Nations* (1776) there are two chapters concerned with urban growth.[3] The reason why it is difficult to provide a definitive answer to the question of who it was that had first called attention to the phenomenon of the spatial cohesion of corporate activities is, as a matter of course, due to the fact that the answer hinges on the definition of the terms "industrial agglomeration" and "cluster". I found an extensive usage of "cluster" in the work of Spencer (1916), who is considered as one of the founders of sociology and a social scientist who applied evolutionary theory to social phenomenon. However, if you take this argument to its extreme, the reason can be attributed to the need to hark back to the definition of "economics" itself.[4]

Generally speaking, I believe that the concept of the classic industrial agglomeration differs from the concept of cluster, since the former does not normally acknowledge business–university alliances and the industrial research and development carried out by universities, public research facilities and research institutes of corporate businesses for the purpose of leading product developments. This is because the term "industrial agglomeration" seems to have paid attention to, in many cases, the phenomenon of the tight geographical convenience of an agglomeration of enterprises, ranging from large to small and medium-sized businesses. For example, a work that is representative of this is Piore and Sabel (1984). Namely, this work draws from observations made of the industrial agglomeration of northern Italy. They argue that the possibility of flexible specialization is mainly driven by small and medium-sized businesses.

Academic interest in the industrial agglomeration was revived by the concept of the cluster proposed by Porter (1990). Henceforth, Saxenian (1994) made a comparison between the Boston area, covered by Route 126, and Silicon Valley, an area covered by Route 101, which links San Francisco to San Jose. In so doing, she had compared a local area led by the national defence, military budget (in the Boston area) and another local area led by private venture capital (in the Silicon Valley). The latter area consequently attracted attention to the collaboration that existed between university and corporate businesses. By paying attention to industrial clusters, Saxenian (1994) emphasized the reality that geographical proximity of specific companies plays an important role in the development of industries.

Porter (1998) states that a cluster is a geographical concentration that connects its constituents through collaboration among corporate businesses, specialized suppliers, service companies, businesses of related industries and associated organizations. After Porter's work (1990, 1998), a large number of geographical research and policy initiatives followed.[5] Porter (1990) explicates the model of the "diamond" when discussing the cluster. This is a schematization of a standard conceptual framework covered in the discipline of economics itself or in the study of industries. It contains the four factors of demand: related and supporting industries, firm strategy, structure and rivalry. Simply for this reason, the factors unexplained in Porter's original account of the "diamond" (Porter 1990), such as governmental policy and social capital, may have been deliberately taken up in detail in Porter's 1998 work. Whereas Porter's 1990 work was seen to be slanted towards economic factors, his 1998 work added economic policy and socio-cultural factors.

The concept of social capital was presented by Coleman (1988). Coleman characterizes social capital (1988, S118) as relationship-based assets. It is a by-product of other activities by concerned parties, arising from social activities. He made comparisons between high school students of private, Roman Catholic institutions, atheistic private institutions and public high schools. He found that private institutions affiliated with the Roman Catholic Church had the lowest rate of expulsions from school. He attributed this data to the fact that parents and children are attached to the social network of religion. Additionally, Coleman makes much of the concept of closure found in social networks. Closure, as defined by Coleman, points to the state showing that nodes connected to a network are not attached to just one other node. For example, the triangle is a closure, but the tree-shaped link is not a closure. When individuals are connected via closure, pressure from connected people is strong. In contrast, in the case when the link is made by an open connection instead, it is said that each individual will come to have unique, independent relationships.[6]

The formation of the cluster is supported by multi-layered human relations labelled as social capital. While this opinion is typically found in relation to Silicon Valley, there are many ambiguous elements in the concept of the cluster itself. As Martin and Sunley's (2003) survey critically shows, plenty of questions arise. These questions are critically important when it comes to the question of making policies on clusters. These questions are about simple indicators. In other words, there were no economists, management scholars, nor any sociologists who came to answer the question of how large an area filled with several companies needs to be in order for it to be recognized as a cluster. This is a fundamental question. Regarding this point, I discuss it in the case study of this chapter as well as in Chapter 7, but I would like to briefly touch upon the point below, regarding, in particular, the theory behind the selection of a production site as a cluster.

Transaction Cost

Generally speaking, the lower the transaction costs are, the lighter the supply parts are, and the lower the chances there will be any changes in design, then it may be said that locations tend to disperse. The concept of the transaction cost was proposed by Coase (1937), for which he won the Nobel Memorial Prize for Economics in 1991. Williamson (1975, 1985) applied the theory of the transaction cost proposed by Coase (1937) to various spheres of research, such as employee–employer relations and anti-trust law. This scholarly theory is generally called "transaction-cost economics".

A transaction cost is defined as the necessary cost incurred when someone is making use of what we call the marketplace. The first is the cost incurred when carrying out a price search. For example, if you make rounds to the offices of real estate agents to make comparisons of properties for the purpose of determining between purchasing a newly built condominium or a used one, you will be giving up the income you could have earned in the time spent making the rounds.

The second transaction cost is the cost of negotiation. Should you buy the condominium at the asking price or should you negotiate a reduced price? On what date should you be able to move into the condominium? If you can set this date to a few days earlier than initially determined, and if you happen to be residing in a hotel, you will end up saving tens of thousands of yen. This is the payoff gained by taking the time to carry out negotiations.

The third transaction cost is the cost incurred to ensure the fulfilment of the agreement. It may be said that this is the cost borne by society as a whole to help the marketplace transaction. In other words, this is legislation, a form of oversight by the judicial system. To illustrate, let us examine a real estate deal. Such a transaction would involve searching for a particular property, negotiating to purchase this property and then drawing up contractual documents. In Japan, to ensure that the terms of the contract are followed, the real estate transaction manager has to have a national licence which allows assisting in the trade of having the buyer and seller stamp their seals of approval on the contract, after explaining important matters to them. This is also one form of a transaction cost.

The fourth transaction cost involves taxes and duties. In particular, it is the consumption tax incurred when using the marketplace. One of the methods for purchasing a product without paying any consumption tax is to purchase the company itself that is selling the finished product. If you obtain the factory through a mergers and acquisitions purchase, you will be able to obtain the finished goods by bypassing the market altogether. Consequently, the need to pay the consumption tax as a transaction cost disappears.

To lower the transaction cost, you should enlarge your business organization. However, on the other hand, if you have to bear the cost to maintain the organization as a result of having enlarged it, your organization may have to become smaller in scale. Then it will turn to outsourcing its operations. In other words, if you enlarge an organization, you will need to spend time and money to make adjustments within the organization. In such a case, you will outsource operations, and by paying transaction costs in a market, lower organizational costs.

Some types of businesses exist because of transaction costs. Examples of these are the real estate brokerages and general trading companies. The general trading company carries out cost searches worldwide, conducts negotiations, executes firmly contracts in an expert fashion, and carries out the task of minimizing customs duty payments. Compared with the organizational expenses incurred when a multinational company enlarges its organization by establishing a foreign subsidiary on its own, the general trading company is a type of business that supports operations by offering the service of reducing transaction costs.

From the perspective of transaction cost economics, you can partially explain the industrial agglomeration effect. Due to geographical proximity, it becomes possible to easily carry out detailed negotiations, and the fulfilment of a contract becomes highly likely. However, on the other hand, even if an industrial agglomeration fails to form, the concept of the transaction cost remains effective as a theory for explaining transactions in general. Due to advancements in Internet technology, the cost of carrying out price searches continues to fall. Regarding transactions for parts in the auto industry, which is an industry that is typical of the manufacturing industry with agglomeration, wide-area logistics covering distances of more than 1000 kilometres and locations adjacent to final assembly manufacturers co-exist with each other. What lies in the backdrop of selecting an adjacent location is also often the

Collective knowledge management

fact that they are factories of parts whose transportation costs are high, such as bumpers, glass and seats. To explain the emergence of a certain geographical framework called the industrial agglomeration, we need to examine in further detail the significance of the act we call price search.

The Need to Compare

Let me explain why a locality emerges. What I mean by locality here is a site accommodating enterprises situated in close geographical proximity with each other. Specifically, it consists of production sites whose distance from each other allow you to leave one site to reach another and then return within a single day, sites that facilitate marketing, sites that facilitate purchasing, and sites that facilitate research and development.

The significance of a locality that affords geographical accessibility to sites lies in the fact that there is a need to make comparisons. It may be said that this is a need to confirm, or more precisely, a need to confirm visually. The need to compare arises from quality differences, and also originally depends on the attributes of a property. The need to compare, at certain times, arises from the need to conjecture the source of a problem an administrative action faces.

It can be said that the marketplace emerges from this "need to compare". In the fish market of Tsukiji, you can compare octopuses from Akashi in Japan with octopuses from Peru. You can compare tuna from the Indian Ocean with tuna from South Africa. There are many examples that show that the marketplace facilitates comparisons between similar products of various kinds, including flowers, green tea, fruits and green vegetables. If "the need to compare" fades, the need of the marketplace as "a place" disappears. Following a transition from a physical place to "a concept", the marketplace transforms into an entity known as the market.[7] In the market, it is not necessary to secure a physical place. Markets such as stock exchange markets, money markets and labour markets are a conceptual construct, and they do not need to be concentrated in a specific space.

When people gather at a certain field to exchange goods and services, they make use of the information provided by this field. When this field is limited spatially, this is in many cases to meet the "need to compare". Within this context of need to compare, people may not share a purpose in common. People are not limited to those who share a common purpose to participate in the field. For example, those who participate in the fish market of Tsukiji may either be proprietors of sushi shops or they may be proprietors of family restaurants. The requirements for participation in the field are lax, compared with shared knowledge, and restrictive, compared with common knowledge. This is the characteristic of local knowledge.

Local knowledge is shared by a limited number of people. For example, in the case of a person who plans to emigrate to Silicon Valley, one requirement becomes moving oneself physically to the field of Silicon Valley.

The need to compare explains the presence of a commercial agglomeration such as the one found in Akihabara, Tokyo. From the viewpoint of the customer, the convenience of being able to compare a large number of commodities within one town is substantial. While the phenomenon of finding manufacturing companies concentrated in a specific location can also be accounted for by the need to make comparisons, there are some factors that account for this need.

The first factor behind the need to compare is proximity for facilitating the transaction of parts. When a malfunction occurs in the production of a part, it is possible to deal with the problem by having an engineer despatched directly from a company nearby that handles assembly.

The second factor behind the need to compare is the need to carry out collaboration from the design and development phase. This is referred to as the sharing of tacit knowledge and it often requires face-to-face meetings. Requirements such as the basic concept of design, transmission of nuance through detailed design, management of design changes and the use of a common language are met by proximity. The strategy known as co-location pertains to selecting a nearby location for developing information systems abroad and, at times, is explained in terms of the concept of tacit knowledge-sharing or information stickiness.[8]

The third is the need to compare organizations. For example, from the standpoint of a final-assembly maker of automobiles, the level of control of a nearby factory can be more easily confirmed than the level of one in a remote location. In the event defective units are produced, it is possible to take prompt action to work out countermeasures for such a situation. If you need to find out the level of motivation of an organization, visiting a nearby factory will provide answers in many cases. In addition, you will see to what extent the priority is attached to your firm by the supplier. In other words, the rank of your company in the supplier's order of priority will be sensed when you visit your supplier.

There are two additional factors which cause agglomeration of firms. The first factor among them is when we see the creation of an industrial complex by the administration or a private enterprise. We can observe a concentration of factories of manufacturing companies caused by the industrial complex. In the case of a developing country, there are facilities called free trade zones, special areas for development and special economic zones. There are times when factory locations concentrate in a particular area due to inducements, such as exemptions from customs duties for exports and the reduction of corporate taxes for a limited period of time after establishing a business. In some cases, there are places, such as Shanghai and Dalian in China, where we see software firms being attracted as a matter of policy.

The second additional factor is the spinoff from a good-standing enterprise, which serves as a local nucleus. This is the case whereby we see the launch of a company after it has honed its technology within a good-standing enterprise. The spinoff is launched when it is deemed that the business is too small in scale to be a start-up venture owned by the good-standing enterprise, but sufficiently large to be a one-person company. In many cases, the entrepreneur of this business or the co-participant of the business already lives with their family in a locality prior to launching the spinoff. For this reason, they have no motivation to relocate. In addition, after launching their business, some of them seek to have the good-standing enterprise, in which they had worked, to be their first client.

Knowledge Resources and the Cluster

When re-reading Porter (1990) while paying attention to the subject of knowledge, you will understand that knowledge creation is categorized under many different descriptions. He preaches the importance of the "factor creation" mechanism (p. 80), which stipulates that technical elements based on knowledge can be created by nations, emphasizing "knowledge resources" alongside human resources, physical resources, capital resources and infrastructure (p. 74).

Porter (1990) points out that in a country where the competition is intensified, the buyer is refined, the level of aspiration rises and the manufacturers, stimulated by the high level of aspiration, turn out to create new and advanced segments (p. 89). In addition, for example, he states that the types of talent on which a country places priority will affect the education and types of jobs selected by individuals with specific types of talent. He cites as an example the period that saw the absorption of superior talent by the aerospace industry in the USA, the chemical industry in Germany and the iron, steel and electronics industries in Japan (pp. 114–15). Like Marshall (1920), Porter (1990) points out that stocks of knowledge and skills are accumulated at the industrial level through the movement of employees between companies (p. 120), and that ideas acquired from studies carried out at universities become industrialized through spinoffs (pp. 122–3).

As mentioned in Chapter 1 of this book, explicit knowledge that has been disclosed has the property of being public goods. It has the property of non-excludability and non-rivalness. Should explicit knowledge be disclosed, then by understanding this knowledge, anyone will be able to obtain it (non-excludability), and therefore knowledge will not decrease (non-rivalness). Seen in this light, the need to compare is nothing more than a drive to obtain tacit knowledge, and the cost incurred in meeting this end is dependent upon physical cost such as travel time and expenses.

The electronics shopping town of Akihabara and the entertainment district of Kabukicho found in Shinjuku in Tokyo can be explained by this need to compare. In Silicon Valley's semiconductor production and in Napa Valley's wine production, tasks such as confirming the design of electronic circuits and required specifications of semiconductors, and the breeding and cultivation of grapes for wine-making become necessary. In the electronics shopping town of Akihabara, you can compare multiple products in many shops prior to purchasing. In the restaurant district of Kabukicho, you can look for the restaurant of your choice by making comparisons to find the one that suits the preferences of individuals gathered at the time. By virtue of having an accumulation of stores in a small town, the cost of carrying out a price search falls. You can obtain various kinds of information, including those on the quality and performance of electronic products, and the contents and prices of a cuisine.

If knowledge remains undisclosed or if it cannot be disclosed due to the fact that it is in the form of tacit knowledge, the properties of non-excludability and non-rivalness will not be established. A person with knowledge can exclude a person without knowledge. If the knowledge leaks from the one who has it, its value decreases. A company that attempts to obtain local knowledge will attempt to pursue a favourable position *vis-à-vis* the aspect of confidentiality and the aspect of openness of such knowledge. Regarding tacit knowhow, if you are nearby, you can acquire it through collaboration. Even in cases where explicit knowledge is offered through a manual for, say, sales engineers stationed at the factory, these sales engineers will help a purchaser understand the usage of machine tools through explaining the manual and subsequently encouraging a trial and error process to obtain tacit knowhow.

To accomplish common goals in a specific company, it is necessary to disclose knowledge within the company. From the viewpoint of the giver of the knowledge, the knowledge is something that has already been understood and does not serve to add any new understanding. On the other hand, from the viewpoint of the receiver of knowledge, the market value of the received knowledge will be discovered when the receiver applies knowledge to opportunities in the workplace. Such examples of knowledge include logical structures of source codes, programming languages, production techniques of products and resources securable from foreign countries. Placing yourself physically in "the company" offers a key opportunity to learn and raise the level of this understanding of disclosed knowledge. If a person acquires such understanding on this type of disclosed knowledge on a trade secret, it is also possible to create a new field of business away from the specific company.

2   CASE EXAMPLES

Cluster Classifications

Fieldwork on clusters reveals that each locality possesses an identity of its own. By establishing two axes, you will be able to classify clusters into four types and reach a sound understanding of them. As seen in Figure 5.1, it is possible to classify clusters into four categories by setting the following axes: in the *x* axis, the classification will be made between manufacturing-

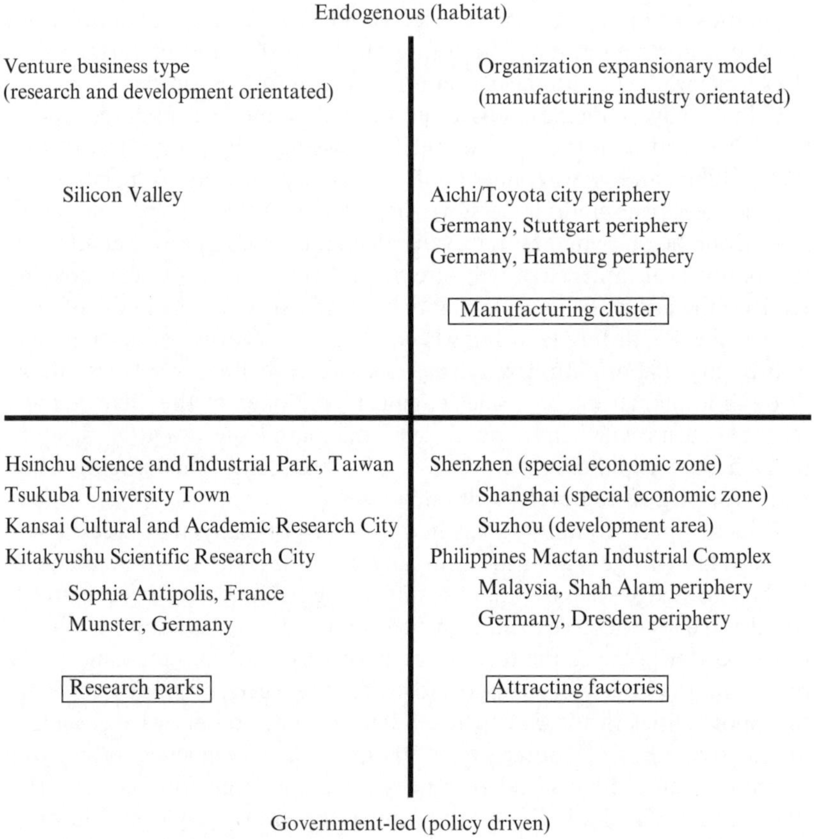

Endogenous (habitat)

Venture business type
(research and development orientated)

Organization expansionary model
(manufacturing industry orientated)

Silicon Valley

Aichi/Toyota city periphery
Germany, Stuttgart periphery
Germany, Hamburg periphery

| Manufacturing cluster |

Hsinchu Science and Industrial Park, Taiwan
Tsukuba University Town
Kansai Cultural and Academic Research City
Kitakyushu Scientific Research City
Sophia Antipolis, France
Munster, Germany

Shenzhen (special economic zone)
Shanghai (special economic zone)
Suzhou (development area)
Philippines Mactan Industrial Complex
Malaysia, Shah Alam periphery
Germany, Dresden periphery

| Research parks |

| Attracting factories |

Government-led (policy driven)

Figure 5.1   Cluster types

industry orientation or research and development orientation, and in the *y* axis, the choice will be between endogenous development or government-led development.[9]

The manufacturing industry orientation involves the tendency to expand the domain of business management, including production, marketing, planning, design, research and development, finance, personnel and information systems by integrating organizational functions. The manufacturing industry orientation carries out management under the notion of integrating these functions of business management in a locality where the headquarters is centred.

Research and development orientation involves activities such as carrying out R&D for chiefly new products and systems, outsourcing to other companies during the mass production phase and permitting the use of patents. There are times the R&D company itself becomes the target of a buyout subsequent to realizing an IPO.

Such a difference in idea between manufacturing industry orientation and research and development orientation may not be clearly put into text as a strategy. When you belong to a certain local community or cluster, as a matter of course, common recognition may be there. For this reason, this kind of idea can be referred to as "tacit strategy". For an organization, this is common sense as it pertains to the management of business organizations. Thus, a tacit tendency for the members in the organization prevails.

Research Parks

The third quadrant in Figure 5.1 shows characteristics of the research park, which is brought about through government-led initiatives. It concentrates on research and development and thus falls under the policy-driven and R&D-oriented category.[10] The university is a typical entrant into a research park. As already discussed in Chapter 4, the policy to foster clusters that revolve around an initiative of an industry–university cooperation has been adopted by various countries in the world,[11] and consequently, local communities have formed world-renowned research parks. These communities in Japan are those such as the Kobe Biomedical Innovation Cluster, the Kitakyushu Scientific and Research Park, the Tsukuba Science City, and the Kansai Science City (abbreviated name: Keihanna). In Europe, there are Sophia Antipolis in the environs of Cannes, France, and Munster in western Germany.[12] Once financial resources of the national government or the provincial government are to be invested, the land is developed, whereupon a research establishment is built and research and incubation facilities for carrying out industry–university collaboration are prepared.

While these research parks are at times called clusters, they only have research and development in terms of the functions of business organizations. With functions of the business organization thoroughly decentralized, this type of cluster differs from the cluster of an industrial agglomeration. In the development of such an area, the provincial government or the national government invests to develop these areas, spending government revenue from tax funds.[13]

Taiwan's Hsinchu Science and Industrial Park is a well-known example of a research park for various business models to have come out of. The Hsinchu Science and Industrial Park was established in 1980, and while having the Industrial Technology Research Institute (ITRI) as a core research facility, it has brought about business models based on a type of business referred to as a foundry, such as TSMC and UMD. The business model of TSMC involves the types of operations that specialize in the fabrication and mass production of semi-conductor prototypes designed and developed abroad, and its linkage with Silicon Valley and Hsinchu is also salient. In Hsinchu, there are universities that have the same names as those in mainland China, such as the Qinghua University and Jiao Tong University. These places are engaged in producing engineers while carrying out industry–university collaborations.[14]

In Singapore as well, there is a university that declares its *raison d'être* to be the creation of innovation based on science and technology, and instead of specializing in operations such as processing and assembly, it remarkably integrates various processes, ranging from research and development to production.[15]

Free Trade Zones and Offshore Production Areas

In the fourth quadrant of Figure 5.1, we can raise the cases of offshore production areas of China and free trade zones, which we typically find in developing countries. We see that factories are established in response to government-led enticements in these cases. While free trade zones were established in Kaohsiung in Taiwan and Masan in Korea, the merit of being located in either of them became lost as wages rose, and their purpose of providing incentives as a free trade zone disappeared. Manufacturing operations are led by the factories of multinational companies, and they behave as "footloose" to locate anywhere advantageous. The presence of preferential tax measures for investments largely forms the attraction for multinational companies.

The fourth quadrant, for the most part, corresponds to "the operational clusters", as proposed by McKendrick et al. (2000). Such clusters differ from the kinds of agglomerations seen in Shanghai, which are formed by manufacturing operations led by factories of multinational companies. This is due to the fact that local communities around Shanghai are transforming rapidly, and research and development by local businesses and universities in China is also making progress. The offshore production area in Shanghai in the 1990s saw a concentration of factories and was perceived to be a foothold for processing and assembly operations. However, in the 2000s, we saw the move towards integrating the functions of planning and design there.[16] I regard the fourth quadrant of agglomerations as localities with concentrations of such manufacturing operations.

Silicon Valley

In Figure 5.1, I raised Silicon Valley in the second quadrant. It is a locality where endogenous development overlaps with a research and development orientation.[17] It is said that Silicon Valley prepares social capital for business promotions. Furthermore, it is also said that successful entrepreneurs, angel investors, venture capitalists, certified public accountants, lawyers/law firms and NPOs that support businesses build a network[18] here and invest in promising entrepreneurs.[19]

Benchmarking competitors and evaluating prototypes benefit from the locational merits of Silicon Valley. Financial support for the newly established venture is made possible in this location. It becomes possible to compare your business plans with those of other companies by being concentrated in a fixed locality that affords short travel times. Through job-hoppers and brokers, you obtain information in the cluster. It becomes easy to observe rival firms. By benchmarking advanced businesses in the cluster, you can come to grasp the direction the industry as a whole is taking. Being located in a cluster, it is possible to reduce the time it takes to evaluate prototypes. Even individuals such as designers and their clients can have face-to-face meetings to affirm mutual understanding. When producing prototypes and evaluating them, if delivery is made from a company located in a remote area, the time loss will be great. In other words, the process of evaluating prototypes and receiving feedback on them can be carried out at a swift pace.

In the history of Silicon Valley, the American military-industrial complex has apparently been seen to wield influence over demand, and in this sense, it turns out that the cluster has had support from the government.[20] Historically, clusters had been receiving the benefits of the military budget prepared by the US government, and so in absolute terms, they are not an entity led by private enterprises. However, unlike free trade zones and offshore production areas, they do not attract businesses through offering exemptions from customs duties or reductions in and exemptions from income taxes. Through spinoffs launched by a large number of entrepreneurs from core firms such as Fairchild and Hewlett-Packard, they have been achieving endogenous development. Regarding Silicon Valley, there are already many studies available, and most of them praise the mechanism that produces a large number of entrepreneurs. However, since the so-called "dot-com bubble" burst at the end of 2000, and since the occurrence of the September 11 terrorist attacks in 2001, the area also underwent a period of recession that saw its population dwindle by 15 per cent in 2004.[21]

Clusters are interlinked with each other. The two clusters, Silicon Valley in the USA and the Hsinchu Science and Industrial Park in Taiwan, are divided into functions of semiconductor design and semiconductor fabrication. However, their human-to-human transactions are lively.[22] At hotels in Hsinchu, you can find numerous businesspeople who appear to be Westerners and Indians. Silicon Valley, rather than pursuing operations ranging from research and development to manufacturing in a consistent fashion, emphasizes R&D activities and design. Manufacturing activities themselves are in many cases consigned to Chinese and Taiwanese manufacturers of semiconductors. It is a common practice and a tacit strategy of Silicon Valley firms to decentralize manufacturing operations that take place in the factory and then to outsource them.

The cluster is understood as some sort of ecosystem. While the ecosystem found in Silicon Valley is one pattern, it cannot be said to predominate in all localities of the world. Just as ecosystems of forests vary by the tropical or subtropical zone, or in the temperate or cold region in which they are found, the growth patterns of clusters vary by country.

Toyota-city and Stuttgart

As endogenous clusters comparable with Silicon Valley, you can raise the periphery of Toyota-city in Aichi prefecture in Japan and the periphery of Stuttgart in Baden-Wurttemberg in Germany. In the paper mainly discussing the former, Amano et al. (2006) pointed to its characteristics and called it "a *monozukuri* (manufacturing) cluster". However, similar characteristics are recognized for the periphery of Stuttgart as well. These characteristics of the manufacturing cluster contain the spontaneity of the developmental process and a high level of manufacturing industry activities. In these localities, there is a division of labour established between corporations, each led by Toyota and Daimler. The tacit strategy of Toyota and Daimler is to prepare in this locality a form of key management as a complete set. On top of this, they have the same functions abroad, and equip the locality with functions that help it to serve as a centre for supporting those functions duplicated abroad.

In localities known as *monozukuri* (manufacturing) clusters, you can find all operations, ranging from research and development to manufacturing and marketing. The R&D activities in these localities have as their aim the heightening of the technical level of the manufacturing industry found in them, and it is thought that research and development is carried out as a component part of the manufacturing industry. If you look back into history, you can see that there was a period that saw the benefits of the government's policy of protecting industrial growth bear fruit, and that industrial growth was supported by the demand fuelled by military needs. However, basically, it may be said that clusters were formed in response to the private sector demand for the production of passenger vehicles.

What the periphery of Toyota-city and the periphery of Stuttgart share in common is the fact that both accommodate factories run by Toyota Motor Corporation and Daimler, which are global-scale, automobile manufacturing firms. Both clusters arose from the need to carry out business-to-business transactions. In these localities, existing enterprises formed a cluster by continuing to expand their factories anew over a long period of time. These processes have vitalized their manufacturing operations.

There are manufacturing operations in the Silicon Valley as well, but much importance is attached to stand-alone companies that focus on R&D activities. Furthermore, the manufacturing operations in the Silicon Valley are transferred to the semiconductor manufacturers of Taiwan and China. And in many cases, Taiwanese manufacturers are also, in turn, outsourced their businesses to their own factories elsewhere such as mainland China or Malaysia. This means that the development of the Silicon Valley basically stems from the production of comparatively lightweight semiconductors. Additionally, the development of an aviation network made low transportation costs possible. This is thought to be a factor to support the business model between Silicon Valley and Taiwan as well as China.

If we compare Figure 5.1's first quadrant and second quadrant, coherent manufacturing processes are differentiated. The weight of automobile is heavier than semiconductors and the former requires "the need to compare" the manufacturing processes.

Figure 5.2 is a map showing the locations of the factories and research and development centres of Toyota Motor Corporation and Denso. Toyota as a group company holds over 212 companies that are either primary suppliers or parts suppliers who participate in the Kyōhōkai, or the name of Toyota *Keiretsu* company group. In addition to Denso, they include companies such as Toyota Industries Corporation, Aichi Steel Works, JTEKT

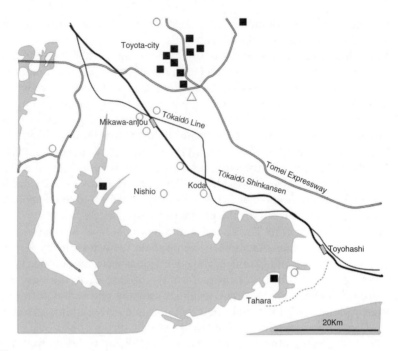

Notes:
■ Toyota's car factory and research institute.
○ Denso's factory.
△ The factory of Mitsubishi Motors Corporation.

Figure 5.2   The locations of the factories of Toyota and Denso around
*   Toyotashi, Aichi*

Corporation, Toyota Auto Body, Aisin Seiki, Toyota Boshoku and Toyota
Gosei. Figure 5.2 shows the locations of the factories of Toyota Motor
Corporation and Denso, but it proves to be too small to reflect the numer-
ous locations of Toyota group companies' factories in their entirety.[23]

Figure 5.3 shows the locations of the factories, service footholds, and
research and development bases of Daimler and Bosch. You can see that
the parts supply system of Bosch has been arranged so as to surround the
two factories of Daimler. Figure 5.3 shows Daimler's factory in Stuttgart-
Untertürkheim for the production of engines, axles, and transmissions,
and the Sindelfingen factory that assembles Mercedes-Benz automobiles.
In addition to these two factories, Daimler has domestic ones located in
Berlin, Bremen, Rastatt and Hamburg, and has more domestic locations
dispersed than Toyota. In addition, the factory in Stuttgart-Untertürkheim
was established in 1904 and the one in Sindelfingen, in 1915. In fact, these

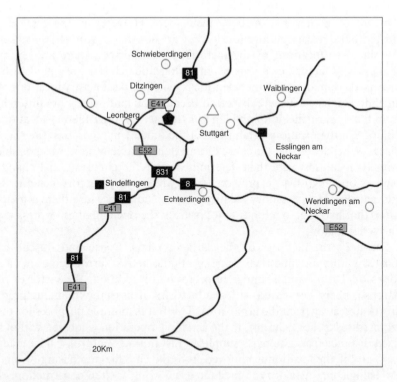

Notes:
■ Daimler's assembly plant.
○ Bosch's business establishment, accommodating more than 100 people.
△ Porsche's assembly plant.
⌂ TRUMPF's factory producing laser beam machines.

Figure 5.3   The locations of the factories of Daimler and Bosch around Stuttgart, Germany

factories have been in operation for around 100 years, even prior to Toyota Motor Corporation's inauguration in 1937.[24]

The Characteristics of the Manufacturing Cluster

The factory location of a manufacturing cluster is seen to exhibit the following characteristics. Primarily, such a location aptly meets the need for securing logistics, such as ports, arterial roads and railways, and therefore, such a location is not necessarily adjacent. In the case of scientific research parks and offshore production areas, because research establishments and factories are lured to a developed site, you can visually confirm the presence of a cluster formed by them there. However, in the case of a cluster that develops endogenously, they are not that obvious to the naked eye since the locations of the factories are dispersed. There are several reasons why factory locations of an endogenous cluster are found to be dispersed compared with the scientific research parks. Factory locations of an endogenous cluster are dispersed because the landowners are different from the ones of the adjoining land of the factory, thus, factory locations differ from the locations established at the time of inauguration for many places. Whereas the net purchase of an extensive area of land was possible initially, locations were then determined after the circumstantial change such as opening of an expressway from which a new factory benefits its convenience. Hence factory locations are separated because there are factories that had been operating since prior to the opening of an expressway and other factors.

Secondly, the factories of the parts suppliers, Denso and Bosch, are located within a diametrical range of 50 kilometres, surrounding the factories of Toyota and Daimler respectively. In addition, the factories of parts suppliers, compared with the factories of assembly manufacturers, are located away from the urban area. This fulfils multiple purposes for the required tasks. For example, if the assembly operation is located within a fixed distance from the parts supplier, "just in time" control will be made easy, and if the location is removed from the city, the purchasing of land for establishing a factory is facilitated, allowing for the construction of spacious plants and buildings. Furthermore, as evidenced when building dormitories for employees, living expenses for them will turn out to be lower than the expenses they would incur if they were in the city.

Thirdly, near Toyota's factory, there is the Okazaki factory of Mitsubishi Motors Corporation, and near Daimler, there is the headquarters factory of Porsche. This set of circumstances can be considered a case example of commensalism in biology, similar to the one introduced in Chapter 2 of this book (see Table 2.2). The use by Mistubishi Motors Corporation and Porsche of the technology of the parts suppliers, who have been responding to large-scale demands from Toyota and Daimler, does not have any negative impact on Toyota and Daimler, but for Mitsubishi Motors and Porsche, such use has a positive impact. This is because these companies would prefer to place supplementary orders to component makers who have been attentive to the technical guidance provided by Toyota and Daimler, rather than take upon the burden of instructing component makers themselves for the purpose of elevating their level of technological standards.

There are also characteristics that a map cannot capture. Firstly, there is the capability to frequently carry out R&D activities and technical collaborations that an adjacent location makes possible. Konno (2007) analysed the situation of joint patent applications made by Japanese car manufacturers and clarifies that Toyota had applied for the most number of joint patents. The assortment of other companies vying for the top position in terms of joint-patent acquisitions consists of Toyota and Denso, Toyota and Aisin Seiki, and Toyota and Toyota Industries Corporation (Toyota Jidou Shokki). Apparently, most joint patents are acquired together with neighbouring group companies in Aichi prefecture.[25]

Secondly, there is the existence of the export market. In a cluster, products are made with a quantity that cannot be absorbed within the environs of the cluster alone. Seen from a historical perspective, there arose companies that succeeded in cultivating the export market, and as businesses that traded with and processed parts for these companies came to be located nearby, clusters began to form. Should overseas local production be carried out to respond to the local needs of the export market, technical support for overseas factories will be carried out as well. Moreover, thanks to technological developments supporting the intellectual advancement of the *monozukuri* (manufacturing) cluster, it is possible to form links and enjoy a cooperative relationship with research and development footholds established overseas.[26]

Such an international reach is partly to do with product developments that are suited to the conditions of demand found in various countries. The impetus behind gaining it also has to do with carrying out technical developments that cannot be made in the home country. So, to summarize the above, the cluster is generated as a phenomenon limited within a country but its existence is supported by an international network. Corporate activities deployed within a global, spatial structure support location-specific geographic proximity.

The third is that industries other than the automobile-related ones are concentrated within the same geographical range. Such a phenomenon can be referred to as the multi-layered attribute of an industrial organization.[27] In the case of the vicinity of Toyota-city, famous industries other than the auto industry are the spinning and ceramics industries. There, on the one hand, you can find companies such as NGK Insulators, Ltd, who produce catalysts for exhaust gas filters to supply to the auto industry, while on the other hand, you can find that NGK Insulators carries out analyses of printer actuators and DNA chips. The reason why such a phenomenon arises is because, firstly, the growth of industry has been transforming. In other words, the phenomenon is, in effect, a reflection of the evolution in the industrial structure. Additionally, the phenomenon arises because the general-purpose technology of machine work, developed in a particular industry, can be adopted in next-generation technological developments.

Matsushima (2005a) traced the transition to maturity of the *pachinko* (Japanese pinball board for gambling) manufacturing industry as it passed through its phases from being a part of the textile industry to being a part of the mechanical industry, describing such a structural transformation of industry as being indicative of the "robustness" of the regional economy. A robust manufacturing cluster such as Toyota-city and Aichi prefecture can be said to be endowed with the multi-layered attribute of an industrial organization.

Geographical Range

Porter (1998) holds a level equal to or less than 200 miles between business footholds to be one of the indexes of the geographic limit of clusters (p. 230). Judging from a Japanese perspective, 200 miles, that is to say 320 kilometres, may appear to be a wide area. The distance covered by the Shinkansen bullet train lines from Nagoya to Tokyo is approximately 366 kilometres, and from Tokyo to Sendai, a major city in Tohoku region, it is approximately 320 kilometres. Additionally, the distance covered by the Shinkansen from Nagoya to Okayama is about 367 kilometres, and from Nagoya to Toyama, it is about 316 kilometres. When you attempt to apply Porter's geographical limitation of clusters to the situation in Japan, it will turn out to include an extensive area containing three to four administrative divisions, called prefectures.[28]

The discrepancy brought to light by Porter's theory of clusters gives rise to two hypotheses. The first hypothesis is that the acknowledgement related to Porter's geographical range is an error as far as Japan is discussed. The cluster range in Japan is defined as far smaller and, in most cases, it tends to be clumped together geographically, and the studies of industrial agglomerations tend to focus on specific local cities or one of the 23 wards of Tokyo. Namely, local cities such as Sanjo city and Tsubame city in Niigata prefecture, Okaya city and the town of Sakaki in Nagano prefecture, Hamamatsu city in Shizuoka, and wards such as Ohta-ku and Sumida-ku in Tokyo. The reason why interest in research is marked at the administrative level is due to the fact that the responsibility for carrying out policies of promoting clusters and industrial agglomeration are shared among administrative divisions, municipalities, prefectures and wards in Japan.

Even in the policy for promoting clusters in France, or *les pôles de compétitivité* (the competitive cluster), 68 bases for cluster areas are designated. This is because the heads of local governments themselves apply pressure on the national government to offer grants to their own municipal areas.[29] On the other hand, as in France's research cluster Sophia Antipolis, there are cases whereby housing complexes of research footholds are developed by wealthy individuals.[30] The will to form an industrial agglomeration may not necessarily be something that should be supported by the government.

The second hypothesis concerning the geographic limit of clusters is that Japanese researchers and policymakers are mistaken in their recognition regarding policy implementation with geographical ranges. In that case, a huge cluster existing within the radius spanning the distance from Tokyo to Nagoya must be recognized. If Porter's geographical span is correct to understand a cluster, the cluster promotion policy in Japan that focuses on a specific city may be too myopic. In other words, it may be too narrow in terms of its geographical scope. Furthermore, in the twenty-first century, the geographic proximity realized through a network of expressways and Shinkansen bullet train lines became a source of great strength as an initial condition for the rise of clusters, giving way to sustain bigger clustering in Japan. I will discuss this possibility in the final chapter of this book.

3   METHODS OF LOCAL KNOWLEDGE

The Role of the Networker in a Cluster

The formation of a cluster typically found in Silicon Valley is basically dependent on the exercise of diffusion (see Figure 4.2 in Chapter 4). There is a company that becomes an axis, then from this company, a spinoff succeeds, and this in turn gives rise to other companies that follow this business approach. The technical level of the axis company in the cluster is high. The employees can acquire a high level of technical understanding and skills. In the event the axis company's strategy differs from the technical orientation of the employees working there, these said employees will spinoff and launch their own business through establishing a spinoff. A large enterprise that becomes an axis in a cluster would be overlooking a business opportunity of small revenue. If a small project has the prospect of achieving a sales figure of 100 million yen, it would be abandoned by the large enterprise. The small project on the other hand would be borne by a start-up venture.

The core activity involving the creation of a spinoff is apparently the movement of employees from one company to another. However, if you view it as an aspect of connecting knowledge, the creation of a spinoff helps in the formation of a network that links bodies of knowledge of varying kinds with each other. Someone who worked at Fairchild may end up working at Intel, someone who worked at Intel may end up working at Hewlett-Packard (HP), and someone who worked at HP may end up working at Google. Such a situation merely involves individuals changing jobs, but nevertheless fulfils the function of forging knowledge links between Fairchild, Intel, HP and Google.

Irrespective of the intent of the individual who had launched the spinoff, this person turns out to have fulfilled the function of a networker. This also applies to the flow of people from a university to a corporation, from a corporation to a graduate school, and from a graduate school to a corporation. The exchanges of information between people are facilitated by sharing the same alma mater in common, such as Stanford University and UC Berkley in Silicon Valley. Local knowledge is accumulated through this exchange of information.

In the case of Japan, rather than advancing businesses through spinoffs, companies have often opted to realize diversification through start-up ventures, which leads to the separation of divisions within their own organizations, triggered by the success of the start-ups. The pre-war *Zaibatsu* (a financial clique) was a diversified family business, and after the war, under the labels of business groups and associated companies, large enterprises adopted the strategy of holding numerous subsidiaries. The existence of *Zaibatsu* is explained by the scarcity of management knowhow, and it was ordered to dissolve after the Second World War. The existence of the business groups of the post-war era are said to be due to the fact that a prohibition had been in place against the establishment of holding companies until 1997. However, I believe there was a more proactive significance.

One hypothesis suggests that there are differences in aim between Japanese business style and Silicon Valley style when running a start-up venture. If your aim is to "be engaged in a sustainable business", one that can serve as an exemplary one in your life, you will be able to carry out substantial work, even without launching a company and going public with the release of an IPO. If your purpose in life is to "be engaged in a sustainable business", even if you do not carry out a flotation by yourself, you may still be able to sufficiently achieve the end by simply initiating a start-up venture within a company. When a new business succeeds within a company, the success would not bring an amount of fortune as enormous as the one you could attain when releasing an IPO. However, with the support of the company's financial resources, you may be able to help grow the new business within the company into a stable one. The research in corporate governance has made it clear that there exists a great difference between the USA and Japan in terms of the amount of executive compensations made. However, the craftsman's sense of values harboured by the Japanese, which makes much of "being engaged in a sustainable business", may have contributed towards stable economic growth.[31]

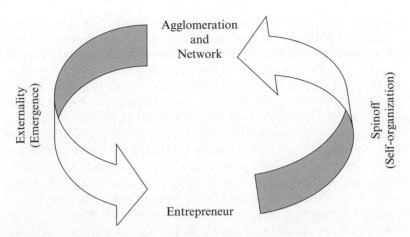

Agglomeration
and
Network

Externality
(Emergence)

Spinoff
(Self-organization)

Entrepreneur

*Figure 5.4   Circulation of local knowledge: a cluster formation case
example*

Benchmarks and the Presence of Mecca

A firm actively managing in a cluster is, in effect, working on building a competitive edge over other firms in the cluster. This is because benchmarking competitors becomes easy, and making comparisons with other capable entities also becomes easy. What characterizes a cluster is the presence of a company that serves as its focal point. Everyone benchmarks a successful company whose business approach comes to be emulated. Prominent firms, including Intel in Silicon Valley, Toyota in Aichi, TSMC in Hsinchu, Taiwan, and Mondavi in Napa Valley, are the ones leading the business world in terms of technology and product quality. Borrowing an expression from game theory, such firms are known as a focal point in the sense that everyone assumes such firms as a point of reference. Borrowing an expression from religion, such firms are analogous to the presence of Mecca. In a Mecca, a large number of talented people gather and compete.

A focal point is a concept that the Nobel Prize winner Schelling (1960) raised as an example of the Nash Equilibrium. The Nash Equilibrium indicates that the strategies of two players are in agreement when one player chooses a strategy by taking into account the strategic choice of an opponent and the opponent chooses a strategy by taking into account the strategic choice of the former. The prisoner's dilemma introduced in Chapter 1 of this book is also a case of the Nash Equilibrium. However, the Nash Equilibrium holds water even when the strategy space is infinite. To put it plainly, the number of strategies does not matter in the Nash Equilibrium. It can be attained no matter how many there are. The concept of the focal point suggests that strategies often arrive at the state of Nash Equilibrium in the end, even when the space is infinite, and that such a concurrence of behaviour is widely observable in our daily lives. In Schelling (1960) we see an example of choosing a meeting place by those who have not decided on a place to meet beforehand. It is reported that two players tend to coincide with the choice of Grand Central Station in New York as a meeting place. In other words, for players, a famous place acted as a focal point. It becomes easy to associate the place with meeting venue. Another example is shown in the case of a game where four by four squares are established, and in which the one who wins is the one who chooses the square the opponent is likely to choose. Then, the players tend to choose one of the squares in the diagonal line in the four by four squares. The squares on the diagonal line become easily selectable. In this case, there is no difference in payoff, no matter which square is chosen. Despite this fact, the reason why the Nash Equilibrium stands is because there inherently exists a potential focal point within human consciousness. While Schelling (1960) calls such a process "tacit coordination" (p. 54), if you put it differently, you can say the focal point pertains to a symbol that functions as a focus of human action.

In a cluster, you can find universities, graduate schools and corporations functioning as this focal point. If you visit the cluster, there is a place inside that anyone would like to visit once. This place is, so to speak, the Mecca, and it significantly fulfils the function of the focal point. Wherever you find first-rate corporations, first-rate universities and first-rate research institutes, you will also find many executives taking the time to confirm such places with their own eyes.

If you examine the actions taken by some Japanese executives in history, you can understand that their pursuit to find a foothold of local knowledge was made swiftly. While Japan was under GHQ's occupation immediately after the Second World War, after the peace conference of the Pacific Wars was held in San Francisco in 1951, the nation returned into the fold of the international community. Upon reading the autobiography of a successful executive, you will see that they had travelled to many parts of the world during the first half of the 1950s. Kohnosuke Matsushita, the legendary founder of Panasonic, travelled to the USA in January 1951 and extended his period of stay there from one month to about three months, during which time he visited GE. In addition, from October through November 1951, he visited Philips in the Netherlands (Matsushita 2001, pp. 47–57). Soichiro Honda, the founder of Honda, went to America in November 1952 to import machine tools (Honda 2001, p. 82). Likewise, in 1952, Masaru Ibuka of Sony, which was then named Tokyo Tsushin Kogyo, visited the USA and obtained information on acquiring a patent for the transistor. And in August 1953, the co-founder of Sony, Akio Morita, left for the USA to conclude the patent contract for the transistor (Morita et al. 1990, pp. 121–4), which was later utilized for the pocket-size transistor radio.

Limitations of Local Knowledge

As Krugman (1991) made a model and showed, the transfer from one type of industrial agglomeration to another occurs in a discontinuous fashion. In some cases, certain industrial agglomerations decline rapidly and shift towards another foothold. An industrial agglomeration arises amid an atmosphere of dynamic disequilibrium and then decline. A city called "business castle town" in Japan went through a phenomenon of rapid industrial hollowing.[32]

The ranking of cities can be made using several indicators. The popularity of corporations and universities found in them and the track record for acquiring patents are the examples of those indicators. One can then gauge local knowledge supporting the cluster. Because these indicators have been accumulated over the years, the ranking is extremely difficult to reverse. Even if it were possible, it would require a long period of around ten years to surpass a superior city. For companies located in small, provincial cities, the initial conditions are poor, and it is difficult for them to even participate in the industry–university collaborations of their choice. Rather, the individual company may wish to find its own segment, or niche, and, if possible, become the proverbial "big fish in a small pond". Another factor hindering the creation of local knowledge is the time horizon for administration. While the policy aiming to engender clusters is global in scale, it takes a considerable amount of time for firms to grow into industrial districts.

4   IMPLICATIONS FOR LOCAL KNOWLEDGE MANAGEMENT

Agglomerate Strategy as an International Business Strategy

Adopting an agglomerate strategy makes it possible to compare between genuine and defective products. To implement the concept of *"genchi genbutsu"* (a Toyota jargon meaning "local goods to be surveyed locally"), an adjacent location is effective. Quality improvement will be attempted not only within the company but also in the local area.

In recent years, ways of overcoming the handicap of a long-distance location has seen remarkable development. With visual transmission through such means as the digital camera, video, Skype and the Internet, you can directly collect as much information as possible from a location and, should there be a problem, you will be able to effectively relay your concern to a large number of people. In order to discover a workplace for *Kaizen* (improvement), however, you need to move the camera to search for problematic places. One must notice that such forms of visual distribution effectively function over a completed network, whereas they function poorly as a means to create a person-to-person network.

A network is not created as a consequence of exchanging business cards, but arises as a consequence of the commitment of people to carry out business transactions. To convert a network into a framework for knowledge creation, it is necessary to have the aim of making comparisons and trying improvements. The knowledge networker of the location is the one who can vie under the severest environment of competition and who can expand their network of acquaintances in a location with the highest level of knowledge. An organization should forge a strategy for continuously promoting such businesspeople. In other words, if the act of making comparisons is essential, the knowledge networkers must be ubiquitous wherever they need to be. Simplifying procedures is a key. The in-house managing department must simplify the procedure without expending much paperwork. It becomes an important support mechanism so that traveling for business all around the world can be accomplished.

Should you aim to secure a global level of competitiveness, it will be effective to establish one foothold at least in a location that's the most leading edge and where the competition is the most intense. In so doing, you can acquire local knowledge that is specific to the location where the competition is the most intense. A strategy should be forged to determine whether to make the foothold a marketing base, a production base or a research and development base. In addition, it is necessary to build a corporate culture that promotes the exchange of information. Such a corporate culture should foster discussion among in-house talents regarding what kinds of cities there are in the world as candidates for being the most advantageous location for their own company. A company should be motivated to search for a city that is distinctively attractive to the company.

Adapting Your Strategy to Fit Cluster Types

When you compare Silicon Valley with the peripheries of Toyota-city and Stuttgart, which are manufacturing clusters, you will see that they vary by whether there are many stand-alone companies run by individuals or many extensions of start-up ventures launched by large enterprises. Because the minimum amount of proceeds acceptable to an organization is low, independent companies run by individuals can aim for projects that are more flexible than can start-up ventures run by large enterprises. Independent companies can change direction quickly in terms of starting an activity. While a venture business has such agility on the one hand, in many cases, such enterprises fall into the "death valley" trap. This occurs when they fail to continue their business due to the widening shortage in the supply of their financial resources for plant and equipment investment. In the case of start-up ventures of large enterprises, it takes time to reach a decision regarding their launch as a matter of corporate finance. However, once the decision is made, it becomes possible to continue a certain level of organizational support over the long term. Whether a certain cluster becomes a Silicon Valley type of cluster or it becomes a manufacturing type of cluster, such as the periphery of Toyota-city, may hinge on the cultural characteristics prevailing in the locality in which the cluster exists.

When the business cycle experiences an upswing, the Silicon Valley model can precisely grasp demand by a company patterned after it, thanks to its ability to respond speedily to the needs of niche markets. However, when the business cycle experiences a downswing, the manufacturing cluster model may prove to be superior. The start-up venture receives the support from the parent company to tide it over the downturn until the business climate recovers. Running an entrepreneurial company seems to be an individualistic behaviour in the sense that you can clearly understand who plays the leading role in the enterprise. However, in the case of running a start-up venture in an existing firm, an organization embedded in agglomeration plays the leading role. To specify who contributes the most towards the launch of the start-up venture is not necessarily easy.

The many research parks built all over the world are at times labelled "clusters", but they completely differ from Silicon Valley and the periphery of Toyota-city. There probably are research parks that cannot even become the second Silicon Valley or the second manufacturing cluster. The rationales of organizations active in the sphere of research parks, such as corporations, government-run research facilities and universities, may merely end up benefitting from the various special privileges offered by the research park. The research parks are set to become the starting point of an endogenous industrial development through spinoffs, but they might simply allow spending government subsidy. It is beyond prediction whether they turn out to be sources of development or not.

A possible scenario of a development revolving around a research park is the emergent fusion of a research park with an industry that has distinctively achieved endogenous development.[33] The reason why I introduce this hypothesis is because free trade zones, offshore production areas or the policy of attracting foreign factories in developing nations have the same principles as those of R&D activities in developed nations. If I see endogenous development from the aspect of the expansion of an organization, the emergent fusion could take place at research parks in developed nations. The *bunkojyo* (a branch factory), lured to an industrial complex, will turn out to rely on the technology and supply of parts/half-finished goods from its parent factory, rather than rely on its links to the local community in developing nations. For fusion with the local economy to take place, it is necessary to meet the long-term condition of having supporting industry situated in an adjacent location.

To encourage spinoffs is to cause the dwindling of the human resources of individual companies over the short term. However, if you aggregate them as a whole cluster, they will generate en masse a diversity of entrepreneurs. Expressions that convey the Japanese mind include euphemisms for ill-natured tendencies, such as "remove the ladder of a person who goes up to the second floor" and "strike the nail that sticks out". Promoting entrepreneurship is a difficult task under such a cultural background. However, when a new entrepreneur emerges from a company, the management, in recognition of this person's future, should promptly be prepared to offer support even after severance. When an employee goes on to launch new start-ups, the company may become your company's competitor, or this company becomes a party your company does business with. It depends on whether there is support or not from the company from which the employee spins off. From the viewpoint of the manager of a big company, it would be rational to recommend a spinoff to be carried out, in the event a certain project's level of risk is deemed high. And an intra-venture business is recommended in the event the risk level is deemed low. At any rate, championing the employee who launches a company will activate an indispensable process in the society of entrepreneurship.[34] Even though you lose employment as a result of setting up a new business, you may well be the first trading partner for those who launch a venture.

NOTES

1. The word "local" has various meanings. The term "local" used here refers to a wide geographic area that covers the argument of industrial collectives and clusters mentioned below.
2. As mentioned in the following chapter, both local knowledge and common knowledge are not purposeful knowledge. See Chapter 6 and relevant example.
3. See Smith (1776), *Part III, Chapter 3, Of the Rise and Progress of Cities and Towns, After the Fall of the Roman Empire*, and *Part III, Chapter 4, How the Commerce of the Towns Contributed to the Improvement of the Country*.
4. It was Marx's *Das Kapital* (1890) that preached the rigid conceptual distinction between

"concentration of capital" and "accumulation of capital". "Concentration of capital" refers to the growth of an oligopolistic company in an industry. "Accumulation of capital" refers to the growth of investment funds in a certain local area. In this sense, a spatial dimension was taken into account in *Das Kapital* (1890) as in classical economics as well. However, there are many economists who firmly appreciate Marx as an author of social thought and do not recognize his works as belonging in the field of "economics".

5. In Porter's work (1998), you can find a detailed reference list. It has continuous influence on cluster creation policy all around the world. For example, Ishikura (2003), Chapter 1, introduces the "Knowledge Cluster Initiative" driven by the MEXT and "The Industrial Cluster Policy" driven by the METI in Japan. Ishikura (2003) mixes the discussion on why cluster emerges and the policy-oriented advocacy on how the government tries to promote clusters through business-science grounds. As explained in detail in Chapters 4 and 5 of this book, policies that are named with the word "cluster" stand on grounds of a completely different mechanism of why the cluster exists.

6. Horaguchi (2008a) reports that a surprisingly high level of output, accompanied by a corner solution, arises in Courtnot's competition tied to the configuration of a free-scale network. The free-scale network falls into the concept of closure as defined by Coleman (1988). Horaguchi (2008a) also reports that only a low-level balanced output arises in a network tied to the hub-and-spoke configuration. This configuration is not a closure. As far as these two configurations are concerned, Horaguchi (2008a) shows an example that a closure can result in a higher level of output than otherwise.

7. The participatory observation in Tsukiji by Bestor (2004) had an impact on Japanese researchers, who tend to be inclined to the manufacturing industry. See Koike and Horaguchi (2006) on Japanese field researchers' experiences.

8. See von Hippel (1994). If the tacit knowledge that Polanyi (1966a, 1966b) points out is important, the exchange of knowledge in a specific local community will become indispensable. The people there gather and directly see and touch the object intended for their activity. This would be essential for producing machines, machine tools, robots and metallic moulds. It would fulfil the need to compare at low cost, since it would be possible to obtain information flexibly. If the need to compare is low, tacit knowledge will be replaced by the checklist prompted by explicit knowledge. Additionally, if a person who has acquired tacit knowledge can move to a remote place, then this corresponds to the mobility of the research worker amid a situation that sees the research and development footholds of a multinational company whose subsidiaries are dispersed globally. In such a case industrial agglomeration cannot be observed.

9. The concept of the cluster itself is not limited to just the manufacturing industry but is broadly applicable to various areas, including the electric town of Akihabara in Tokyo, the theatres and businesses of Broadway in New York, and the wineries of Napa Valley in California.

10. Kubo, et al. (2001) report the current nationwide conditions of research parks in Japan. In Chapter 8 of this book, Okamato (2001) discusses the importance and role of the coordinator in research parks, and questions the low level of recognition given to this position in Japanese society.

11. Kitagawa (2004) carried out international comparison of industry–government–university collaborations seen in research parks. She calls it "the local innovation system". I am hesitant to say, however, that industry–government–university collaborations are something you can refer to as an "innovation system". As I observed the operation of research parks, there were cases that the research and development there were not innovative at all. Performance evaluations were made possible by benchmarking the activities in research parks.

12. The records of my visits appear in appendix Table 1 and Table 2 found at the end of Horaguchi (2009b). My visits include all of 18 designated places of the Knowledge Cluster Initiative in Japan and 25 clusters in various countries. I visited the place of the Knowledge Cluster Initiative a few times when it was considered as innovative.

Observation and interview in Japan started in 2004 and it resumed in 2009. Interview research in foreign industrial parks started in 1992. Here, I include records of visits I made prior to having arrived at any critical ideas that led to the authoring of this book. This is because some of my thoughts were not crystallized until I made comparisons with past information.

13. If you compare research parks with spontaneous clusters, you see some fundamental differences among them. Some research parks are not equipped with the conditions of business linkage which leads to the access for export markets. In a world of Japanese media some sort of public spending is called "administration to build boxes" (*hakomono gyosei*), which refers to inefficient buildings set up for spending public budget. In such cases one can observe agglomeration of inefficient public buildings such as research facilities in research parks. How do you measure the cost performance of a research park? What can be the indicator of performance measurement? Are patents and papers sufficient as the measurement? Many questions remain to measure performance of research parks.

14. In addition to the visits I made that appear in the appendix Table 2 of Horaguchi (2009b), I presented an invitational lecture at the Institute for Information Industry, Market Intelligence Centre in Taiwan on 15 October 2007. I also attended an international convention held by the Taiwan Institute of Economic Research from 21–22 August 2008. Thereafter, I was granted an interview with the director of the Industrial Technology Research Institute (ITRI) of Taiwan and with a professor at Tsinghua University in Taiwan who was formerly a managing director at ITRI.

15. On 17 March 2006, Horaguchi interviewed Mr Patrick Kwang-Peng Chan, the Technopreneurship Program Manager of The National University of Singapore Entrepreneurship Centre. He said that there was a plan in place to hold a business plan competition for entrepreneurs from the USA, Southeast Asia, Europe and Australia. He added that industry–university collaborations initiated by the professors of the department of engineering were being actively carried out as well.

16. I visited the Shanghai Jiao Tong University on 27 February 2006 and noticed that the research and development centres of Toray, Intel and Kao were located in the science and technology park district found in the adjoining land of the university. China's cluster promotion policy seemed to be shifting from the fourth quadrant of Figure 5.1 to the third quadrant.

17. The second quadrant of Figure 5.1 is close to the technology cluster as conceived by McKendrick et al. (2000). However, the manufacturing cluster in the first quadrant also boasts a high level of technology.

18. Kanai (1994) investigates a network of entrepreneurs revolving around the Massachusetts Institute of Technology (MIT). He presents noteworthy issues, including the point of speaking highly of the network of the Boston area. This view is in contrast to the one which was assessed slightly negatively by Saxenian (1994). Kanai (1994) made an application of the network theory by Granovetter (1973), and recognized that support networks for entrepreneurs vary from "the forum type" to "the dialog type". These points are characterized by participatory observations.

19. See Kenney (2000) and Lee, Miller, Hancock and Rowen (2000). I conducted field research in Silicon Valley with my collaborators in September 2004. The work features interviews with failed entrepreneurs, venture capitalists, venture businesses invested by Japanese-owned companies, and individuals belonging to large American enterprises and law firms. In addition, we conducted interviews with Stanford University researchers Marguerite Gong Hancock, Professor Henry S. Rowen, and Professor Daniel Okimoto, and Professor Annalee Saxenian at the University of California, Berkley.

20. See Lécuyer (2000).

21. At the time the authors carried out the survey in 2004, the dot-com bubble that began at the end of 2000 had burst, and the world was going through a recession that followed in the aftermath of the simultaneous terrorist attacks of September 11, 2001. The Japanese economy saw the burst of an economic bubble at the end of 1989 and in 1997 the

Hokkaido Takushoku Bank and Yamaichi Securities failed. Horaguchi, Amano, Kim, Konno, and Yaginuma (2005b) speculated that American financial institutions would fail around 2008, which is seven years after 2001. In this report of theirs, it is written as follows.

"Since the 'simultaneous terrorist attacks of September 11, 2001,' the Silicon Valley had fallen into a period of a severe business slump. Not only did bankruptcies see a rise, but it became clear that venture capitalists were finding it difficult to gather funds. In addition, the venture funds established around the year 2000, which was prior to the burst of the bubble in Silicon Valley, were expected to see their recovery around 2007 through 2008, considering that a venture capital's cycle, from its establishment to recovery, lasts for a period of around seven to eight years. At that time, ventures unable to acquire the next investment capital and venture capitalists who fail to establish funds will be screened. It was at the end of 1989 that the Japanese bubble economy had burst, and consequently, it was in 1997 that we saw the Hokkaido Takushoku Bank, Sanyo Securities, and Yamaichi Securities going bankrupt. If we recall these facts, we can predict that the IT slump of Silicon Valley will continue for several more years (p. 28)."

In September 2008, Lehman Brothers, a major American investment bank, met with failure. While the failure of the financial institution is attributed to the bad debts of subprime loans for homes and the net deficit of credit extended to businesses, it remains to be seen which one of these factors had played a substantial role in causing the downfall.

22. Saxenian (2000) introduces a case example of Taiwanese entrepreneurs who make linkages between Taiwan and California to develop business. Their educational backgrounds are of high calibre and they are well versed in scientific knowledge.

23. Matsushima (2002) offers an overview of the characteristics of 33 metalworking systems suppliers to Toyoda Iron Works, the secondary parts supplier to Toyota Motor Corporation. Just one company is located in Osaka, while 32 companies are located in Aichi. In addition, Matsushima (2005b) carried out a questionnaire survey of the suppliers to Futaba Industrial and Toyoda Iron Works, and made it clear that many of them were small to mid-sized businesses operating with around 100 employees and a capital of 10 million yen, and their founders had become independent by spinning out from metal working manufacturers.

24. See Daimler AG edition's *Mercedes-Benz Cars at a Glance: 2008 Edition*. This booklet was available for download from Daimler AG's homepage.

25. Horaguchi (2013b) analyses patent strategy of aircraft manufacturers in Japan. The number of jointly owned patents is small in the aircraft industry.

26. Regarding the above-mentioned argument, refer to Amano, Kim, Konno, Horaguchi, Matsushima (2006) and Porter (1986, 1990).

27. Applying the concept of "the fusion of industries", Uekusa (2000) discusses the process of how a new industry is created.

28. I already made this point in footnote 22 in Chapter 4 of this book.

29. This is based on interviews carried out on 11 and 12 September 2006, in Grenoble, France.

30. This is drawn from interviews carried out on 12 and 13 September 2005, in Sofia Antipolis, France.

31. Differences in risk evaluations are key issues when starting an entrepreneurial business.

32. See Horaguchi (2001a, 2002, 2004c).

33. Depicting such scenarios are authors such as Yamasaki and Tomokage (2001) and Yamasaki (2003), who describe a design for turning Kyushu into a "silicon island". It is necessary to carefully monitor future trends, and to this end, economists are asking some questions that reflect their overall viewpoints on policy administration. The first question they are asking is, can you expect a research park to develop into a manufacturing cluster through the attempt of forming and managing the Kitakyushu Science and Research Park? The second question is, how do you measure the performance of a research park? The third is, how can the factories of IC-related industries, spreading

throughout the entire Kyushu area, differentiate from the factories in Shenzhen and Shanghai in China in terms of quality? Appraising performance is a key challenge, and if a viable means to this end is unavailable, evaluating the cost performance of an infusion of governmental funds will not be possible.

34. See Burgelman and Sayles (1986).

6. Common knowledge

1 PRINCIPLES

Necessity of Information Exchange

Common knowledge is synonymous with common sense. It can be defined as a fact that can be assumed to be understood by two parties within a mutually interactive framework whereby interchanges of certain information are possible. It is something that is known mutually, as it were, even though both parties may not confirm the fact. In game theory, such a definition of common knowledge is known by economists as a condition that gives rise to the Nash Equilibrium. In a more general sense, common knowledge means a notion that is commonly understood by all the constituent members of a certain society. However, the common knowledge possessed by a speaker may not necessarily correspond with the expectations of someone listening to the speaker. There are many examples where the common knowledge differs between generations, between man and woman, and between regions.

Regarding the spread of knowledge in society, as a classic theoretical consideration, there is the work of Tarde (1895). Tarde (1895) states that "advancement is a kind of collective thinking" (translation in Japanese, p. 217), and emphasizes that imitation gives rise to relations between individuals. Tarde (1895) discusses innovation in several places, and in that respect, has passages in common with Schumpeter (1926), whom he precedes. For instance, Tarde (1895) argued that in the course of the development of a production driven by the steam engine, various inventions and imaginative ideas would be triggered and that, before long, one definitive machine emerged. Subsequently, various improvements revolving around this machine will be made and any other inventions and machines will come to be forgotten (translation, p. 217).

Common knowledge as one category of collective knowledge signifies not only a certain type of knowledge that is widespread, but also one that becomes the foundation for subsequent knowledge creation processes once it spreads. The following discussion comprises the first principle of how common knowledge spreads. Common knowledge as collective knowledge refers to a moving body that traces two processes, namely invention and imitation.[1] The structural outline shown in Chapter 2's Figure 2.1 also applies here. The dissemination of knowledge works as an exercise of self-organization affecting individuals existing in a society. Subsequently, the knowledge that becomes widespread emerges as a framework for thinking in common. If we were to only observe the process of how knowledge spreads, the research concerning the speed of its dissemination will not differ from an inquiry into the dissemination of pathogens, or disease-causing germs. What is important to note here is that the knowledge that has finished spreading acts as a foundation for the conception of the next stage of creating knowledge. The basic principle concerning the formation of common knowledge is primarily the necessity of information exchange carried out by humans. People have a need to exchange information for the purpose of realizing communication, or mutual understanding.[2] Natural language is one of the forms of collective knowledge and people have to learn this natural language, which they are supposed to have created them-selves, under the subject heading "national language". Furthermore, there is the fact that people obtain pleasure through the act of exchanging infor-mation. Information exchange is carried out not only when it is deemed useful, but also when it is deemed useless, as long as the act is perceived to be pleasurable.[3] Within a playful state of mind, language usage, which diverges from its practical usage, develops and gives rise to a new type of grammar.[4] Cultures derived from common knowledge in many cases are frowned upon by the older generation and this is indicative of the fact that such cultures are dependent upon the enjoyment attained through the act of information exchange.[5]

The second principle concerning the formation of common knowledge is the emergence of a socially recognized form of knowledge when a certain type of innovation has finished spreading.[6] *Ex post facto*, this can be referred to as common knowledge. While shared knowledge, symbiotic knowledge and local knowledge each transform the shape of knowledge locally, when such innovative changes spread out into society, common knowledge emerges. When technology developed as shared knowledge of a particular company is offered to other companies belonging to another industry through alliances between them, a new symbiotic knowledge comes into existence. It becomes local knowledge when transaction spreads and labour moves within the local area. The process by which this knowledge spreads further into society as a whole can be referred to as the spread of innovation as stated in Rogers (1995 and 1962, first edition) or in Drucker (1993). Common knowledge emerges in a process whereby the shared knowledge that was embodied in a form of goods within a cor-porate organization transforms into a societal, universally common form of knowledge. The reason why shared knowledge, symbiotic knowledge and local knowledge spread is because, along with the profit motive of enterprises, people exchange information to seek properties and services that help them enjoy at a lower cost a higher level of convenience and a higher level of pleasure. At the same time, the enterprise obtains feedback[7] about the products or services offered to customers and makes further improvements based on such feedback. The market for a product is formed through evaluations of sales promotions and "word-of-mouth" by customers.

The third principle concerning common knowledge is the existence of state power. The domains such as a legal system, official language, education and regulation on the marketplace are controlled by the state. National power can prescribe language usage and establish the subject and content of compulsory education. The migration of people is restricted by nationality and emigrating from one's home country to a foreign one is difficult since it involves assimilation to a different linguistic area. The contents that can be covered in public education, such as particular novels or prose originating in certain languages, are all decided by the state. It is also the role of the state to arrange for the uniformity or the standardization of language notations. This role of the state is irrespective of whether or not it has adopted a democratic style of government.

The Spread of Innovation

Common knowledge indicates the state where innovation has spread. Although an enterprise's shared knowledge may have been public goods property only within the enterprise, with the creation of symbiotic knowledge as a reflection of inter-organizational relations, and after extending into local knowledge as a reflection of a local community network, the common knowledge is found to be in a state where it has spread into society. You can confirm public goods property in the characteristics in common knowledge.

The essence of innovation is described in a single phrase. The creativity of persons is actualized in corporate activities. When something new actually emerges out of people's intellectual ideas and is also supported by profitability, it is recognized as an innovation. Regarding the spread of innovation, there is research that has been carried out by Rogers (1995, 1962 first edition). I review in the following that the spread of innovation follows the pattern of the logistic curve. The spread of commodities resulting from innovation means that there is 100 per cent spread in accordance to time. To show changes in certain variables over time, we use a differential equation.[8] By solving Bernoulli's differential equation, we can

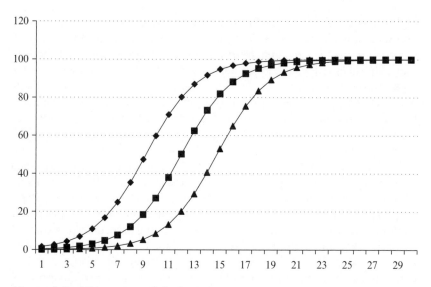

Figure 6.1   Illustration of the logistic curve

obtain equation (15) shown on page 167, where this chapter's supplement provides the derivation process. The shape of this equation is called the logistic curve.

$$x(t) = \frac{A}{1 + Be^{-Ct}} \tag{15}$$

The results of the simulations carried out by entering suitable values in the parameters of the above-mentioned equation (15) are shown in Figure 6.1. In all the three curves of Figure 6.1, the parameters are A = 100 and C = 0.5. As for B, the values of 100, 400 and 1600 respectively have been assigned from the left curve. As for t, the values from 1 through 30 have been assigned.

Some interesting facts can be observed from this simulation. Firstly, since it is defined as $B = A/x_0 - 1$ (derived from this chapter's supplement section), the smaller the initial value at the time of introduction of a new product x_0 in comparison with market scale A, the slower the rise of the curve becomes. Secondly, the slowness of this rise does not mean a time delay at the time of the new product x_0's introduction *per se*. Although the time of introduction of the new product x_0 is the same for all three curves, it appears that the speed of spread is delayed due to the fact that the value of parameter B is big. This signifies that the size of the initial value x_0 is small.

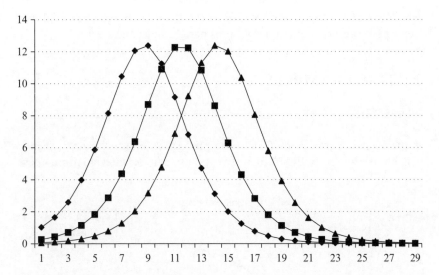

Figure 6.2   Graph capturing the differences found in the logistic curves

Regarding B, since each curve from the left has been assigned the values 100, 400 and 1600 respectively, if the -1 in $B = A/x_0 - 1$ is disregarded, then based on $A = 100$, it is approximately equal to assigning x_0 the initial values of 1, 0.25 and 0.0625. If we check the point where the product diffusion level exceeds 80 per cent, it shows $t = 12$, 15 and 18 respectively. Provisionally, if $t = 1$ denotes one year, with this parameter setting, when the initial value is 1/4 small, it manifests as an approximately three-year delayed product diffusion.

An attractive interpretation regarding the size of the initial value is that it can be comprehended as the scale of a cluster. When a cluster wields substantial influence, or in other words, when the network that can be connected from the cluster is large and information on new product developments spreads extensively, you can expect to see the speed of diffusion becoming fast.

Figure 6.2 is a graph that captures the difference in the curves shown in Figure 6.1. The greatest change is seen during the growth period and the rate of change becomes almost zero during the introductory and declining periods. In marketing theory, people who show a positive attitude towards purchasing new products are called early adopters and they are vividly responding to market segmentation.[9] Granovetter (1973) points out that innovation spreads more rapidly when individuals among early adopters connect other groups through "weak ties" (pp. 1367–9).[10] When the curves in Figure 6.2 were backed by empirical data, economists and management scholars attached great importance to the data as being substantial and went on to present them under various names they conceived.[11]

2   CASE EXAMPLES

Internet Sites

If the logistic curve is applied to the process of Internet spread, then it will be as shown in Figure 6.3. Two points can be inferred from these

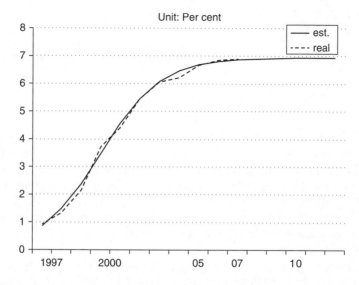

Notes:
1. An Internet user is defined by Soumusho (Ministry of Internal Affairs and Communications) to be someone above 6 years old who has experienced using the Internet within the past year. Their Internet connection equipment includes a PC, a mobile phone, a personal handyphone system (PHS), an information terminal and a game device.
2. Estimations were prepared by the present author. Refer to Satō (1984) regarding the method of estimation applied.
3. Actual-value data available are for those until the end of 2007, and the graph representing the time period thereafter depends on the estimate.

Source: The definition of actual-value data and the above-mentioned note 1 depends on a single page of the "Results of the 2007 Communication Usage Behavior Study" and the explanatory note for the said page. This data appears in a PDF file available from http://www.soumu.go.jp/s-news/2008/pdf/080418_4_bt.pdf.

Figure 6.3   Transitions in the Internet population diffusion rate

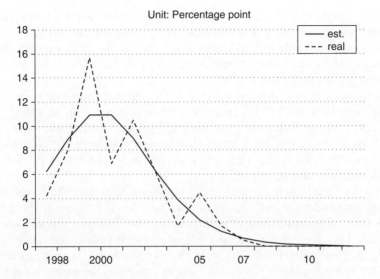

Unit: Percentage point

Figure 6.4   Differences in the increase of the Internet population

measurement results. Firstly, the logistic curve shows a slowdown in the rate of diffusion, and the spread of the Internet is seen to be entering a stage of maturity. The quantitative growth is approaching its peak and is about to transition into the mature stage, wherein we see usage becoming more sophisticated and demand shifting for software and hardware replacements.[12] Secondly, the period spanning from the start of the growth stage until the slowdown in growth is observed is approximately ten years if I set the starting point at the point from when statistics become available. Since the growth of industry is rapid, the period of growth is short. Figure 6.4, which shows differences between the logistic curves, helps us understand that the curves tend to lack the data of early diffusion rates and tend to fluctuate from theoretical values on a bi-yearly basis.

A typical representation of common knowledge on the Internet is Wikipedia. This system of common knowledge is grounded in a social infrastructure that is the Internet.[13] Although Wikipedia is an encyclopaedia, users are able to set their own categories and post descriptions on the site of the encyclopaedia itself. While users can post incorrect information or deliberate lies on Wikipedia, if there are many people making revisions to correct such errors and falsehoods, the site will turn out to become a repository of correct information. In terms of the aspect of information accumulation, Wikipedia is a mechanism that promotes the participation of the readers to the site. In this respect, it differs from other search sites, such as Yahoo and Google. In the sense of retrieving information stored on the Internet, search sites also function as sites that extract collective knowledge. However, it is not necessarily the case that the readers of the information are able to participate in the process. If a site you launch is ranked low in the display of search results by the search site, the site will turn out to be neglected in effect.

Examples of sites I want to refer to as common knowledge sites are spreading over time. While sites that publish answers to questions are typical, there are other sites that offer information on bargain prices for various products, ranging from gasoline to cosmetics, sites that offer music and movie reviews, sites that facilitate cuisine with recipes and sites to exchange job-hunting information.

Though there are many useful common knowledge sites, there are some questionable ones as well. As a professor who lectures at universities, one site I felt to be remarkable in particular was the "Happy Campus" site in Japan. This site lets undergraduate students upload and sell reports on subjects they study. In this site, a user can search by keywords and collect multiple reports. While there are voices by professors lamenting the rise in reports created by simply cutting and pasting from web pages, such reports were easily discernible because of the differences in writing style. However, it becomes more difficult to make such discernments when the reports are bought in the "Happy Campus" and are authored by undergraduate students themselves. In effect, this involves not copying a classmate's report, but downloading one written by a student of another university in a distant location, changing its font and then submitting it.

Thus the traditional educational practice at universities of making the submission of reports for term-end examinations is facing a crisis of existence.[14] To avoid such deeds, you can have students carry out research by themselves and have them create reports with photographs of the research. Alternatively, you can adopt the method of assigning a reading list containing a number of the latest literary sources and have them write up a report within a short time.

Motivations Behind Participating in Collective Knowledge Sites

There is a pioneering study regarding the reasons why people participate in what I call common knowledge sites on the Internet. Miura and Kawaura (2008) call a virtual community, whose purpose is information acquisition, a "knowledge-sharing community". They classify them into two kinds: one is the "encyclopaedia-model community", as represented by Wikipedia, and the other is the "Q&A community", which facilitates mutual teaching among users. As representatives of the latter, in Japan, there are "Oshiete! Goo" (Teach Me! Goo), "Jinriki Kensaku Saito, Hatena" (Manpower

Search Site, I Wonder?), "Yahoo! Chie Bukuro" (Yahoo! Brains), and abroad, there is "Yahoo! Answers". After starting in December 2005, "Yahoo! Answers" managed to attract 60 million users in one year. In turn, it is said, these users contributed a total of 160 million responses. In addition, in "the Q&A community", there are considered to be two types of questions: one is the type of question with a pre-existing correct answer and the other is open-ended, or one without a determinate solution.

Miura and Kawaura (2008) carried out a factor analysis by collecting the questionnaires from 2513 users who had posted answers on "Yahoo! Chie Bukuro (chiebukuro.yahoo.co.jp)" and concluded that people who post responses on these sites are "motivated by the urge to help" by the respondents of the questionnaire. Specifically, when asked why they answered questions on these sites, their responses, showing high factor loadings, included: "I wish to solve the questioner's problem" or "it's natural to help a person in difficulty or a person who wishes to learn." It is worth noting that responses such as "because I like Yahoo! Chie Bukuro", "because I wish to liven up Yahoo! Chie Bukuro" and "because the act of answering itself is fun" were not rated high in terms of the factor loadings. These answers are grouped and labelled by Miura and Kawaura (2008) as "social motives". As Miura and Kawaura (2008) clarified, if the motives to participate in the online activities of Q&A community sites are to be explained, even partially, by the motive of compassion, as reflected in the response "I wish to solve the questioner's problem", or the site is supported by entertainment motives, as reflected in the response, "because the act of answering itself is fun", this will mean that Q&A community sites are supported by factors that are universal among human beings. If this is the case, we can expect to see Q&A community sites becoming more salient over time in terms of social universality.

Laser Welding and the Industrial Robot

Even in the field of mechanical engineering, we can observe examples of technologies that have become widespread as universal technologies for industrial use. At the beginning of the twentieth century they remained mere theoretical possibilities which were just being debated. Unlike Internet sites, laser welding cannot be used easily by the general public, but for industrial engineers, technological difficulty is not the issue.

I visited laser welding machine manufacturers. One is Mitsubishi Electric's Nagoya factory in Japan and the other is TRUMPF in Stuttgart, Germany. I received explanations regarding CO_2 lasers and YAG lasers.[15] Consequently, I learned that Mitsubishi Electric was found in 1921 and TRUMPF was found in 1923. The former company had initiated in 1967 basic research into the technology of laser processing while the latter initiated laser applications for manufacturing in 1964. Since 1982, Mitsubishi Electric has started production of two-dimensional laser processing. In addition, Mitsubishi Electric is carrying out production of "The LD Excitation YAG Laser Oscillation Machine".

Their real issue in manufacturing application is rather the question of striking the right balance between cost and benefit. I visited the Nissan Shatai Hiratsuka Factory and the Toyota Motor Corporation Motomachi Plant, and conducted interviews regarding welding lines. In the course of these interviews, both companies stated that their level of automation of automobile welding lines had reached 94 per cent.[16] The one-armed industrial robot performs spot welding, arc welding and laser welding. In addition, at Nissan Shatai,[17] the tasks of robotic-parts recognition and transferring to welding lines were being carried out.[18]

According to an engineer of a major German car-body producer, which joined a tour to the welding lines of Toyota's Motomachi Plant, the places where laser welding are performed differ for Toyota and European manufacturers. As far as you can tell by looking at bodies displayed at Toyota's Motomachi Factory, laser welding is performed for areas hidden by the seat's shadow. However, in the case of European cars such as the Jaguar and Land Rover, it is said that laser welding is applied for the exterior of the body as well.[19]

Learning a Language

In this section, I would like to step away from case examples of specific industries, such as the Internet and laser processing with industrial robots, and instead consider the characteristics of common knowledge found in the domain of cultural elements that are tightly woven into the fabric of our day-to-day lives. Elements such as the language of a certain country, gestures shared in common among people or the understanding of the connotations of symbols all fall under the designation of common knowledge.

A language is merely a tool of everyday life. It comes in handy in situations for the native speaker born in the country in which the language is spoken. For the foreigner, however, it is knowledge that should be learned and acquired. The power of collective knowledge as common knowledge can be evidenced in the formation of a language. The language is created through self-organization process. Once it emerges, people have to learn the language. While there is no academic preparation necessary to carry out the task of speaking your native language, once you attempt to acquire a language that is foreign to you, you will be reminded that such a language includes bodies of knowledge such as grammar, usage, conjugation and idioms. By remembering non-routine knowledge, you will turn out to be a foreign language speaker.

Human beings are educated to acquire common knowledge from the moment they are born. This common knowledge evolves by country and by local community. In Japan, for example, the particular common knowledge of bowing one's head when greeting another with the Japanese word for hello, "konnichiwa", is learned. In no other parts of the world can anyone find this practice. Another example concerns the structure of a passage. After you read the passage written by the Japanese Nobel Prize winner Yasunari Kawabata, "After passing through the tunnel, it was snow country there," which appears in his famous novel *Yukiguni*, or Snow Country, you learn the beauty of the sentence without a subject. The sentence does not specify exactly who or what is passing through the tunnel, prompting you to presume from the tenor of the sentence that the subject is the train on which the protagonist is.

As I discussed in Chapter 3, shared knowledge is knowledge that arises in the process of specializing and subdividing such common sense. Or in other words, such common knowledge is shared in a limited place by limited participants. A university's specialized curriculum is based upon common knowledge so that intellectual students can choose before they learn a particular subject. In the course of deciding what to study from the curriculums offered by the university, the students learn specialized subjects are subdivided into a special field of category. By that time the students are immersed by each body of shared knowledge in the curriculums. For example, it is the task of the discipline of linguistics to point out that the subject of the sentence is missing in the sentence, "After passing through the tunnel, it was snow country there."

The youth in Japan, especially high school students, are known to create vogue phrases. This is one example of a self-organizing system. A Japanese word "*yabai*" is a typical example of this. Up to the 1980s, it clearly meant "chancy" or "immoral". In the 2000s the word "*yabai*" can mean "something tremblingly good" or "awesome". It involves transforming a known word into a new word and then distributing it. When this distribution exceeds a fixed threshold, the process of emergence begins. At this point, a state of mind that makes you feel "shameful if you don't know" forms. A state power then follows the trend to include the word into their educational standard.

A language is considered as a body of collective knowledge. Then linguistics is regarded as the comparative study of collective knowledge. Linguistics works on extracting various forms of logic common to various languages. In this sense, it is an academic field that has been pursuing the study of collective knowledge.[20] Since this field compares a multiple number of bodies of language as collective knowledge, it may be appropriate to describe the linguistic approach as one distinctive to a form of meta-collective knowledge.

The activity of maintaining a standardized form of language is universally assumed to be the role of the nation. There are cases when linguistic endeavours should be shouldered throughout the nation, such as the establishment of the standard language, the prevalence of traffic signs and the rules of law adopted by the nation. However, things such as gestures and a sense of values cannot readily become the objects of a nation's conscious efforts. They are forms of common knowledge self-organized from interactions among people.

Education

It is interesting to see that Drucker (1986) points out an example of innovation. It was popularization of the textbook as an educational gimmick (p. 31). Since common knowledge enlarges the knowledge base of a society, it has an influence on the level of new knowledge arising from there.

In October 2006, in the Japanese city of Takaoka located in Toyama prefecture, news broke that the subject of world history was not being taught at high schools. Following this revelation, critics began to point out that high schools all over Japan were facing a similar problem.[21] It therefore turned out that a massive number of high school graduates had not learned world history. On the other hand, private universities in Japan have set a standard for entrance examinations, which requires examinees to take three subjects, such as English, Japanese and elective subjects such as world history, Japanese history or mathematics. Some of them even allow students to take examinations for only one to two subjects, making the decline of common knowledge clearly attributable to this requirement. Consequently, such a state of institution is giving rise to a fragile society, where a knowledge base shared in common by its people is non-existent.

Education level speaks of a form of knowledge that society as a whole can presume. In times when the percentage of students pursuing higher education was low, there were many who joined the workforce soon after graduating from junior high school out of dire economic necessity. Apprenticeships and shop manufacturing systems played an important role then, but they are continuing to see a decrease in present-day Japan. These systems used to absorb the part of the workforce made up by people whose level of education stopped short at the junior high school level.

Since we have seen a rise in the ratio of students who go on to become college undergraduates over time, their aptitude rests on those of high school students of the past. In this respect, the level of Japanese education may be falling in crisis. When the knowledge level of "an undergraduate whose level of education is at the same level of a high school student of the past" does not meet the level of aspiration in a modern knowledge society, you can readily expect to see the emergence of a group of young people who are unable to gain employment.

The reason why a company should attach great importance to enriching education for primary and junior high school students by way of contributing to the local community can also be found here. The company employs school graduates and helps them carry out knowledge management. To this end, we must not forget that reducing the number of pupils per class in schools that carry out compulsory education and secondary education will raise the level of students' understanding, ultimately leading to the heightening of the overall education level. I must also emphasize that individuals are able to acquire a form of knowledge on their own. This includes the ability to comprehend foreign languages, mathematical aptitudes, common understanding of history and science, and capabilities for operating information technology, which comprise, in effect, what we call computer literacy. As long as we see the prevalence of continuing adult education, we probably should not be too pessimistic about the future of education.

Cuisine in Culture

Ethnic cuisine cultivated in specific countries, such as Japanese, Chinese, Italian and French cuisine, falls under the category of common knowledge. People rarely enquire about the origins of these cuisines, and while it may be impossible to find an answer, there are dishes that are widely shared in common in the country. Just as you can easily distinguish Italian cuisine from French cuisine, so can you similarly distinguish Chinese cuisine from Japanese cuisine.

Be it French cuisine or Japanese cuisine, it will become necessary to have the type of cuisine training. To prepare a particular country's cuisine, the training has as its main aim the acquisition of tacit knowledge. Chinese cuisine breaks down into categories that are differentiated by local communities in China, such as Sichuan, Guangdong and Hakka, and in many cases you can find large differences among the different styles despite the fact that the said styles belong to the same country. The cuisine of each country differs by northern and southern localities and by seaside and mountain locations.

Individual restaurants are in competition with each other. In every Chinese restaurant, you are sure to find fried rice served, and each individual restaurant should be attempting to offer "delicious" Chinese fried rice. However, as long as a dish named "fried rice" is offered in the menu, the restaurant is not categorized as an authentic Japanese restaurant, a French restaurant nor an Italian restaurant. This is a difference in terms of cuisine-based specialties. Here is an example of common knowledge. By definition, common knowledge entails that everyone knows about it. However, it is precisely because everyone knows that you will not see any French restaurant offering fried rice, nor would there be anyone with such an expectation.

While I have discussed in detail in the argument concerning symbiotic knowledge in this book, I refer to such a specialty as "the dimension of knowledge". If you combine French and Chinese cuisine it might create symbiotic knowledge in the field of non-traditional cuisine. Two of the dimensions of knowledge would be combined in such a case.

Story and Religion

Myths, traditions and fairy tales are not presumed to have been recorded by one single individual. It may thus be possible to consider them as one form of common knowledge. The formation of the academic discipline known as ethnology, which involves the collection of folktales, stands on the grounds of common knowledge. The ways in which stories are presented vary by the times and by the country. Some are presented through word of mouth as part of an oral tradition, some are presented in the form of prose and some are left as lyrics in a song.

As examples of the modern format, we find various genres, such as novels, comics, video games, exclusive game consoles, movies, DVDs and YouTube. The formation of a certain genre is dependent on the number of people participating in the genre. In Japan, you can find traditional genres that enjoy only a handful of creators today. Such genres include *Renga* (linked verses), *Nishikie* (colour woodblock prints) and *Ukiyo-e* prints.

Religion is considered as another example of common knowledge. Japan is a country with many new religions. We can cite dozens of religions and denominations that came into existence in the twentieth century. It may follow therefore that people may be choosing religions out of their own free will. In many cases, the religious choices people make are largely influenced by what religions their own parents follow. Children are influenced by their domestic circumstances and share in common a faith in the same religion. While there are gradual historical changes, a certain religious sphere historically establishes itself.

Religion offers business opportunities. In countries that have already seen capitalist development, various observances and events that stem from religious ceremonies become commercialized. Christmas, Valentine's

Day and Halloween are observances that have already become firmly established in Japan, and they have become a battleground for trade wars. While Weber (1919) attempted to portray through his book, *The Protestant Ethic and the Spirit of Capitalism*, the idea that the sudden rise of capitalism was triggered by religion, the argument was criticized by followers of Judaism from the outset (p. 19, translation, note 4). The development of capitalism in nations such as Japan, China and Korea challenges the proposition of a single religion triggering the development of capitalism.

Play and Sports

Play and sports are a gold mine of tacit knowledge-cum-common knowledge. In Japan, there are traditional games, such as *Otedama* (beanbag), *Ayatori* (cat's cradle) and *Origami* (paper craft). With play and sports, in most instances, people learn their methods through imitation. You will also find traditional sports, such as *sumo, karate, kendo* and *judo*. There are deep-rooted supporters for exercises known as radio calisthenics broadcasted through NHK television and radio.

This is illustrative of the transmission of tacit knowledge. To execute a volley shoot in soccer, you will need to work on observing someone else performing this action and then imitating the moves. Verbal explanations are merely auxiliary. Common knowledge is created through play and sports which spread at a societal level, and are acknowledged to have been experienced at least once by everyone. While this is at times supported by education, there are many cases when it solely prevails throughout the domain of private enterprises. In addition, sports have the conspicuous consumption effect.[22] It triggers the feeling in other people of following suit. Those who can perform something being envied is considered to be a characteristic of the so-called "leisure class", which comprises people who have free time on their hands.

As touched upon in Chapter 1 of this book, in games that involve thinking, such as *go, shogi* and chess, the tradition of *anzan*, or mental arithmetic, lives on. While the aspect of thinking is inherent in games that use video and gaming devices, a large aspect of playing games on such platforms entails play by pushing buttons and reacting by moving sensors. In such cases, the emphasis is placed on reacting, rather than thinking. Games such as *go, shogi* and even *mahjong* have developed into competitive Internet-based games, having, in effect, evolved into a form that facilitates matches between players who are remote in distance from each other. Play and sports have been affected by the innovation known as the Internet, too.

3   CONTROLLING COMMON KNOWLEDGE

The Role of the Gatekeeper

Wikipedia has a practice of prohibiting entries when they reflect too many varying perspectives. A person who plays such a role is called the gatekeeper. Just like the committee establishing ethical codes for television broadcasting, this gatekeeper fulfils the role of establishing standards that determine the level of common knowledge society should tolerate.

The legal system can become a gatekeeper that determines society's common ideas.[23] The legal system itself is important as common knowledge, and those who establish concepts of "public order and morals" are inspectors and jurors (citizen judges). Their role is characterized as a gatekeeper as well. What determines the quality of common knowledge as a form of collective knowledge is the ethical outlook of the people who become gatekeepers. Examples of social systems supported by a legal system would be an election system, a tax system, accounting system and pension system.

The Market as a Gatekeeper

The market mechanism includes the function of a gatekeeper. There is a competitive mechanism that realizes the survival of the fittest. A simple example is found in a Japanese cuisine such as *sushi*. It is unknown when and by whom the type of *sushi* called the *California maki* (the California roll) was created. However, the product that implemented the idea of placing avocado into Japan's traditional sushi-roll entree was probably offered by a *sushi* restaurant in California, and was met with approval by people who like sushi there. In abstract terms, this means that people who like sushi comprise the "sushi market" and the California roll appears to have survived through a process of selection in this market.

Once it was established as a marketable product and its recipe became known, the California roll came to be offered as a marketable product in Japan as well. In other words, the California roll's recipe emerged in a macro society and came to affect the sushi shop as a micro entity. This is a case example of self-organization and emergence. Common knowledge is sometimes produced as the form of a fad or fashion. The role the mass media plays is large. The mass media creates huge demands in the market. The number of people who are able to realize circulation of information through media such as the television and newspaper still remains more than the number of people who have a connection to the Internet or those who browse it. While the influence of the Internet is predicted to surpass that of television and newspapers in the future, the impact of the mass media continues to be substantial in terms of shaping the market. In the legal system, one can observe gatekeepers we know as judges, but in the market, we cannot identify individuals as gatekeepers. While in some cases connoisseurs can appreciate a certain scarce product, its production is terminated depending on the criteria of the profitability of the company offering the product.

The Culture Business and Its Strategy

What characterizes common knowledge is that it is impossible to manage it over the short term.[24] Common knowledge cannot be changed overnight. From the perspective of an individual entity – a human being or a business enterprise – common knowledge changes slowly. If you take about five to ten years, however, common knowledge surely changes. Yet, it is difficult to predict who the subject of change will be, and what kind of common knowledge will appear in the end after the change. This is because emergence is set into action from this point onwards (see Figure 6.5).

Communication via mobile phones and communication via text messaging became the standard in Japanese society around 2000. If you look back, text messaging by mobile phone was rare in 1990, and what facilitated communication via mobile phones around that time was a technical standard called the personal handyphone system (PHS). Around 2010, Internet communications appear to be moving in the direction of being

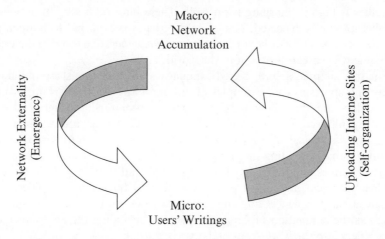

Figure 6.5   Circulation of common knowledge: an Internet case example

incorporated into the mobile phone. Even though only a small number of letters can be displayed on its screen at one time, the use of the device, as a handy tool, has been spreading. This resembles the downsizing of products and the reactions of users in the early phase of product innovation that Christensen (1997) observed transpiring in the hard disk drive (HDD) market. When the HDD miniaturized, there was scepticism regarding its possible applications, but following discoveries of new uses, the product overwhelmed the market as a case of "disruptive innovation". The orientation of the technical foundation of the Internet is shifting from PC use towards mobile phone use.

Common knowledge changes slowly yet steadily. Established common knowledge is understood as culture and it is tolerated in a society. If a product developed through shared knowledge becomes a company's hit product, and turns out to be an innovation that spreads throughout society, this would then mean that culture would have changed at this point. The body of common knowledge changes as a result of innovation, giving birth to a new one in the process.

Seen from a global viewpoint, products and services that have become part of the body of common knowledge in Japan can go on to become innovative products and services in other parts of the world. This is because the speed of innovation diffusion in one country varies from the one in foreign countries. In particular, it takes time for content to spread. This is because, in comparison with physically movable products and simple services, contents that require a certain level of understanding by users need ample time to become common knowledge. And if copyright can be maintained, the cost for duplication becomes low. The level of profitability is high if charging is possible. There have been sectors in which global growth is expected. Namely, this growth is expected to happen as contents originating in Japan such as *karaoke*, *manga* (cartoon) and games become widespread throughout the world.

In this chapter, I have raised language study, cuisine, story, religion, play and sports as case examples of common knowledge. It is important to understand that these industries can be promoted through national strategy in the context of what I call collective knowledge management. In other words, in such areas, you will find business opportunities in overseas propagation. Spreading anything distinctive to Japan such as language, cuisine, games and martial arts abroad could lead to prosperity in culture industry abroad, making it possible to form a huge tourism. There are many areas for which government authorities should offer assistance, such as the cultivation of Japanese teachers, including the acceptance of foreigners into the work front of Japanese cuisine.

4 IMPLICATIONS FOR COMMON KNOWLEDGE MANAGEMENT

The Organic Strategy as an International Business Strategy

Plainly speaking, what an enterprise can do to gain from common knowledge is to strive towards nurturing innovation. The enterprise cannot know beforehand what will actually become an innovation. However, it is possible to assume subsequent circumstances, and a company can engage in the following activities. The first activity of a company is to create new products by managing shared knowledge and developing technology elements based on prevalent common knowledge. The second activity is to exceed the limits of what was considered impossible in the past by managing symbiotic knowledge. The third is to make initial conditions favourable by adopting an agglomerate strategy and utilizing local knowledge. In particular, deciding which cities in the world will serve as bases for the deployment of strategy is a key strategic issue.

Products and services offered by companies themselves become an important constituent of common knowledge in society. If we were to call this process innovation, it would follow that a company would be unable to intentionally trigger it. However, an internal screening process enquires as to whether a product offered by a company will be one that will be respected by future generations, or whether a service offered by a company will have the qualities that will be appreciated by the present generation. And this is the reason why executives need liberal arts as understanding culture. In the fortunate event that a new product is accepted by society, the executive will have changed people's common knowledge by the product they created.

The Codification of Common Knowledge into Language

Knowing liberal arts is a prerequisite for understanding how stylish common knowledge should be. The foundation of next-generation product developments is based on existing culture in society.[25] This, in effect, is the cultivation of the ability to predict the results of product diffusion. An example is found if a particular junk food prevails in society, for example, people's health would suffer due to an unbalanced diet. As it were, executives carrying out international activities should become international sophisticates. Besides so-called traditional disciplines of medicine, biology, law, literature, mathematics, economy and engineering, we should have respect for various domains such as music, painting, sports, ethics, religion, domestic affairs, parenting, educational approaches, language and psychology.

The respect we pay for these domains establishes the direction of a company's philanthropy and eventually the common knowledge of one country. Corporate social responsibility (CSR) should be understood not as a minimum level of a moral code that is required to be observed, but as a proactive way to engage in the wide domain in which the intellectual culture of a company manager is reflected. The so-called global environmental problem is an example that has important significance as a touchstone for gauging a company's level of intellect.

The executive should speak about their own "perspectives on value" to employees, clients and shareholders. It is necessary to repeatedly preach the answer to the question, "What are the set of values we can offer through our business?" The common knowledge transmitted by philanthropy and the product cannot sufficiently explain corporate activities. In addition, it does not even achieve accountability, or responsibility to explain the particular conduct of the company. The enterprise manager needs to send messages beyond business policies that are reported at general shareholder meetings. These messages go beyond transactions mediated by money and product. Geared towards the next generation, these messages will convey "feelings and wishes" that help clarify the meaning of common knowledge in a society.

To convey a message, a common language is necessary. One activity that helps realize the sharing of language is education. Aiming for an original educational approach that is adapted to your company will help widen the common knowledge base. You will find that the company is endowed with foundational elements that help create shared knowledge. The shared knowledge needs experience and individual knowledge, exchange of opinions and acquisition of basic technology in order to convert them into common knowledge. You will need to consciously pursue universality in shared knowledge so that you can convert it to common knowledge. It is essential not only to be mindful of basic behaviours,[26] such as the manner in which executives and employees conduct themselves, the honorifics they use and the way they greet, but also to acquire an attitude that encourages putting themselves into another's shoes when attempting to solve problems. The person who is enthusiastic about raising the level of a society's cultural standards is the one who should become the gatekeeper.

Dangers of Common Knowledge: the Deterioration of Societal Culture

My visit to the baroque city of Lecce in Italy had an unforgettable impact on me.[27] The rows of stores and houses on the streets made of stone in the fifteenth century created beautiful cream-coloured streets, but I found many places had been mercilessly tarnished by doodles. These American-style doodles known as graffiti undermine the townscape not as the manifestation of one individual's ignorance, but as ignorance of a collective body who reside in and around Lecce. In places where education in ethical views is found to be lacking, doodles see a rise. The significance of attaching great importance to common knowledge is weighty.

The society that fails to manage common knowledge will decline. Any society that neglects the pursuit of common knowledge will deteriorate. Common knowledge should serve as ideals in the society of humanity. In other words, we call it stylishness and intelligence when we see a city or a country pursue acquiring a high standard of common knowledge. For a case in point, we do not need to look back into Roman history nor examine modern Italy for that matter, since I believe that even twenty-first-century Japan is rapidly going down this slippery slope. Apparently, the "good tradition" of artisans that had been enduring in Japan appears to be disappearing.

In a society where common knowledge is decaying, the knowledge base will also collapse. This author is concerned about such an outcome. Since 2000, Japanese society has seen much evidence of deterioration. Residential buildings fraudulently designed as earthquake proof,[28] stock lots of rice accidentally tainted with pesticide residues put up for resale,[29] beef with fraudulent designations of localities sold,[30] a high-class traditional Japanese restaurant serving the leftovers of previous customers,[31] high schools certifying course credits for graduation without teaching world history,[32] tests for recruiting high school teachers passing unsuccessful candidates and qualifying them for employment,[33] companies offering official employment promises to third-year college students,[34] the practice of bribery in bureaucratic institutions being exposed,[35] information systems of national pension records malfunctioning,[36] and furthermore, a portion of those records being tampered with by the Social Insurance Agency.[37] Japanese society seems to be losing its sense of morality, and absurdity has become the norm.

It is hard to believe that these matters came into existence coincidentally at the same time. Excessive priority on brands and the deception of quality behind them are the characteristics common to the various scandals mentioned above. These can be said to be the results of intentional acts carried out by members of organizations with particular specialties under the assumption that outsiders will not understand their acts. Rather than driven by malice, these wilful goings-on are rather indicative of being negligent about following the guidance of a moral compass. In a sense, it shows the lack of ability to evaluate the degree of earthquake-resistance of a fraudulently designed quakeproof building. We may be living in a society in which this evaluation role needs to be played by people outside of organizations. Japan had once attained the world's second largest GDP, but the nation turned into a country in which companies and official organizations have frequently committed scandals.

Whether it be an independent administrative organization or an ombudsman appointed by a citizen group, the task of evaluating the effectiveness of an earthquake-resistance setup by an entity outside of an organization will prove to be very costly. If business ethics and bureaucratic organizational ethics are established by internal people and if you can establish standards of conduct that can serve as good examples for the world, you should be able to evade such oversight costs. The border between collective knowledge and collective folly is marked by moral standards.

SUPPLEMENT: DERIVATION OF THE LOGISTIC CURVE

Bernoulli's differential equation form is used to derive the logistic curve.[38] That is, it is in the form of the following equation.

$$x' + a(t)x = b(t)x^n \tag{1}$$

x' represents $\frac{dx}{dt}$. Thus we solve the equation as follows.

$$\frac{dx}{dt} + a(t)x = b(t)x^n \tag{2}$$

If we assign the values $a(t) = -kA$, $b(t) = -k$, and $n = 2$ and revise the equation, we get the following result.

$$\frac{dx}{dt} - kAx = -kx^2 \tag{3}$$

If we note the value $x' = \frac{dx}{dt}$, then the equation becomes $x' - kAx = -kx^2$. If we sum up this equation in relation to k, we can rewrite it as follows.

$$x' = kx(A - x) \tag{4}$$

Equation (4) is a basic equation that shows the marketing performance of new products and services. Here, x' indicates the speed of a certain product x, which is indicative of current sales figures. k is a proportional constant that rests on the present state of x, and in respect to a certain value of k, the larger the value of x is, the larger the value of kx becomes. A represents the theoretically possible total number of buyers, comprising the total demand. Therefore, $(A-x)$ is the number of people who still do not have the product, and when the value of x grows, the value of $(A-x)$ shrinks.

If we transform equation (4) to $x' - kAx = -kx^2$, and divide both of its sides by x^2, we arrive at,

$$\frac{x'}{x^2} - \frac{kAx}{x^2} = -\frac{kx^2}{x^2} \qquad \text{or } x'x^{-2} - kAx^{-1} = -k$$

Furthermore, we make a change of variables here. If we replace $y = x^{-1}$, we attain,

$$\frac{dy}{dt} = \frac{dy}{dx}\frac{dx}{dt} = \frac{d(x^{-1})}{dx}\frac{dx}{dt} = -x^{-2}\frac{dx}{dt}$$

$$= -x^{-2}x' \tag{5}$$

Therefore, if we replace with $y' = -x^{-2}x'$ and $y = x^{-1}$, into the following equation $x'x^{-2} - kAx^{-1} = -k$, then you can get

$$y' + kAy = k \tag{6}$$

To solve this differential equation, we multiply e^{kAt} to both sides. We arrive at,

$$e^{kAt}(y' + kAy) = ke^{kAt} \tag{7}$$

The left side of the equation (7) can be rewritten as follows:

$$\frac{d(e^{kAt}y)}{dt} = e^{kAt}\frac{dy}{dt} + ykAe^{kAt} \tag{8a}$$

In other words, it is equivalent to differentiating $e^{kAt}y$ with respect to time t. Then, we link the right side of equation (7) again with an equal sign, and conclude with:

$$\frac{d(e^{kAt}y)}{dt} = e^{kAt}\frac{dy}{dt} + ykAe^{kAt} = ke^{kAt} \tag{8b}$$

If we gather up only the left and right sides of equation (8b) above, we can arrive at:

$$\frac{d(e^{kAt}y)}{dt} = ke^{kAt} \tag{8c}$$

or

$$(e^{kAt}y)' = ke^{kAt} \tag{8d}$$

Here, we solve the differential equation by integrating equation (8c). If we integrate each of equation (8c)'s left and right sides with t, then we arrive at the integration of left side,

$$\int \frac{d(e^{kAt}y)}{dt} dt = e^{kAt}y \tag{9a}$$

and right side of equation (8c) is integrated as

$$\int ke^{kAt}dt = \frac{e^{kAt}}{A} + c \tag{9b}$$

Here, c is an integration constant. We can confirm that equation (9b) stands good, if we differentiate it conversely.

$$((e^{kAt}/A) + c)' = ke^{kAt}$$

turns out to be valid. If we connect equation (9a) with equation (9b) once again with an equal sign, then we arrive at

$$e^{kAt}y = e^{kAt}/A + c \tag{10}$$

If we assign $t = 0$ as an initial value, then we arrive at,

$$y = 1/A + c \tag{11a}$$

While we can revise the equation to $c = y - 1/A$, since we made a variable change to $y = x^{-1}$, when t = 0, if we take note of $y(0) = x_0^{-1}$, we can write the equation as

$$c = 1/x_0 - 1/A \tag{11b}$$

Since with this calculation, we are able to attain the value of integration constant c, if we were to assign $e^{kAt}y = e^{kAt}/A + c$ to this, then we attain,

$$e^{kAt}y = \frac{e^{kAt}}{A} + \frac{1}{x_0} - \frac{1}{A} = \frac{x_0 e^{kAt} + A - x_0}{Ax_0} = \frac{(e^{kAt} - 1)x_0 + A}{Ax_0} \tag{12}$$

If we divide both sides of equation (12) with e^{kAt} (taking note of the difference between e^{kAt} and e^{-kAt}), then we get:

$$\frac{e^{kAt}y}{e^{kAt}} = \frac{(e^{kAt} - 1)x_0 + A}{Ax_0e^{kAt}} = \frac{(1 - e^{-kAt})x_0 + Ae^{-kAt}}{Ax_0}$$

the most left-hand side of the equation above is none other than y, and if we rearrange the most right-hand side with e^{-kAt}, then we can revise the equation as follows.

$$y = \frac{x_0 + (A - x_0)e^{-kAt}}{Ax_0} \tag{13}$$

Once again, if you take note that we had made a variable change to $y = x^{-1} = 1/x$, then in place of equation (13), we attain,

$$y = \frac{1}{x} = \frac{x_0 + (A - x_0)e^{-kAt}}{Ax_0}$$

$$x = \frac{Ax_0}{x_0 + (A - x_0)e^{-kAt}} \tag{14a}$$

To eliminate x_0 from the numerator of equation (14), we can divide the denominators and numerators with x_0, and revise the equation as follows.

$$x(t) = \frac{\dfrac{Ax_0}{x_0}}{\dfrac{x_0 + (A - x_0)e^{-kAt}}{x_0}} = \frac{A}{1 + (A/x_0 - 1)e^{-kAt}} \tag{14b}$$

While equation (14b) is the equation of the logistic curve, it can be simplified further. To this end, if we place:

$$B = A/x_0 - 1$$
$$C = kA$$

we will be able to revise the expression as follows.

$$x(t) = \frac{A}{1 + Be^{-Ct}} \tag{15}$$

This equation (15) is the equation expressing the logistic curve.

To verify whether equation (15) works as the solution for differential equation (5), if we differentiate with time t, we attain,

$$\frac{dx}{dt} = \frac{ABCe^{-Ct}}{(1 + Be^{-Ct})^2}$$

(The differential law of the quotient. If we differentiate A, we attain zero.)

$$= C\frac{A}{1 + Be^{-Ct}}\frac{Be^{-Ct}}{1 + Be^{-Ct}}$$

(Decompose the numerators and denominators properly)

$$= Cx\frac{1 + Be^{-Ct} - 1}{1 + Be^{-Ct}}$$

(x is assigned from equation (15). Add one and subtract)

$$= Cx\left(1 - \frac{x}{A}\right) \tag{16}$$

Additionally with respect to $\left(1 - \frac{x}{A}\right)$ found on the right-hand side of equation (16), if we revise equation (15) $x(t) = \frac{A}{1 + Be^{-Ct}}$, we can express it as $\frac{x(t)}{A} = \frac{1}{1 + Be^{-Ct}}$.
Consequently, we can confirm this from the fact that it becomes the following expression.

$$\frac{1 + Be^{-Ct} - 1}{1 + Be^{-Ct}} = \frac{1 + Be^{-Ct}}{1 + Be^{-Ct}} - \frac{1}{1 + Be^{-Ct}} = 1 - \frac{1}{1 + Be^{-Ct}} = 1 - \frac{x}{A}$$

Since we defined as $C = kA$, if we assign it to equation (16), we will be able to eliminate $\left(\frac{x}{A}\right)$. Consequently, we attain

$$x' = kx(A - x) \tag{17}$$

This is none other than equation (4). Since equation (4) was a differential equation, you can see that its solution is offered by equation (15).

NOTES

1. The difference between imitation and invention is discussed in Chapter 8 of Tarde (1895). An imitation can be carried out by skipping over certain logical development stages, whereas an invention has to go step by step through a series of irreversible stages (translation, pp. 494–5). Certainly, the former is a fact that is often observed in the pattern of introducing foreign technology into developing countries and the latter is a point that serves as an explanation for the practices carried out by scientists.

2. Refer to Chapter 6 of Tarde's 1895 work (translation pp. 285–90). A baby needs to show hunger, bowel movements or sleepiness through the act of crying in order to live. When a human being acts as a human being, language becomes necessary. Since the scope of circulation of a language as information is limited to a particular age cohort, a language that is unique to that age cohort is created.

3. The facilities of information exchange, namely telephone, email, and so on, are not only used when necessary. In fact, a very strong reason for their use is that one can attain enjoyment out of them. These facilities are enjoyable in themselves.

4. Puzzles, verses, word games, onomatopoeia, amusing novels, pictographs on mobile phones, and so on, are cases in point.

5. Veblen (1899) explained the conspicuous consumption of the leisure class but it is perhaps the behavioural pattern of the general masses to incur expenses for the purposes of flaunting their wealth or because they observe and attempt to imitate the consumption habits of others.

6. Tarde states in his 1895 work that "innovation that does not depend upon imitation does not exist in society" (translation, p. 219). Since the term imitation can be defined broadly, this statement can be interpreted in multiple ways. However, in Tarde's description, we find many elements that are relevant to the twenty-first century. Many parts of his statements are so novel that it becomes difficult to believe that the work is a nineteenth-century one. Rogers (1995) admires Tarde (1895) and cites from his work.

7. Von Hippel (2005) calls such a process user innovation.

8. The explanation in this chapter is dependent on Satō (1984). The procedure by which the logistic curve is obtained from the differential equation is explained in this chapter's supplement.

9. See Kotler (1999) and Kotler and Armstrong (1996).

10. Discussions on social capital introduced by Coleman (1988) and by Putnam (1993), and discussions on "weak ties" by Granovetter (1973) introduced in Chapter 2, note 13, and in Chapter 5 of this book, and Watts' network theories (2003) introduced in Horaguchi (2008a) are all common in respect of their proposition that interpersonal relationships are supported by trust. Yasuda (2004) analysed the number of co-authored books and joint papers in Japan according to the network theory and deduced the correlation that if network density is high the productivity of dissertations also rises.

11. Akamatsu (1956) pointed out that a certain industry of a country passes through the stages of import, domestic production and export, and he refers to this development as the "wild-geese-flying pattern". If we graph the foreign trade statistics and production figures of the machinery and appliances industry, the spinning machine industry, the bicycle industry and the electrical machine industry since the Meiji period, we will see imports grow as a leading indicator and then move towards a decline before long, and then we will see domestic production grow, and as it does so, a part of it becoming exports. Akamatsu (1961) schematically shows that Japanese economic data forms a wild-geese-flying pattern when graphed, while referring to Kondratiev's long-term economic cycle and Schumpeter's (1939) business cycle theory. Vernon (1966) graphed the trend of foreign direct investments and proposed the theory of the product lifecycle. Kotler, Kartajaya and Den Huan (2006) discuss marketing techniques that use the wild-geese-flying pattern in ASEAN nations. Suehiro (2000) surveys many studies regarding the industrialization pattern of developing countries.

12. There are approximately 90 million users and, as expected, the rate of diffusion is considered to be approaching the upper limit.

13. Segaran (2007) introduces programming related to collective intelligence.

14. This author knows a Japanese student who had used a piece of translation software to help the said student understand summaries of the English readings included in MBA case studies. The importance of the Socratic dialogue lives on in the twenty-first century. Of course, those who have developed their aptitude for practising the principles of the Socratic dialogue have been found all over the world, including Confucius, Mencius and Baigan Ishida, a Japanese philosopher in the Edo era.

15. I visited Mitsubishi Electrics's Nagoya factory on 7 March 2006 and TRUMPF on 8 January 2007.
16. The author visited Toyota Motor, Motomachi factory on 6 March 2006 and Nissan Shatai, Hiratsuka factory on 10 March 2006.
17. The prevalence of industrial robots is an example that is in line with laser welding. In car manufacturing, industrial robots are used for manufacturing processes such as moving of press parts, painting, welding and assembly of glass fixtures. On a visit to the production line of car air conditioners at the Nishio factory of Denso, I observed industrial robots automatically manufacturing aluminium fins for air conditioners. These robots were developed by Denso Co. and are said to have been in use for the past ten years since 1996 (visited on 7 March 2006). In Horaguchi (2006), I collected business cases that attempted to realize innovation by focusing on the development of technology elements.
18. This author visited Volkswagen on 7 September 2005 and received explanations on the uses of computer-aided design (CAD) and digital processing in die processing, and on the welding process by laser. As for automobile body welding, arc spot welding has been used, but it is said that cases of laser welding have seen a rise. On 9 September 2005, I visited the welding line of Audi in Ingolstadt, Germany. Here, there were larger-sized robots than the robots made available for visitors at the Toyota and Nissan Shatai plants. These larger-sized robots were transporting bodies with their arm, while performing welding. Between Japan and Germany, the concept of production line design varies considerably. While apparently in Japan production machines are installed by giving top priority to striking the right balance with cost, in Germany, it seemed that people attached greater importance to street-credibility of technology. When I interviewed auto manufacturers of Japan and Germany and asked them to confirm this point, I generally received affirmative responses.
19. This was an observation made by a senior executive of Thyssen Krupp. However, since our observations at Toyota's Motomachi factory of the scene of welding and of car models displayed for visitors were restrictive, I cannot help but say that doubt remains as to the accuracy of this observation.
20. The academic presentation delivered by the linguist Ikegami in September 2008 at the European Association for Japanese Studies was extremely interesting. The gist of it conveyed that Japanese people are accustomed to having the subject omitted in the language, which is an aspect that is difficult for the non-Japanese to grasp. This suggests that Japanese transmit connotation through a missing symbol. In such a case, it would turn out that even though we may carry out thinking by using symbols, as Peirce (1868) pointed out, we do not linguistically transmit the symbol itself. In other words, we can presume missing symbols from the context.
21. "As the issue of students not studying required courses came to light one after another throughout high schools all over Japan, investigators discovered on the 26th that students in high schools of Aichi and Gifu were also not being taught required courses, including world history, and therefore it was feared that these students lacked the necessary units to graduate. On the same day, the same problem was ascertained to be occurring in high schools of Hokkaido, Tokyo, and Fukuoka, among others, raising the nationwide total to 213 schools in 35 administrative divisions of Japan. The number of third-year students possibly unable to graduate amount to more than 20,000 at least." *Nihon Keizai Shimbun*, Nagoya morning edition, 27 October 2006 (city news), p. 21. This was retrieved through the NIKKEI Telecom 21 database.
22. See Veblen (1899). In Chapter 10 of this classic book, *Theory of the Leisure Class: An economic study of institutions*, he discusses sports under the title of "Modern Survivals of Prowess". Veblen (1899) has asserted that "addiction to sports . . . in a peculiar degree marks an arrested development in the man's moral nature" (p. 167, Oxford University Press, the USA).
23. Regarding the people who played active roles as innovators to introduce the legal system into Japan and for a historical background of this event, refer to Horaguchi with the collaboration of Research Institute for Innovation Management (2008).

24. In the area known as contingency theory, which is found in the theory of management, much importance is attached to a company's external environment.
25. Culture is referred to as liberal arts, and it is a subject that should be fostered in a university.
26. The practice of insolent politeness in which problems are deferred with polite speech is deep-rooted in Japanese culture. The standardized practice of management advocated by a manual is fraught with such danger. A manual cannot assure the way in which people can improve the practice of the workplace.
27. In September 2008, I delivered a lecture at the international conference of EAJS, European Association for Japanese Studies, upon invitation.
28. "Fraudulent design for earth-quake proof 21 Residential buildings: Pressure to curb costs by registered architect Aneha." *Nihon Keizai Shimbun*, 18 November 2005, evening edition, p. 17.
29. "Senior partners of *Mikasa* Foods to be prosecuted next month on suspicion of fraudulently reselling accidental rice," *Nihon Keizai Shimbun*, 21 December 2008, morning edition, p. 35.
30. "The Ministry of Agriculture, Forestry and Fisheries issues advisory in Hida Gyu (Hida Beef) fraud case, recommending the meat company '*Maruaki*' to correct its label," *Nihon Keizai Shimbun*, 29 July 2008, evening edition, p. 23. In 2008, in addition to this incident, there were cases of mislabelling related to the designation of the production areas of *Hinaidori* chicken and eel products, among others.
31. See footnote 14 found in Chapter 1 of this book.
32. See *supra* note 21.
33. "Corruption in the employment practice of teachers in Ooita, 'Test scores for more than 30 candidates padded' for 2 years, Board of Education councillors testify that they were mandated by superiors," *Nihon Keizai Shimbun*, 8 July 2008, morning edition, p. 43. In addition, an article appears on page 38 of the morning edition of *the Nihon Keizai Shimbun* dated 29 November 2008 titled, "A total number of 43 reports from the administrative divisions of Japan on the teacher-employment controversy alert on foul play." According to this article, the Assembly for Government Regulation Reform solicited information on foul play in teacher employment practices and also solicited suggestions for improving the situation. The Assembly asked for responses to be sent via mail and the Internet with the subject heading, "Education Complaints Box." In total, they received 238 contributions from 43 prefectures' administrative divisions, pointing out controversies in 42 administrative divisions. The practice of using the complaints box as an incentive to anonymously disclose information, as mentioned in footnote no. 9 found in Chapter 3 of this book, lives on even to this day.
34. Universities in Japan require four years of education. "Question: Is the official employment promises received by students in their third year at University a breach of the charter of the Federation of Economic Organizations? Answer: They are breaching the charter but are nevertheless valid (correspondence from the student employment personnel department)," see *Nihon Keizai Shimbun*, 20 October 2008, morning edition. According to the report, 20 per cent of the respondents had received unofficial employment promises in March of their third year in university. This would mean that companies do not rely on scholastic evaluations made by educational institutions we know as universities. In addition, cancellations of unofficial employment promises made to college students were recognized as a social issue. The cancellations occurred along with the business downturn that began from the end of 2008 through March 2009. "Business downturn, increasing instability of employment: Unofficial employment promises are cancelled one after another, verbal notifications only, universities enraged," see *Nihon Keizai Shimbun*, 28 November 2008, evening paper, p. 23.
35. Amid a large number of reports filed on this subject, one example is "Ministry of Economy, Trade and Industry is criticized for letting alone the 'unexplainable budget fund controversy': External fact finding committee reports, 'Ex-Director under suspicion of committing embezzlement'," *Nihon Keizai Shimbun*, 27 August 2005, morning

edition, p. 1. "Disgraceful affairs, including those involving collusion and bribery occur one after another, self-governing body, feel for reform: Akita, Tottori move toward total abolition of private tenders," *Nihon Keizai Shimbun*, 18 December 2006, morning edition, p. 29. "False accounting controversy, Aichi prefecture, purpose for the spending of 3 million yen unclear, suspicion of embezzlement, prefectural police alerted," *Nihon Keizai Shimbun*, 20 October 2008, morning edition, p. 39. "Fraudulent accounting reported in 12 prefectures: Self-governing bodies pressed for explanation, 'Apology to citizens of prefectures'," see *Nihon Keizai Shimbun*, 19 October 2008, morning edition, p. 35.

36. "24,000 pension record errors, 20% of inquirers: Social Insurance Agency, careless management," *Nihon Keizai Shimbun*, 26 October 2006, morning edition, p. 1. "Dissolution of Social Insurance Agency: Inherits pension system and pension-record problem, 12 million cases untouched," see *Nihon Keizai Shimbun*, 11 February 2009, morning edition, p. 3, etc.

37. "Pension manipulation, 'Social Insurance Agency involvement,' 426 people replied, 69 staff identified by name," see *Nihon Keizai Shimbun*, 10 February 2009, morning edition, p. 5.

38. The following explanation is based on Satō (1984).

7. Collective knowledge and collective strategy in the intelligent society: extension for the international business strategy

1 THE ROLE OF THE KNOWLEDGE ADMINISTRATOR

Typology Revisited

I refer to the person who assumes responsibility for "managing collective knowledge" as a knowledge administrator. The role that the knowledge administrator fulfils varies by the collective knowledge that should be brought about and by the strategy adopted for bringing it about. In this book, I wish to refer to the different types of knowledge administrators as knowledge managers, knowledge coordinators, knowledge networkers and knowledge gatekeepers. They have already appeared in Chapters 3–6 of this book, and each deals with the following four types of knowledge: shared knowledge, symbiotic knowledge, local knowledge and common knowledge.

Table 7.1 presents a summary for four typologies of knowledge administrators that respond to four forms of collective knowledge. For shared knowledge by confederate strategies, the role of the knowledge manager applies; for symbiotic knowledge by conjugate strategies, the role of the knowledge coordinator applies; for local knowledge by agglomerate strategies, the role of the knowledge networker applies; and for common knowledge by organic strategies, the role of the knowledge gatekeeper applies.

These four roles each have their own characteristics. The assertion I wish to make through this book is this: corporate managers run into the needs for each of the four strategies and they need to carry out these four different roles as occasion demands. The activity of managing knowledge requires not only managers who are professionals specializing in management, but also professionals who can fulfil the role of connecting people (networking), carry out the task of making adjustments between people (coordinating) and carry out the task of cutting off unnecessary information (gatekeeping).

The business entrepreneur needs to go beyond their role of a typical manager and play the roles of a networker, a coordinator and a gatekeeper. By doing so, the manager will be able to make a breakthrough from a mature state of business management. This is the strategic proposition inferred by the previous chapters of this book. I have elaborated on the principles and case examples supporting this proposition and specific management tips in Chapters 3–6.

Table 7.1 offers a summary of the above-mentioned viewpoints. Based

Table 7.1   *Types of collective strategies and collective knowledge*

		Interdependent forms	
		Commensalistic	Symbiotic
Types of association	Direct	(Confederate) Shared knowledge 1 No anonymity 2 Limited participation 3 Manager 4 Intra-company project, workplace team, QC circle, suggestion scheme 5 Leadership	(Conjugate) Symbiotic knowledge 1 No anonymity 2 No prior limitation of participants 3 Coordinator 4 New business collaboration, business–university–government cooperation, interdisciplinary activities 5 Recognition
	Indirect	(Agglomerate) Local knowledge 1 Anonymity 2 Prior limitation of participants 3 Networker 4 Network in Industry, local community network, spinoff 5 Fame	(Organic) Common knowledge 1 Anonymity 2 No limitation of participants 3 Gatekeeper 4 Network with an interest in intelligence, virtual community, diffusion of innovation 5 Popularity

Notes: 1 is participant anonymity, 2 is whether limitation exists through requiring qualifications to participate, 3 is the personality of the knowledge administrator, 4 indicates case examples of the strategic types, and 5 is the talent a knowledge administrator needs to have to effectively recruit participants.

on these contents, I will now summarize the special features of a knowledge administrator. As explained in Chapters 3–6, collective knowledge is something that links the following two associations: self-organization and emergence. Therefore, collective knowledge is not something that can possibly be managed by a knowledge administrator. While shared knowledge, symbiotic knowledge, local knowledge and common knowledge are each expected to emerge as a consequence, it is futile to predict concretely what form of knowledge will eventually take shape. What is possible to manage is collective strategy. Depending on what kind of collective strategy is adopted, the form of collective knowledge varies. With emergence, not only can you discover knowledge you had aimed to discover beforehand, but also come across unimaginable discoveries in the form of accompanying results. In the world of science, this is called serendipity and it is understood as good fortune that arises amid a state of prepared readiness.

The knowledge administrator is capable of managing the choices of people suited to participate in each of the collective strategies. The challenge here is in considering what types of people should be allowed participation or in determining who should be invited to participate. Dealing with this challenge helps the collective strategy to develop. In general, the more capable a person is, the more this person will tend to be busy, making it difficult for this person to participate in projects. Therefore, to promote participation of such people, the ability to recruit them becomes necessary.

Barnard (1938) explained that the right balance needs to be struck between inducement and contribution to effectively recruit people into an organization. When the motivation to participate in an organization is greater than the contribution demanded from the person who participates, this person will remain in the organization. In addition to the financial motive, aspects such as the name of the company and the sense of accomplishment that comes from engaging in work function as motives. When you stand on the side of recruiting people, you need to present such motives. Capabilities to recruit people also correspond to collective strategies. Leadership, recognition, popularity and fame are examples to describe such capabilities. Let us look at this point in detail in accordance with the type of knowledge administrator.

The Role of a Knowledge Manager

The knowledge manager exists to manage confederate strategy that functions as a collective strategy designed to give rise to shared knowledge. Mintzberg (1973), in his famous book *The Nature of Managerial Work*, investigates the manager's allotment of time, but the argument lacks any discussion of how to manage knowledge. While it is ideal that knowledge managers acquire leading-edge scientific knowledge at an exhaustive level, practically speaking, this is impossible. Scientists specializing in subdivided areas of specializations are working together all over the world, night and day, aiming to make new discoveries in competition. A knowledge manager cannot hope to understand all knowledge produced by such scientists. Even if such knowledge were limited in scope by one's company's business field, it would also prove challenging to comprehensively understand the bodies of knowledge of various areas related to just this business field. As the argument posed by Hayek (1945), which I introduced in Chapter 2, explains, this is because knowledge evolves every day at the scene of management. Then, how should a knowledge manager manage knowledge? To repeat, what is possible to manage is the choice-making of people who should participate there. If we aim to acquire people who will continue to contribute knowledge creation over the long term, we can select them through evaluations over this time horizon, including the level of their technical skills, communication abilities and patience. Japanese enterprises are adept at fostering the expertise of their employees and selecting from a pool of graduates seeking employment.

If we were to raise the aim of bringing about shared knowledge, we would need to adopt a confederate strategy. A characteristic of the confederate strategy is that it is commensalistic and that, with this strategy, it is possible to impact in a direct manner. It is commensalistic because of the following conditions; when a company offers its employees a place in the company to realize problem-solving and when it also offers the opportunity to make use of knowledge, the company benefits and the employees avoid suffering any disadvantages in the process. In this sense, it is commensalistic that no one suffers disadvantage, and that a direct form of communication via the workplace is carried out. Some excellent employees who attain rewards clearly benefit. In this way, when aiming to improve workplace organization, employees and the management need to forge an alliance and deal with the task of problem-solving together. The knowledge manager needs to safeguard the promise that no employees will be fired due to improvements made possible through the suggestion scheme. It is in this sense that the confederate strategy is commensalistic.

In the case of a confederate strategy that involves the forging of a project team, success or failure hinges on how you go about choosing the participants of the project team. It also depends on who should be appointed as the leader of the project team, and on who should be appointed as supporters. Should the leader be the one who will be most interested in the challenges the project team faces? It is necessary to know such prior information. Japanese enterprises have plenty of middle managers who are expert at drafting and implementing confederate strategies. For example,

Carlos Ghosn, who dealt with the restructuring of Nissan Motor, attached great importance to the kind of project team that could straddle across different divisions within a company. This was the so-called "cross-functional team".[1] In other words, with respect to managing the production workplace, the confederate strategy was neatly implemented by Japanese companies. *Kaizen* (improvement activities) via the small group used to be the kind of collective strategy that Japanese enterprises were good at performing, but it turns out that in the cross-functional team that operates at a companywide level, there remains room for more gimmicks. While the creation of shared knowledge has supported the competitive advantage of Japanese enterprises, this practice of cross-functional teams needs to be further improved.

Confederate strategy is functionalized by positive evaluation for participation. In the case of Japanese enterprises, in many cases, it used to be that participation was something urged through peer pressure, or in other words, through tacit pressure from peers. There were also cases whereby there were no clear rewards indicating participation, and it was uncertain as to whether the participation was used as a measure to determine promotions over the long term. Even the quality control circle, which is the mechanism that forges the shared knowledge of Japanese enterprises, was carried out within Japan as unpaid overtime work in some cases. For this reason, it is said that when Japanese enterprises advanced into Asia and attempted to carry out small group activities, the reaction they first received from local employees came in the form of a complaint. They enquired as to why they had to engage in activities for which they would not be compensated monetarily.[2] In Japan, it turns out that the sense of rivalry among employees is strong, and there exists the carrot and stick of expectation for a promotion (carrot) over the long term and peer pressure (stick). In an environment devoid of such conditions, functionalizing small group activities will prove to be difficult.

The Role of the Knowledge Coordinator

Collective strategies vary depending on what modes of networks can be found behind them. This attribute is a key in understanding the characteristic of a collective strategy. It also helps to control the course of action as collective knowledge evolves. Shared knowledge is knowledge shared among the members of a certain organization. If you wish to go beyond the members of an organization and give rise to a new form of knowledge, you must adopt a different strategy.

At this point, the knowledge administrator needs to carry out activities that deviate from what is expected from the in-office title of manager.

In conjugate strategy for creating symbiotic knowledge, activities carried out through the capacity of a knowledge coordinator become key. In Chapter 4, I had sketched the role of a knowledge coordinator in the case example of the business–university–government (BUG) collaboration that took place in Toyama.

In Chapters 3 and 4, I explained that the differences are found between the types of tasks performed by supervisors of a production workplace and the types of tasks performed by knowledge coordinators of the science and technology field. They correspond to the differences between shared knowledge and symbiotic knowledge. In supervising a production workplace, you will need a production manager capable of bringing together executives, planning engineers, experts on machining, people in charge of distribution and the procurement of materials, and a network of workers involved in production. Since the number of capable experts is limited in any company, you will have a comparatively small number of experts to offer advice on solutions. These experts will be in a position to know each other's reputations.

The task of a knowledge coordinator for symbiotic knowledge is more wide ranging than the task of a production manager of a production workplace. This difference resembles the one between a movie director and a movie producer. A movie director needs a network of people who are essential for producing a work of cinema. Such people include scriptwriters, photographers, lighting professionals, costume designers and assistant directors. The network the producer has is much wider than the director's network, and when seen from the criteria of movie-making, the network is an assembly of diverse industry types and talents. For the serious work of raising funds, associating with advertising agencies, sponsors and financial institutions becomes necessary, and for the purpose of realizing distribution, negotiations with a film distribution company become necessary.[3]

The knowledge coordinator is active in a place that lies beyond the boundaries of an organization called the company. Thanks to this fact, the knowledge coordinator can incorporate into an organization those people who have solutions from a dimension that is inaccessible from within a company. Symbiotic knowledge, among experts of different fields, is a form of participation realized through mutual recognition. In this sense, as I have shown in Table 7.1, popularity among experts becomes key. The type of knowledge coordinator who makes people feel that "it would be an honour to work with this person," will be able to connect (conjugate) people, and in the process lay the foundation for giving rise to symbiotic knowledge formed by diverse bodies of knowledge.

The concept of open innovation posed by Chesbrough (2003) is one that advances a conjugate strategy. It encourages using resources found outside of a company, but the methods applied for acquiring participants for such a strategy are vague. It appears as if Chesbrough (2003) stresses the idea that participants with specific technical interests are automatically attracted. To functionalize conjugate strategy, a knowledge coordinator needs to exhibit an attractive personality. This attractiveness involves discovering capable participants and offering solvable challenges through concrete efforts.

The Role of the Knowledge Networker

A typical knowledge networker for agglomerate strategy, who helps bring about local knowledge, is the entrepreneur active in Silicon Valley. Ultimately, activity to widen the human network for the launch of a venture business is nothing but "activities to receive investments". This can also be expressed as a covert search for investment opportunities. If you are able to obtain funds from investors known as angels or venture capitalists, you will have received something tantamount to a scholarship, which does not oblige you to make any repayment. Only if the business succeeds, you will be paying dividends, and by doing so the value of the shares sees a rise.

The agglomerate strategy adopted by Japanese enterprises has aspects that contrast with the aspects of the agglomerate strategy adopted by firms in Silicon Valley. In Japan, there is an active drive to raise the level of technology of existing enterprises through auditing factories and providing on-site guidance. On the other hand, however, it is rare to see any promotions after launching a spinoff, which is a large factor that supports local knowledge in the case of the Silicon Valley model. A more salient feature of the Japanese model is found in the fact that there are only a few employees who leave their company and go on to launch their own business, which means that there are only a few managers who have experience of launching a business after leaving their company. For managers of large enterprises in Japan, the role of the knowledge networker, which is to discover new needs by connecting diverse individuals to each other, is rather an exceptional activity. In the case of Japanese enterprises, with long-term activities revolving around parts suppliers and sales outlets, there is a demand to respond to existing demand. Like shared knowledge, the difference in the grounds from which local knowledge originates is huge.

Seen from the eyes of an investor searching for investment opportunities, investing in venture businesses is not a low-risk matter. To discover an appropriate investment outlet, an investor will personally meet with an entrepreneur and enquire about their business plan and, when necessary, the investor will aid in launching their business in a hands-on way. In the case of institutional investors, there are cases where they replace an entrepreneur who established the business in the early phase. The entrepreneur resigns as the company's CEO so as to be replaced by an individual with reliable administrative ability.

The knowledge networker works on more open targets than the knowledge manager. A knowledge coordinator creates a network for the creation of symbiotic knowledge primarily in cases when interest in technology overlaps. However, in the case of the knowledge networker who gives rise to local knowledge, action is motivated by having an interest in new businesses and wishing to evaluate them. When we follow the path of activities taken by the knowledge networker, we can discover there a relationship referred to as social capital. To make a business succeed, it is necessary to obtain the cooperation of people of various occupations, including lawyers, patent attorneys, accountants, administrators of incubation facilities, engineers, sales executives and partners who can help expand overseas market channels. The knowledge networker is a person who carries out activities to connect such people together.

The Role of the Knowledge Gatekeeper

The role of the knowledge gatekeeper in organic strategy is a passive one. Common knowledge includes a process that sees the diffusion of new ideas throughout society in general. The knowledge gatekeeper of such common knowledge will be obliged to adhere to minimum regulations. In terms of managing a website, the role entails adherence to rules, deleting illicit posts, maintaining and upgrading the system and processing claims. However, the knowledge gatekeeper determines the structure of the site and will bear a strategy underpinning this stage. The success or failure of the site will be determined by the conceptual architecture of the site – how sound it will be planned in shaping the site.

The knowledge gatekeeper will also be obliged to advocate moral standard. If mobile phones spread, the question of usage etiquette will become an issue, and if cars spread, people will turn out to face issues such as the problem of exhaust gas emissions, car accidents and traffic congestion. Fortunate companies that can offer goods and services that can become common knowledge will turn out to shoulder a substantial social responsibility. Whether to establish codes of business conduct that go beyond existing regulations and establish new societal norms, or whether to pass through loopholes in existing regulations and profit by engaging in activities that evade the law depends on the businessperson's sense of morals and aesthetics for all intents and purposes. What is necessary for a knowledge gatekeeper to have is a balanced sense of morals and sensitivity to society's ethical needs.

2   THE ATTEMPTS OF JAPANESE ENTERPRISES: OMRON

I wish to introduce the case example of OMRON as a case example of managing collective knowledge.[4] In short, OMRON creates four different types of collective knowledge through composite management. As representing a company that has been promoting organized R&D and seriously searching for optimal methods of evaluating research workers active in research institutes, the R&D management of OMRON seems to have a strategic direction. By sketching the attempts made by a Japanese enterprise, I wish to record the management method of a research and development oriented Japanese enterprise.

OMRON's Research and Development Base[5]

OMRON was founded by Kazuma Tateishi, and as of 2005 his son became the chairperson. In 1948, the company became OMRON TATEISI ELECTRONICS, and in 1960, the firm established a central laboratory in Nagaokakyo in Kyoto prefecture. The mainstay item then was the contact-less switch. The company changed its name to OMRON in 1990 and went on to open the Keihanna Innovation Centre in 2003. The company has factories in Shanghai and Shenzhen also; the factory in Shanghai carries out the production of conventional goods, while the one in Shenzhen carries out cellular phone-related product manufacturing.

In the OMRON Keihanna Innovation Centre, the company is developing state-of-the art "sensing and control" devices. In the Okayama Development Centre, tone instruments are being developed. In the Komaki In-Vehicle Business Centre in Aichi, the development of the laser radar is being carried out.[6] The sensing device that measures the distance between cars is undergoing development there. This device was available as an option for passenger vehicles in 2005. In Kusatsu, Shiga, in the sector of electronics and mechanical components, the company handles products related to finance, station services and roads. As for finance, OMRON handles it together as a joint venture with Hitachi. The backlight module adopted in liquid crystals brings annual sales of 10 billion yen, and its consignment production is outsourced from the Kusatsu Business Centre. In Mishima, Shizuoka, the company handles programmable controllers and factory automation. In the Ayabe Business Centre in Kyoto, the company handles sensors and sensing equipment. In the Minakuchi factory in Kouka-gun, Shiga, the company handles the production of semiconductors. The company produces an array of microlenses, which are used in bipolar ICs, micromachines and liquid crystal projectors.

Positioning of the OMRON Keihanna Innovation Centre

The OMRON Keihanna Innovation Centre is positioned as "a core base of the global R&D collaborative creation strategy" and attaches great importance to "the atmosphere of harmony" and "collaborative creation". It is advancing joint research projects between companies and cutting-edge research facilities, such as universities under the concept of "collaborative creation". It was established in May 2003 in the Keihanna Gakken city (officially known as Kansai Cultural and Academic Research City), which was modelled after the Tsukuba Research and University Town. Prior to that, there were research institutes found in Nagaokakyo, Tsukuba and Kumamoto. These three research institutes were merged to establish the current research institute of the OMRON Keihanna Innovation Centre and then they were discontinued thereafter.

In the area of devices and sensing, the institute has secured a place to facilitate discussions on collaborative creation among members. The research institute is 71 834 square meters and has four stories, measuring 60 meters by 200 meters. It accommodates 400 staff members. On the first floor, there is a laboratory that includes a cleanroom, on the third floor, there is an office, and a mezzanine can be found as well. The research laboratory is managed by "the technical headquarters". There used to be four sections: the Planning Office, the Sensing Department, the Research Institute for Advanced Devices, and the Research Institute for Control. In 2005, however, only the three sections, the Planning Office, the Research Institute for Sensing and Control, and the Research Institute for Advanced Devices remained with minor change, and the new Research Institute for In-Vehicle Uses was established.

Under the Research Institute for Sensing and Control, there are: the Technology Marketing Group, the Pictorial Image Sensing Group and the Light and Electric Wave Sensing Group. Under the Advanced Device Laboratory, there are: the Technology Marketing Group, the Micromachining Group and the Microphotonics Group.

The process of establishing the research and development theme is a bottom–up process. A theme will be proposed as one endorsed by the organization, and a decision by headquarters will be pushed for. Every year, the technical chief of headquarters and the manager of research carry out fiscal-year policy explanations. Each personnel under managers draws up plans in a process that can be characterized as bottom–up. "In accordance with the macro-policies declared from the top, specific themes are proposed from the bottom," an interviewee explained. The roadmap is created within the company, and its revision work is carried out on a constant basis.

In the short-range plan with the target period set from 2005 through 2007, output is sought after, but in the long-range plan with the target period set from 2005 through 2010, there is no such demand. For the short-term plan covering the period until 2007, requests made within the company need to be met. This is because the short-range plan is requested by not the technical headquarters, but is, instead, demanded by the so-called "business company system". As for newly developed products that can be contributed as devices, including state-of-the-art machine facilities and objects for in-vehicle use, funds will be allocated from the company or the Management Strategy Room. This is possible because needs are so clear that the company can pick up the needs to carry out the short-term plan.

In the long-range plan that aims to cover ten years, the work of "product development based on the concept of seeds" is carried out and hypotheses on needs are verified. However, there are cases when needs come from the company. While the Management Strategy Room becomes central in this case and carries out the allocation of research funds, in some cases, research funds are allocated by the company. The carrying out of industry–university collaborations also falls within the purview of the long-range plan.

Industry–University Collaborations of the Advanced Device Laboratory

The Advanced Device Laboratory in OMRON acquires its grants from the Ministry of Economy, Trade and Industry (METI). This grant is not under any industry–university collaboration scheme. In the field of micro-electro-mechanical systems (MEMS), the laboratory receives half of its research funds as aid. This project's final year is 2005.

In the area of joint research projects with universities, in the nanotech cluster forged by Kyoto University and an industrial cluster policy, aid in the amount of 17 862 000 yen has been received for the "development of next-generation terabit light-electron memory". With the cooperation of Kyoto University's Professor Shizuo Fujita and Professor Kazuyuki Hirao, the total sum amounts to 50 578 000 yen. To raise the memory level to the tera level, the technology is being developed to realize control at the level where three-dimensional space plus the length of the wavelength of light are adopted.

In the Knowledge Cluster Initiative of the Ministry of Education, Culture, Sports, Science and Technology (MEXT), with the Kyoto Advanced Technology Laboratory Foundation playing a central role, the research fund has been received for "the development of next-generation optoelectronic devices adopting nanotechnology". It is a collaboration among several professors, including Professor Shizuo Fujita of Kyoto University.[7] Since the project director who was in charge of business integration until 2004 left in the midst of the project, the vice president of OMRON, Tatsuro Ichihara, became the project director in charge of business integration in place of him. From OMRON, there were several researchers involved in the Knowledge Cluster Initiative. Barbecue parties were held at Professor Fujita's home, apparently to broaden the network of acquaintances for OMRON's researchers. In addition, a link was also made with the International Fusion Field, to which Professor Fujita belongs.

In the field of high-frequency micro-electro-mechanical systems, a system was started to facilitate the despatch of people from OMRON to the laboratory of Ritsumeikan University and have them acquire a doctorate to qualify as researchers in OMRON. With Doshisha University, there is an association in the area of biological research, and in the area of microphotonics, four people, among whom one is the group leader, are carrying out research at the laboratory of Osaka University. While experience of collaborative research with universities in Tokyo and its surrounding areas is minimal, OMRON did not even consider communicating with universities until there was a research laboratory at Keihanna. At times, people are transferred for one year to study at universities abroad. This is made feasible, as long as it falls under the purview of the financial year's policy and OMRON's budget limits. There are professors who are on familiar terms at UC Berkeley. OMRON pays UC Berkeley for the research cost and it secures research meetings on a regular basis. So OMRON sends people who meet there approximately once every six months. Another cooperation has also been initiated with China's Qinghua University.

Researcher Performance Evaluation

OMRON does not have a rigid performance evaluation system as of 2005. However, as output, the company attaches great importance to the following three Ps: (1) paper, (2) patent and (3) product. With these three points, OMRON determines overall evaluation of the researchers.

1. With regard to the scholarly paper, papers submitted to academic associations and at international conventions also count. Papers submitted at international conventions receive higher appreciation if it is one written as an invited speaker. With an academic paper, the impact factor (the rate of citations) is also considered. In other words, the impact factor reveals whether the paper is appearing as a well-known literature in an official journal of a scientific society. Papers without much substance are not evaluated. However, companies with head

offices in Kyoto, including OMRON, Murata Manufacturing, and ROHM, make only a small number of presentations to academic societies as compared with the companies located in Tokyo, such as Toshiba.

2. Patents are ranked into the following in-house categories: S, A, B and C. The number of applications is also taken into account, and a percentage of the sales is allotted to the developer as patent royalty income. In this way, acquiring patents has become a financial incentive. With respect to patents, since the developer's name will be entered, the equity will also be determined at this stage.

3. In the case of products, at the level of the department head during the beginning of the financial year, people argue over which of the following stages a particular product belongs: design, theory, manufacturing trial or product development. For example, in the case of the Minakuchi factory, it belongs to the group of semiconductor companies, and the new products move toward the mass production process after a consensus is reached among the corporate director, the development director, the chief project manager and the factory superintendent. As a development step, each step is discussed in a conference to ascertain its procedures. The convening body then carries out product commercialization and mass production trials, and reports their results to an operating division. When the conclusion is attained, they will enter into individual consultations with the factory to carry out mass production. There are cases when development engineers attend the initiation of mass production. And in the case of a certain researcher, after developing optical devices, he was transferred to the Minakuchi factory, and then after being placed in charge of enlarging sales as well, he was assigned once again to the central laboratory. Consequently, after one and a half years of working at the Kusatsu business establishment, he was assigned to the Keihanna Innovation Centre. However, such a case is rare, in which researchers leave and return to the laboratory twice.

The development objective schedule does not follow a normal scheduling process for manufacturing products. However, since researchers assert the development objective schedule themselves, it has similar significance. The career ladder of researchers usually comprises office staff positions, starting from staff (*shain* in Japanese), superintendent (*shuji*), chief examiner (*shusa*), chief leader (*shukan*), counsellor (*sanji*), councillor (*sanyo*), director (*riji*) and executive director (*torishimariyaku*). Positions found above chief leader form the manager class, and councillors are division heads. When the "professional system" was established around 2004 and certain technical specialties came to be recognized, qualifications corresponding to the status of a manager came to be offered. As of 2005, fewer than ten people have received the recognition of professional system, and professions in the area of "information engineering" received recognition most.

Among the 400 people working in OMRON's Keihanna Innovation Centre, the number of those who graduated from postgraduate schools is around 50, and others are almost all university graduates. Previously, OMRON stayed away from employing postgraduates, but from around 2003 through 2005, the company began to employ as mid-career employees those who had completed their PhD. It accepts internships from two laboratories of Kyoto University and from one laboratory of Ritsumeikan University in Kyoto. The average age of employees at OMRON research laboratories is low, averaging in the early thirties. One of the reasons for this is due to the fact that a considerable number of older people had left when early-retirement preferential treatment used to be in place. After being transferred from a laboratory to a business establishment, it is rare that employees return to the laboratory. OMRON research laboratories do not accept researchers from outside companies. While there are times they cooperate with companies, there is the issue of confidentiality.

This concludes the summary of the interview findings regarding OMRON's Keihanna Innovation Centre in 2005.

Case Interpretations

We can interpret the R&D activities of OMRON by looking at their activities within the context of collective knowledge management. In this case, the role that collective knowledge fulfils is great. OMRON has positioned the Keihanna Innovation Centre in Keihanna Gakken City (the Kansai Cultural and Academic Research City) and actively promotes industry–university collaborations. For two- to three-year projects, priority is given to satisfying the needs stipulated by the operating division, while the in-house research organization is placed in charge of the projects. Collaborations have also been initiated with UC Berkeley and Qinghua University in China by reinforcing ties with universities in the Kansai area with Kyoto at its core. For long-standing research themes lasting around five years, the industry–university cooperation approach was taken, and joint research with university researchers considered external from OMRON's perspective was advanced. Despatching researchers to university laboratories and providing them with education were also part of such programmes. This is the symbiotic knowledge creation approach.

In the Toyama case example introduced in Chapter 4, companies were passive participants in the area of industry–university collaborations. Companies themselves did not take the initiative and elaborate a collaborative industry–university plan, but merely participated for one reason or another in the industry–university cooperation scheme planned by the MEXT. While many Japanese companies had carried out collaborative projects with university researchers, they negotiated directly between companies and laboratories. Therefore, in the event the researcher moved to another university, the fellowship grant followed to the laboratory with the researcher's consent. A research programme was carried out on an approximately three-year project basis and was discontinued if the company deemed the laboratory unattractive and chose to end any associations with it. This functioned as a system of how companies absorbed knowledge from universities.

Evolution comes about in common knowledge when a global-scale framework and its overriding idea are implemented. Many Japanese companies attach great importance to R&D and seek a new perspective. They establish research bases in various countries other than advanced countries, and build strategies that tie into market development in those countries. Japanese enterprises used to set their supreme directive to achieve cost reduction and acquire market share. They have now evolved to the companies that make use of a home base within Japan to pursue intensive R&D. They are aiming to spread out its innovative capacities into the world.

3   METHODS FOR CREATING COLLECTIVE KNOWLEDGE

The Reason Why Collective Knowledge is Superior to Individual Knowledge

By analysing the materials found in Chapters 3–6, you can understand the reason why collective knowledge is superior to individual knowledge. Just like Surowiecki (2005), who was introduced in Chapter 2, there is the possibility that a nameless yet superior expert is lost in the masses. However, this answer is as naïve as the premise of the proposition that the intellectual masses are superior to an individual. It acquiesces in the argument that the individual is superior to the masses, even though the masses conceal the individual. Surowiecki's argument is feeble because superior knowledge is created only when the masses are the kind in which a superior individual participates.

As a reason why collective knowledge is deemed superior to individual knowledge, I would like to restate below the two reasons found in this book.

The first reason is that having many people act together as a mass will help you detect problems that could be solved. While each individual only has limited problem-solving abilities, it is possible to look for solvable problems through a combination of individuals that acts as a group and actually solves the problems. The fact that a group has such a problem finding function raises the possibility of bringing about "superior collective knowledge".

I wish to summarize the case examples raised in each chapter of this book from such a point of view. The typical case example of shared knowledge in Chapter 3 is improvement suggestions made by small group activities. Improvement suggestions in small group activities are evaluated only once after improvement has been made (see Chapter 3, Figure 3.2). Those case examples that were recorded, evaluated and commended as the fruits of *kaizen* (improvement activities) were limited to only those where improvement was possible. *Kaizen* activities are not performed for problems that are absolutely impossible to improve upon, but problems where improvement is possible. Improvement suggestions are made when people see this possibility. Those problems that are impossible to solve remain to be dealt with in the future.

The typical example of symbiotic knowledge in Chapter 4 was the BUG collaboration project. The BUG collaboration project, which saw the successful product development of lymphocyte analysis, the biochip, went on to bear fruit as a new business. Now, what is noteworthy here is that the focus on lymphocytes, the research objective at that time, was essentially a focus on a solvable problem. It was not a case of suddenly attempting to tackle a challenge deemed insolvable at the present time, such as cancer and leukaemia, bird flu and new types of influenza. The challenge of analysing lymphocytes, on the other hand, was carefully chosen as a solvable problem. This power of investigative imagination, in effect, helped lead the project to its success.

Chapter 5 covered local knowledge, and I took up Toyota and Denso located around Toyota-city and Daimler and Bosch located around Stuttgart as exemplars of the manufacturing cluster. I found that cooperation is easier to carry out when there are multiple companies existing in one cluster. We can see similar forms of cooperation taking place within the relationships between entrepreneurs of venture businesses and large companies in Silicon Valley. A cluster is the result of finding the most advantageous location *vis-à-vis* the question of where to locate a firm. In effect, a cluster is recognized on the map as the proximity of companies that have survived and have achieved growth. This is also a case example that the solution of a collective strategy was offered subsequently.[8]

In Chapter 6, we saw that common knowledge is typically the spread of new products. The maker attempted to develop new products that would exceed the expectations of users. While users have good command of these new products, they can choose between whether to continue using the product or switch to a different brand. This choice will be expressed as support or the lack thereof for the product and maker. In the process of one technical product's spreading, many companies suggest usages of the product that are unintended until present. And then they compete. Only the product that wins approval survives.

In this way, if we observe the way collective knowledge works, we can summarize as follows. Human beings possess the ability to find solvable problems while they respond in diverse ways *vis-à-vis* subjects. For example, two outstanding officials may discover problems related to healthcare for the elderly. However, a single youth may discover a problem after facing an elderly person with dementia. The latter would have so much of hidden reality as a problem that should be solved, and may attract many people. If it is a pre-existing problem, such as the problem-solving of a question on the past appearing in a university entrance exam, the two outstanding officials, more than the single youth and the elderly person with dementia, will undoubtedly be able to discover a large number of correct answers much faster by far. Nevertheless, what should be searched as new knowledge is a solvable problem rather than an answer to a pre-existing problem.

Collective knowledge is not the act of a group solving a difficult problem that any individual would find insurmountable to solve. When the mass is endowed with a problem-finding ability that is unimaginable to achieve by a single individual, and when the mass includes people who can evaluate what problems are solvable among the various problems discovered, the presence of collective knowledge becomes subsequently recognized, or recognized after the fact. When a loop of self-organization and emergence forms, the problem has been discovered, and there are participants who can solve the problem. The knowledge administrator is a person capable of bringing together people who are able to find problems. The knowledge administrator also brings together individuals capable of carrying out solutions to problems. This impetus paves the way to the creation of the soil upon which knowledge is brought about. Collective knowledge is created by a process whereby someone among the masses discovers a solvable problem as an important problem that should be solved.

The Second Reason

The second reason why collective knowledge is superior to individual knowledge lies in the fact that people improve new abilities. When taking a certain point in time, as mentioned in the first reason, the act of problem-finding precedes. Then problem-solving will be carried out immediately with existing abilities. However, in the case of taking a certain amount of time and evaluating, there are cases when problem-solving abilities become cultivated through investing some time.

As introduced in Chapter 1 of this book, Polanyi (1966) discusses problem-solving by quoting Plato's "Meno". If the problem is one that nobody can solve, the problem is insolvable, and if it is a problem that "anyone" is able to solve, the problem would not exist as a problem. Therefore, the discovery that entails a solvable problem is dependent on tacit knowledge, which is knowledge we know, yet cannot put into words. This is Polanyi's assertion (p. 22).

In collective knowledge, however, there is a function for facilitating the questioning of just who the "anyone" is. Within the group comprising participants in which "nobody was able to solve the problem", one of the participants may become able to solve the problem. Or it may be that someone who improved new abilities will discover a solution that cannot be solved by others. This is the main reason why collective knowledge management is effective in broadening individual knowledge. And the second reason is based on the fact that a problem that nobody was able to solve at one point in time becomes solvable one day, thanks to an extension of someone's ability in a group or a community.

In Chapter 3 I gave a case example of a *kaizen* suggestion, or improvement suggestion. A production engineer who has a deficiency of a production process pointed out may notice a disparity between what was learned through planning and the reality of the workplace. The small group activity is a typical example of an organization that continues to learn. It gives the opportunity to practically learn the state of production management through *kaizen* (improvement activities) and to understand solution patterns. At this point, the workplace's problem-solving ability improves. The reason why we can conjecture this is because the data over several years have shown that the ones occupying the top rank in terms of suggestion numbers have been specific superior enterprises.

In Chapter 4's case example of symbiotic knowledge, the resin treatment manufacturer producing a body part for cellular phones acquired a new processing technique to accommodate the production of biochips, which demanded precision at the nano level. To participate in projects that involve industry–university cooperation, the company needed to raise its level of technological capability. Then, this new technology led a further development of fuel cell parts. A company will also need to develop new abilities when making its entry into a research park with aspirations to carry out research and development activities that will yield superior world-class results.

In Chapter 5's case example of local knowledge, I offered the example of supplying automobile parts. By being located in a cluster, a company will be demanded by its clients, the car assembling companies, to deliver high-quality products, and to this end, the need will be created to raise the level of the effectiveness of factory management. Geographical proximity enables synchronization and imitation in production processes and it enables collaborative R&D with interlocking organizational culture. Inventory reduction through just-in-time production and frequent delivery assumes an extension of the problem-solving ability with the parts supplier and assembly manufacturers, signifying the local cooperation found in ability development.

In Chapter 6, I covered common knowledge and raised various case examples that were realized through the collective action of people. The propagation of common knowledge depends on the information-processing equipment humans have at the time. In effect, common knowledge has been traditionally conveyed via conversations, papers, books, printed materials and radio waves. We now have the Internet and mobile phones. As of the present age of the twenty-first century, even with respect to information-processing equipment that people use in the course of their everyday lives, if we go back 20 years, we would see that the use of such tools was permitted to only an extremely limited number of people. For example, the ability to launch a website is becoming something even an elementary school student can acquire. However, in retrospect, if we look back to the point immediately prior to the birth of the Internet, we can clearly see that this ability had at one time been considered a specialized skill. A knowledge base in our society comes into place to simplify the ability of launching a website. It becomes possible for anyone to acquire this knowhow. We see clearly a typical example of the emergence of common knowledge in our society.

Creative Reflex

The phenomenon of the creation of new knowledge amid the interaction of diverse individuals can possibly be called creative reflex.[9] This is one of the functions of intellect. You can find the validation of this theory of creative reflex that runs through shared knowledge, symbiotic knowledge, local knowledge and common knowledge. In other words, this means that humans have a latent ability to reflexively respond to intellectual acts. Conditional reflex is the psychological reaction that people unconsciously have, but creative reflex indicates the act of contributing through deed or thought to creative thinking in the reflexes people experience. An encounter between one youth and an elderly person with dementia would, in certain cases, evoke conscious reactions and numerous unconscious reflexes in the youth. The conscious reaction of the youth would already be controlled by a sense of purpose, and this sense of purpose would depend on his intellectual level. Among the various reflexes the youth exhibits in response to encountering the elderly person with dementia, the one which ties into intellectual activity is the creative reflex. This resembles the situation of an individual who makes uses of Internet networks for acquiring information and then responds to many websites by showing his own ability.

The diversity of creative reflexes is brought about by the broad development of human ability. In the case of such ability development, if we focus our attention on individuals within a group, we can see that what is being developed is the ability of the individual and the knowledge of the individual. In this case, however, the improvement in ability is realized by belonging to the group. This is illustrative of how collective knowledge functions. As to what type of creative reflex is attained will depend on the participants of the group. Depending on whether an official joins the group of the youth and the elderly person with dementia, or whether a care manager or a homemaker or a grade-school child joins this group, the creative reflexes of the members of the group may vary. These creative reflexes may lead to the discovery of problems that should be solved, or they may lead to the discovery of the problem-solving methods themselves. This field in which creative reflex can be gained gives the chances of capability development for problem-solving. This type of knowledge creation process would not exist for an individual if the said individual did not belong to a group.

Why do Entrepreneurs Emerge in a Clustering Fashion?

Collective knowledge secures the multifaceted aspects of problem-finding ability and then functions to raise the level of problem-solving ability. Rather than the individual taking action on their own, it becomes possible to discover various problems by taking action as a group. Rather than just extending the ability held by an individual independently, the development of various individual abilities become possible in the case of the group. When we understand the function of collective knowledge in this way, we can offer a new answer to the question that Schumpeter observed. As I mentioned in Chapter 2 of this book, it is, namely, the question of why entrepreneurs appear in a clustering fashion.

When a certain person discovers a new problem through the creative reflexes of another person, we can expect a chain reaction to this creative reflex to occur. This chain reaction is induced by a third party's presence, which is sparked off by contact with the one who made the discovery. The creative reflex can then be transmitted. The reaction of the third party may in turn impact further by having a retroactive effect on the first and the second persons. If people who have the ability to react in a superior way can gather together, we can also assume that from this potential state there will be the occurrence of a chain reaction that goes beyond the threshold of a certain point in time.[10]

Entrepreneurs appear in a clustering fashion because creative reflex leads to a chain reaction for a new type of collective knowledge. Behind "the new combination" that Schumpeter exemplified, there is the association of knowledge. The combination of knowledge is accumulated so that new knowledge is brought about as the result of mutually contacting people and mutually reacting to the actions or the ways of thinking of another person. In this book, I called this collective knowledge. Launching a business is the confederate strategy of the people carrying it out, and it is founded on shared knowledge. A conjugate strategy is adopted when shared knowledge encounters an insolvable problem and it acquires a new dimension called symbiotic knowledge. By this stage, after the launch of new business, selection has already taken place[11]. And if we observe successful cases of agglomerate strategies in this context, we will see entrepreneurs growing in clusters. Agglomerate strategy is the strategy of locating near a successful company and acquiring local knowledge. If a technical development is pushed forward as the result of a collective strategy made possible by the act of mutual contacting, and if it is then spread throughout society through an organic strategy, new common knowledge becomes established. One can call such an overall process innovation.

Superior Japanese Enterprises in Historical Perspective

Although this book did not adopt a historical approach, if you read the annals of Japanese business, you will see that entrepreneurs have at times sought the assistance of university professors. The entrepreneur Kokichi Mikimoto, who aspired to realize the cultivation of pearls, requested Tokyo Imperial University's Kakichi Mitsukuri to teach him about the habits of the Pinctada fucata martensii, or Akoya Pearl Oyster. It was 1890 then. The commercialization of *Ajinomoto*, a synthetic seasoning, is attributed to businessman Saburosuke Suzuki, who in 1908 visited Tokyo Imperial University's Professor Kikunae Ikeda. Suzuki acquired Kikunae's grant for his patent. Soichiro Honda, the founder of Honda, for three years from 1937, audited classes at the Hammamatsu High-Grade Industrial Technical School (currently known as the Faculty of Engineering, Shizuoka University), where he learned metallurgy and engaged in the development of the piston ring.[12] The founder of Murata

Manufacturing, Akira Murata, in 1947 took charge of the production of barium titanate ceramics in parallel with the study of the material tackled by Kyoto University's Department of Engineering's Testuro Tanaka. The barium titanate ceramic material was developed into an oscillator used as a component in fish detectors.[13]

In Chapter 5, I mentioned that Japanese entrepreneurs had already ventured out to search for local knowledge. Kohnosuke Matsushita visited GE and travelled around the USA in 1951, and in the same year, he made a visit to Philips Corporation in the Netherlands. Soichiro Honda went to the United States to import machine tools in 1952, and Masaru Ibuka of Sony visited the USA too and obtained information about the patent of the transistor. Subsequently, in 1953, Akio Morita, the co-founder of Sony, concluded the patent contract for the transistor in the USA.

These companies used to actively view the USA as an export market and acquire shares of the market as such, while actively carrying out local production in the USA. Furthermore, they used to also actively pursue the establishment of research and development bases in the USA. The brands of each of these companies have become pronouns for product names and become generalized as a result. If the company is superior and is globally active, the company is then very likely to have passed through the process of creating on its own shared knowledge, symbiotic knowledge, local knowledge and common knowledge. Further historical research remains and it is possible to gather more concrete instances in the twenty-first century.

The Possibility of the Megacluster

If we consider the characteristics of a locality in Japan that contains local knowledge, we can understand that there is a serious contradiction in what Porter (1998) stated regarding the measure of the geographic limit of a cluster. Namely, he had said that such a limit would be marked by the fact that business bases would be spread to one another by a distance of less than 200 miles (p. 230). Two hundred miles, or in other words, 320 kilometres, roughly encompasses the distance between Tokyo and Nagoya, which is approximately 360 kilometres. Several regions in Japan completely fit into this 200-mile range. They include the financial district of Marunouchi in Tokyo, the machining district of Ota-ku in Tokyo, and the ferrous metal product, ship-building, car-related industrial district spanning from Kawasaki to the Tokyo Bay coastal line, the area around Odawara and Atsugi with a group of factories serving the electric equipment, automobile parts related industries, the area around Hamamatsu-shi, Shizuoka, accommodating the factories of Suzuki, Yamaha and

Honda, and manufacturing industries supporting Toyota around Toyota-city, Aichi.

Researchers on cluster have focused on the peculiarity of Japanese clusters that may be marked by the fact that they can be accessed by car within 30 minutes or less than an hour, as shown in Chapter 5's Figure 5.2. These clusters are far smaller than those defined by Porter (1998). However, if clusters exist in multiple layers within the 200-mile range in Japan, which is the range that supposedly accommodates only one cluster, then what this would signify is the remarkable tenacity of Japanese clusters. In other words, Japanese industrial clusters have a high density, while also having diversity. In such a case, even if industrial growth stagnates in one cluster, the industrial growth of another cluster may be accelerated while it absorbs the surplus resources of the declining cluster. The new cluster may be regarded as the one existing on the periphery of the old cluster. As such, we may be able to call the cluster a megacluster in the sense that there are multiple clusters combining to form one huge cluster. The Pacific Belt zone in Japan is a candidate for a megacluster and observing this region as a whole will prove to be essential in drafting a regional policy.

Products produced in a cluster cannot be consumed with the demand of its surrounding area alone. It is impossible to consume the products produced in a megacluster within Japan. While there are politicians who promise to build up domestic demand in Japan when the world economy turns sluggish, this would be impossible unless megaclusters are made to collapse. To sustain the activity levels of existing megaclusters, there is no other option but to rely on external demand. What is possible in terms of policy is to cultivate the markets of countries other than those of advanced countries, and to that end, a qualitative change will be sought in the concept of official development assistance (ODA). Basic human needs (BHN) functioned as the driving idea behind ODA and supported irrigation, medical care and measures to counteract poverty. While the BHN approach for the least less-developed countries (LLDC) is still effective, for the less developed countries (LDC), I believe aid packages that meet basic knowledge needs (BKN) are necessary. Along with government-run aid for such areas as elementary education and preventive medicine, programmes may be carried out and specialists despatched to teach technical skills in particular areas such as language study, production management, accounting, distribution and logistics management, and information systems. To carry out such activities, private non-profit organizations (NPO) could also play a role. Ultimately, though, to cultivate markets of countries outside of advanced ones, an understanding of common knowledge is a prerequisite, as it will contribute towards elevating the effectiveness of the various activities of BKN.

Paradigm Shift for Knowledge Creation

The state of knowledge that Kuhn (1962) called paradigm is itself one of the forms of collective knowledge. As I explained in Chapter 1, a paradigm is supported by a wide range of people and it becomes a faith. Those who believed in the Ptolemaic theory were not just the Catholic Church, but the public of the time in general as well. If a paradigm becomes widespread throughout society, the paradigm acts as common knowledge and, in this sense, it includes the faith of the people who are not purposeful.

The paradigm shared by a group of people who work with a purposeful coercive drive is shared knowledge. Paradigm can refer to basic knowledge shared by members participating in certain laboratories of certain universities or by members of specified enterprises. If there is faith shared in industrial collectives such as Silicon Valley and manufacturing clusters, these then are also paradigms. According to this book's terminology, they comprise local knowledge. With such significance, the differences between shared knowledge, local knowledge and common knowledge lie in the differences between the people who understand them in terms of range and degree.

In this book, I have explained four patterns of collective knowledge: shared knowledge, symbiotic knowledge, local knowledge and common knowledge. What should be noted here is that among these different forms of knowledge, you cannot state one is more outstanding than the other. However, one can assert that symbiotic knowledge has the biggest possibility to overturn existing paradigm as a superior form of knowledge. Because creating symbiotic knowledge requires diversity in talent and it adopts a diversified view, it may lead to the construction of a new way of thinking.

This is not an easy task to accomplish. However, if you are able to afford well-motivated talent, your company can attempt all four forms of creating collective knowledge. It is obviously a superior enterprise that can concurrently secure a QC circle within the company and create shared knowledge, participate in industry–university collaborations and bring about symbiotic knowledge, create local knowledge together with regionally associated companies, and heighten the level of common knowledge through CSR and philanthropy.

The theory of knowledge creation surveyed in Chapters 1 and 2 was limited in scope within the company. The concept of user innovation by von Hippel (2006) suggested that the participation of people utilizing a new device triggers innovation, extending innovation's point of emergence. The message suggested from the analysis of the entire contents of this book is, however, much more profound. In other words, the point is that in the creation of symbiotic knowledge, even knowledge from people who are not users can possibly function effectively. It may be that knowledge creation gains a new dimension when knowledge from various, dispersed and independent people are aggregated and when there are people who acquire tips from this aggregation. For example, in the case of environmental problems such as global warming, you cannot even define who the users are. However, a solution is nevertheless demanded. In such a scenario, not only will the viewpoints of governmental authorities of various countries in the world and numerous experts be effective, but also very likely the knowledge on the "wisdom of life" cultivated in different cultures and the viewpoints of various peoples going about their everyday lives, including children and the elderly. If the knowledge management strategy of multinational enterprises were to demonstrate its viability in such a problem domain, the enterprises create collective knowledge from diverse people around the world. The time has come to heighten the level of the knowledge management strategy by moving away from the practice of the suggestion system and *kaizen* (improvement activities), implemented by operating personnel in factories, to the building of a global suggestion system. Such a concept will go a long way towards enriching the international business strategy of a knowledge-based society.

NOTES

1. See Ghosn (2001) and Ghosn and Riès (2003).
2. This part is based on an interview survey in preparation for the work by Horaguchi (1991, 1992, 2002).
3. On 5 November 2012 I interviewed Mr Ben Harris, Assistant Director, Producers Program, UCLA Department of Film, Television and Digital Media.
4. Horiba Ltd, an automotive emissions measurement systems manufacturer, was earnestly intending to realize industry–university collaborations. For the record, I would like to state that the 22 February 2005 interview with the doctor of science, Mr Koichiro Matsuda, who serves as the Project Leader and Director of the New Technology Project Division at the Development Centre of Horiba Ltd, is full of valuable suggestions. For a clear picture of the management executives of this company, I would like to recommend the book by Horiba (2001).
5. This is based on the interview conducted on 16 June 2005 at the OMRON Corporation Advanced Device Laboratory.
6. In May 2010, OMRON Automotive Electronics Co., Ltd in Japan was established.
7. On 22 February 2005 I interviewed Professor Shizuo Fujita of the Kyoto University International Innovation Centre. I was informed that the centre was helming and advancing joint research programmes with companies such as NTT, Pioneer, Hitachi, Mitsubishi Chemical Corporation and ROHM.
8. Even in foreign direct investments, we can likewise recognize the difference between strategic decisions made beforehand and those made retroactively. What is observable as an economic phenomenon is not prior intent but results attained after the fact. See Horaguchi (2004b).

9. Feeling sceptical about this claim, or upon reading the phrase, "creative reflex", is an act of creative reflex itself and feeling the possibility of application is an example of creative reflex as well. Needless to say, conditional reflex is an expression that derives from the phenomenon known as "Pavlov's dog", in which a fixed reaction is made in response to a particular stimulus.
10. The facts shown in Horaguchi (2008a) can be interpreted in terms of such a case example. Additionally, in many cases, education is carried out collectively. We are apt to forget this because it is too obvious.
11. Timmons (1990) is a standard textbook on venture businesses. Chapter 17 touches on the crisis of bankruptcy into which start-up companies fall.
12. Regarding the above-mentioned Mikimoto, Suzuki and Honda, see Udagawa and Sangyō Jōhō Center (1999). In addition, on the Japan Patent Office's website, you can find a listing of the patent applicants whose inventions were selected as the top ten Japanese inventions that contributed to industrialization.
13. Inoki and Umezaki (2004, pp. 51–5). As cautioned in Chapter 3's explanatory note, oral history serves as a powerful tool of analysis in attaining historical testimony pertaining to enterprise management. As a guide to research technique, refer to Mikuriya (2007). While the large question of how to analytically make use of oral history remains, you can expect to see a further enrichment of the field research approaches. See also a compilation by Koike and Horaguchi (2006).

References

Akamatsu, Kaname (1956), 'Wagakuni sangyō hatten no gankōkeitai: Kikai kigu kōgyō ni tsuite' (Flying geese pattern of our country's industrial development: On machinery and equipment industry), *Hitotsubashi Ronsō (Hitotsubashi Review)*, **36** (5), 68–80 (in Japanese).

Akamatsu, Kaname (1961), 'A theory of unbalanced growth in the world economy', *Weltwirtschaftliches Archiv*, **86** (2), 196–215.

Akashi, Yoshihiko (1996), 'Nihon kigyō no hinshitsu kanri yōshiki, shōshūdan katsudō, teian seido: Jidai kubun teki kōsatsu' (Quality control patterns, small group activities and suggestion system of Japanese firms: Historical development approach), *Kikan Keizai Kenkyū (Quarterly Economics Research*, Osaka Ichiritsu Daigaku Keizai Gakkai, Osaka City University, Faculty of Economics), **19** (1), 29–70 (in Japanese).

Amano, Tomohumi, Yongdo Kim, Yoshinori Konno, Haruo Horaguchi and Shigeru Matsushima (2006), 'Monozukuri kurasutā no tokushusei to fuhensei: Globalization to chitekikōdo-ka' (Particularity and universality of monozukuricluster: Globalization and up-grading knowledge intensity), *Keiei Shirin (The Hosei Journal of Business)*, **43** (2), 73–97 (in Japanese).

Ansoff, Igor H. (1965), *Corporate Strategy: An Analytic Approach to Business Policy for Growth and Expansion*, New York: McGraw-Hill.

Antonelli, Cristiano (2007), 'The system dynamics of collective knowledge: From gradualism and saltationism to punctuated change', *Journal of Economic Behavior and Organization*, **62** (2), 215–36.

Arrow, Keneth J. (1994), 'Methodological individualism and social knowledge', *American Economic Review*, **84** (2), 1–9.

Asaba, Shigeru (2004), *Keiei Senryaku no Keizaigaku (Economics of Management Strategy)*, Tokyo: NipponHyoronsha (in Japanese).

Asanuma, Banri (1997), *Nihon no Kigyō Soshiki: Kakushin-teki Tekiou no Mechanism (Corporate Organization of Japanese Firms: Mechanism for Innovative Adaptation)*, Tokyo: Toyo Keizai (in Japanese).

Astley, Graham W. (1984), 'Toward an appreciation of collective strategy', *Academy of Management Review*, **9** (3), 526–35.

Astley, Graham W. and Charles J. Fombrun (1983), 'Collective strategy:

social ecology of organizational environments', *Academy of Management Review*, **8** (4), 576–87.

Avis, James (2002), 'Social capital, collective intelligence and expansive learning, thinking through the connections: Education and the economy,' *British Journal of Education Studies*, **50** (3), 308–26.

Axelrod, Robert M. (1984), *The Evolution of Cooperation*, New York: Basic Books.

Axelrod, Robert M. and Michael D. Cohen (1999), *Harnessing Complexity: Organizational Implications of a Scientific Frontier*, New York: Free Press.

Bara, Venkatesh and Sanjeev Goyal (2000), 'A Noncooperative model of network formation', *Econometrica*, **68** (5), 1181–229.

Barabasi, Albert-Laszlo (2002), *Linked: The New Science of Network*, Cambridge, MA: Perseus Publishing.

Barabasi, Albert-Laszlo and Reka Albert (1999), 'Emergence of scaling in random network', *Science*, **286**, 509–12.

Barnard, Chester I. (1938), *The Functions of the Executive*, Cambridge, MA: Harvard University Press.

Barney, Jay B. (1997), *Gaining and Sustaining Competitive Advantage*, Reading, MA: Addison-Wesley.

Bestor, Theodore C. (2004), *Tsukiji: The Fish Market at the Center of the World*, Berkeley: University of California Press.

Boder, André (2006), 'Collective intelligence: A keystone in knowledge management', *Journal of Knowledge Management*, **10** (1), 81–93.

Bruun, Steffan and Mosse Wallen (1999), *Boken om Nokia, Bengt Nordin Agency AB* (translated into Japanese by Yumiko Yanagisawa as *Nokia: Sekai Saidai no Keitai Denwa Meikā*, Tokyo: Nikkei BP Syuppan Sentā, 2001).

Bresnahan, Timothy F. (1981), 'Duopoly models with consistent conjectures', *American Economic Review*, **71** (5), 934–45.

Bresser, Rudi K.F. (1988), 'Matching collective and competitive strategies', *Strategic Management Journal*, **9** (4), 375–85.

Bresser, Rudi K. and Johannes E. Harl (1986), 'Collective strategy: Vice or virtue?' *Academy of Management Review*, **11** (2), 408–27.

Brown, Phillip and Huge Lauder (2000), 'Human capital, social capital, and collective intelligence', in Stephen Baron, John Field and Tom Schuller (eds), *Social Capital: Critical Perspective*, Chapter 13, pp. 226–42.

Burgelman, Robert A. and Leonard R. Sayles (1986), *Inside Corporate Innovation: Strategy, Structure, and Management Skills*, New York: Free Press.

Chandler, Alfred D. (1992), 'Organizational capabilities and the economic history of the industrial enterprise', *Journal of Economic Perspective*, **6** (3), 79–100.

Chesbrough, Henry W. (2003), *Open Innovation: The New Imperative for Creating and Profiting from Technology*, Boston, MA: Harvard Business School Press.

Christensen, Clayton M. (1997), *The Innovator's Dilemma: When New Technologies Cause Great Firms to Fail*, Boston, MA: Harvard Business School Press.

Clark, Kim B. and Takahiro Fujimoto (1991), *Product Development Performance: Strategy, Organization, and Management in the World Auto Industry*, Boston, MA: Harvard Business School Press.

Coase, Ronald H. (1937), 'The nature of the firm', *Economica*, **4** (16), 386–405, reprinted in R.H. Coase, *The Firm, the Market, and the Law*, University of Chicago Press, 1988, pp. 33–55.

Coase, Ronald H. (1960), 'The problem of social cost', *Journal of Law and Economics*, **3**, 1–44, reprinted in R.H. Coase, *The Firm, the Market, and the Law*, University of Chicago Press, 1988, pp. 95–156.

Coleman, James S. (1988), 'Social capital in the creation of human capital', *American Journal of Sociology*, **94** (Supplement), S95–S120.

Collins, H.M. (1974), 'The TEA set: Tacit knowledge and scientific networks', *Science Studies* (Social Studies of Science), **4** (2), 165–85, reprinted in Barry Barnes and David Edge (eds), *Science in Context: Readings in the Sociology of Science*, Chapter 3, MIT Press, 1982.

Diestel, Reinhard (1997), *Graph Theory*, New York: Springer.

Dollinger, Marc J. (1990), 'The evolution of collective strategies in fragmented industries', *Academy of Management Review*, **15** (2), 266–85.

Drucker, Peter F. (1986), *Innovation and Entrepreneurship: Practice and Principles*, New York: Harper & Row, reprinted in Harper Business, 1993.

Eco, Umberto (1976), *A Theory of Semiotics*, Bloomington: Indiana University Press.

Engeström, Yrjö (1987), *Learning by Expanding: An Activity-theoretical Approach to Developmental Research*, Helsinki: Orienta-Konsultit.

Fudenberg, Drew and Jean Tirole (1991), *Game Theory*, Cambridge, MA: MIT Press.

Fujimoto, Takahiro (1997), *Seisan Sisutemu no Shinka-ron: Toyota Jidōsha nimiru Soshiki Nouryoku to Sōhatsu Purosesu (Evolutionary Theory of Production System: Emergency Process and Organizational Capacity in Toyota)*, Tokyo: Yuhikaku (in Japanese).

Fujimoto, Takahiro (2003), *Nouryoku Kouchiku-kyōsō: Nihon no Jidōsha-sangyō wa Naze Tsuyoinoka (Capacity Building Competition: Why is Japanese Automobile Industry Strong?)*, Tokyo: Chuōkōron-shinsha (in Japanese).

Fukuda, Kensuke and Satoshi Kurihara (2003), 'Network no kagaku' (Science of network), *Jinkō Chinō Gakkai-shi (Journal of Japanese Society for Artificial Intelligence)*, **18** (6), 716–22 (in Japanese).

Ghosn, Carlos (2001), *Runessansu: Saisei eno Chousen (Renaissance: Challenge for Regeneration)*, translated by Haruko Nakagawa, Tokyo: Daiyamondosha (in Japanese).

Ghosn, Carlos and Philippe Riès (2003), *Carlos Ghosn Keiei wo Kataru (Carlos Ghosn Talks about Management)*, translated by Yu Takano, Tokyo: Nikkei (in Japanese).

Gibbons, Robert (1992), *Game Theory for Applied Economists*, Princeton NJ: Princeton University Press.

Goto, Akira and Hiroyuki Odagiri (2003), *Nihon no Sangyō Sisutemu 3: Saiensu-gata Sangyō (Japan's Industrial System 3: Science-driven Industry)*, Tokyo: NTT Publishing (in Japanese).

Goto, Akira and Sadao Nagaoka (2003), *Chiteki Zaisan Seido to Inobeishon (Intellectual Property System and Innovation)*, Tokyo: University of Tokyo Press (in Japanese).

Gourlay, Stephen (2006), 'Conceptualizing knowledge creation: A critique of Nonaka's theory', *Journal of Management Studies*, **43** (7), 1415–36.

Goyal, Sanjeev and Jose Luis Moraga-Gonzalez (2001), 'R&D networks', *Rand Journal of Economics*, **32** (4), 686–707.

Granovetter, Mark S. (1973), 'The strength of weak ties', *American Journal of Sociology*, **78** (6), 1360–80.

Greene, William H. (1993), *Econometric Analysis*, 2nd edition, Englewood Cliffs, NJ: Prentice Hall.

Greenhut, Melvin L., George Norman and Chao-Shun Hung (1987), *The Economics of Imperfect Competition: A Spatial Approach*, New York: Cambridge University Press.

Haak, René (2004), *Theory and Management of Collective Strategies in International Business: The Impact of Globalization on Japanese-German Business Collaboration in Asia*, Palgrave Macmillan.

Hachiya, Yoshihiko (1999), *Shūdan no Kashikosa to Orokasa: Shōshūdan Rīdāshippu Kenkyū. (Cleverness and Foolishness of Groups: A Research on Small Group Leadership)*, Tokyo: Mineruvashobō (in Japanese).

Hamel, Gary and C.K. Prahalad (1996), *Competing for the Future*, Boston, MA: Harvard Business School Press.

Harary, Frank (1969),*Graph Theory*, Reading, MA: Addison-Wesley.

Hayek, Friedrich A. (1944), *The Road to Serfdom*, Chicago: University of Chicago Press.

Hayek, Friedrich A. (1945), 'The use of knowledge in society', *American Economic Review*, **35** (4), 519–30.

Hayek, Friedrich A. (1946), 'Individualism: True and False', The twelfth Finlay Lecture, delivered at University College, Dublin, on December 17, 1945. Published by Hodges, Figgies & Co., Ltd., Dublin, and B.H. Blackwell, Ltd., Oxford, 1946; in *Individualism and Economic Order*, London: Routledge & Kegan Paul Ltd., 1949, Chapter 1, pp. 1–32, also reprinted by University of Chicago Press in 1996.

Hayek, Friedrich A. (1973), 'The place of Menger's Grundsätze in the history of economic thought', in J.R. Hicks and W. Weber (eds), *Carl Menger and the Austrian School of Economics*, Oxford: Clarendon Press, Chapter 1, pp. 1–14.

Hendricks, Ken, Michele Piccione and Guofu Tan (1995), 'The economics of hubs: The case of monopoly', *Review of Economics Studies*, **62** (1), 83–99.

Hofstede, Geert (2001), *Culture's Consequences: Comparing Values, Behaviors, Institutions, and Organizations across Nations*, 2nd ed., Thousand Oaks, CA: Sage Publications.

Honda, Souichirou. (2001), *Honda Souichirō, Yume wo Chikarani: Watashi no Rirekisho (Honda Souichirō, Dreams for Power: My Biography)*, Tokyo: Nikkei Business Bunko.

Horaguchi, Haruo (1991), 'Firippin no jōyōsha-shijōkōzō to nikkei assenburi meikā no yakuwari: Genchi chōtatsu buhin hinmoku ni kansuru nihon, thai tono kokusai hikaku' (Japanese multinationals and market structure in Philippines passenger car industry: An international comparison with Thailand on local content), *Asia Keizai (Asian Economy)*, **32** (12), 2–24 (in Japanese).

Horaguchi, Haruo (1992), Nihon-kigyō no Kaigai Chokusetsu Tōushi: Ajia heno Shinshutsu to Tettai (Foreign Direct Investment of Japanese Firms: Investment and Disinvestment in Asia), Tokyo: University of Tokyo Press (in Japanese).

Horaguchi, Haruo (1996), 'The role of information processing cost as the foundation of bounded rationality in game theory', *Economics Letters*, **51** (3), 287–94.

Horaguchi, Haruo (1997a), 'Gaibusei' (Externality), in Masu Uekusa (ed.), *Shakai Kisei no Keizaigaku (Economics of Social Regulation)*, Chapter 5, Tokyo: NTT Publishing, pp. 100–130 (in Japanese).

Horaguchi, Haruo (1997b), 'Sannyū, taishutsu to soshiki no sai-hensei: Amerika ni okeru nikkei takokuseki kigyō no jigyō keizoku to soshiki-teki shinka' (Entry, exit, and reorganization: Survival and evolution of Japanese multinational subsidiaries in the United States), *Mita Gakkai Zasshi (Mita Journal of Economics)*, **90** (2), 282–310 (in Japanese).

Horaguchi, Haruo (1998), 'Futatsu no shakai-kagaku no 20seiki: Keieigaku to keizaigaku' (Two Social Sciences in the 20th Century: Management and economics), *Shakai Kagaku Kenkyū (Journal of Social Science)*, **50** (1), 3–27 (in Japanese).

Horaguchi, Haruo (2000), 'America jidōsha meikā, big surii heno intabyu chousa gaiyou: 1997nen 9gatsu, Shimokawa Koichi kyōju ni doukoushite' (A summary of interview survey to the big three in American automobile industry: Accompanying with Professor Koichi Shimokawa in September 1997), *Keiei Shirin (The Hosei Journal of Business)*, **36** (4), 95–108 (in Japanese).

Horaguchi, Haruo (2001a), 'Kokusai keiei: Sangyō shūseki' (International business: Industrial agglomeration), in Hiroyuki Fujimura and Haruo Horaguchi (eds), *Gendai Keieigaku Nyūmon: 21seiki no Kigyō Keiei (Introduction to Modern Management: Business Management in the 21st Century)*, Chapter 8, Tokyo: Mineruvashobō, pp. 198–217 (in Japanese).

Horaguchi, Haruo (2001b), 'Kakou kumitate-gata sangyō ni okeru kanagata koukan jikan no kansatsu: Kokusai bijiness kenkyū ni okeru aratana jirei bunseki houhou no tankyū' (Oberservations on changing dies for injection molding machines in a Malaysian manufacturing company: A new approach for field work of international business studies), *Kokusai Bijinesu Kenkyū Gakkai Nenpou: Nihon Kigyō to Kokusaiteki Saihen (The Annual Bulletin, Japan Academy of International Business Studies: Japanese Firms and International Restructuring)*, **7**, 57–68 (in Japanese).

Horaguchi, Haruo (2002), *Globalism to Nihon Kigyō: Soshiki to shiteno Takokuseki Kigyō (Globalism and Japanese Firms: Multinational Enterprises as Organizations)*, Tokyo: University of Tokyo Press (in Japanese).

Horaguchi, Haruo (2003), 'Chiiki tougou to takokuseki kigyō: EU shijō ni okeru jidōsha, denki, denshi, tsūshin sangyō no doukou' (Regional integration and multinational enterprises: Field research on automobile, electrical, electronics, and communication industry in EU market), *Keiei Shirin (The Hosei Journal of Business)*, **40** (3), 103–15 (in Japanese).

Horaguchi, Haruo (2004a), 'Nihon no sangyō kūdōka to chishiki shūyaku kurasutā no sōzō: Tairyō seisan sisutemu no mirai to sangakukan renkei no genzai' (Hollowing-out of Japanese industries and creation of knowledge intensive clusters: Mass-production system in the future and alliance among industry, academia and government at present), *Inobeishon Manejimento (Innovation management)*, **1**, 1–23 (in Japanese).

Horaguchi, Haruo (2004b), 'Takokuseki kigyō no riron to ningen koudou no koujun' (Theories of multinational enterprises and axioms of human behavior), in Nihon Keiei Gakkai (Japan Academy of Business Administration) (ed.), *Globalization to Gendai Kigyō-keiei, Keieigaku Ronshū 74shū. (Globalization and Modern Business Management,*

Bulletin of Business Administration vol. 74), Tokyo: Chikura Publishing, **74**, 19–29.

Horaguchi, Haruo (2004c), 'Takokuseki kigyō to keizai seisaku: Senryaku teki sozei seisaku no tayousei to nihon no sangyō saisei' (Multinational enterprises and economic policy: A multiplicity of strategic tax policy and redevelopment of Japanese industry), *Kokusai Bijiness Kenkyū Gakkai Nenpou, Nihon no Sangyo to Kigyō no Saisei: Guroubaru Pāsupekutibu (The Annual Bulletin, Japan Academy of International Business Studies, Industry in Japan and Rejuvenization of Firms: Global Perspectives)*, **10**, 1–8 (in Japanese).

Horaguchi, Haruo (2004d), 'Japanese foreign direct investment in China: From export-oriented production to domestic marketing', in René Haak and Dennis S. Tachiki (eds), *Regional Strategies in a Global Economy: Multinational Corporations in East Asia*, IUDICIUM Verlag GmbH, Chapter 5, pp. 119–35.

Horaguchi, Haruo (2006), 'Youso gijutsuno inobeisyon: Seizōgyō ni okeru kenkyū kaihatsu no hōkōsei' (Innovation of factor technology: R&D direction in manufacturing industry), The Research Institute for Innovation Management, Hosei University, working paper, **17** (in Japanese).

Horaguchi, Haruo (2007a), 'Chiteki kurasutā sousei jigyō kōdineitā heno ankēto chousa: Shūkei kekka to kaitou no tokuchou' (Questionnaire survey for coordinators in Knowledge Intensive Cluster Initiative: Some characteristics on survey results), The Research Institute for Innovation Management, Hosei University, working paper, **28** (in Japanese).

Horaguchi, Haruo (2007b), 'Economic analysis of free trade agreements: Spaghetti bowl effect and a paradox of hub and spoke network', *Journal of Economic Integration*, **22** (3), 664–83.

Horaguchi, Haruo (2008a), 'Economics of reciprocal networks: Collaboration in knowledge and emergence of industrial clusters', *Computational Economics*, **31** (4), 307–39.

Horaguchi, Haruo (2008b), 'Collective knowledge and collective strategy: A function of symbiotic knowledge for business-university alliances', Working Paper Series **57**, Research Institute for Innovation Management, Hosei University.

Horaguchi, Haruo (2008c), 'Shūgōchi to shūgō senryaku: Innovation hassei riron no tankyū' (Collective knowledge and collective strategy: Quest for genetic theory of innovation), *Nihon Keiei Gakkai-shi (Journal of Business Management)*, **21**, 15–26.

Horaguchi, Haruo (ed.) (2008d), *Fakarutii Diberopumento: Gakubu Zemināru hen. (Faculty Development: A Volume for Undergraduate Education)*, Tokyo: Hakuto-Shobo (in Japanese).

Horaguchi, Haruo (2009a), 'Keiei ni okeru chishiki to nōryoku: Anmokuchi no kikensei to shūgōchini kansuru joronteki kōsatu' (Knowledge and capability in management: Risks from tacit knowledge and some preliminary survey for collective knowledge), *Keiei Shirin (The Hosei Journal of Business)*, **45** (4), 67–78 (in Japanese).

Horaguchi, Haruo (2009b), *Shūgōchino Keiei: Nihon Kigyō no Chishiki Kanri Senryaku (Management of Collective Knowledge: Knowledge Management Strategy of Japanese Firms)*, Tokyo: Bunshindō (in Japanese).

Horaguchi, Haruo (2013a), 'Hardy-Weinberg equilibrium and mixed strategy equilibrium in game theory', *Theoretical Economics Letters*, **3** (2), 85–9.

Horaguchi, Haruo (2013b), 'Aircraft industry in Japan: Niche construction and patent portfolio strategy', *Journal of Modern Accounting and Auditing*, **9** (6), 908–21.

Horaguchi, Haruo and Bryan Toyne (1990), 'Setting the record straight: Hymer, internalization theory and transaction cost economics', *Journal of International Business Studies*, **21** (3), 487–94.

Horaguchi, Haruo, Hisashi Yaginuma, Shigeru Matsushima, Yongdo Kim, Yoshinori Konno, Tomofumi Amano, Seiki Yukimoto and Ruixue Li (2007), *Sangyō Kurastā no Chiteki Kōdoka to Gurōbarizeishon*, Heisei 16(2004)nendo-Heisei 18(2006)nendo Kagaku kenkyūhi hojokin kiban kenkyū (A) kenkyū-seika houkokusho, Kadai bangou 16203022, Heisei 19(2007)nen 4 gatsu. (*Up-grading Knowledge Intensive Cluster and Globalization*, 2004–2006 Grant-in-Aid for Scientific Research(A), JSPS Grant number 16203022, final report) (in Japanese).

Horaguchi, Haruo, Tomofumi Amano and Yongdo Kim (2005a), *Kitakyūshū, Fukuoka nimiru Chiteki Kurastā Sousei Seisaku no Doukou: 2004nen 8gatsu chousa (A Report on Knowledge Cluster Initiatives in Kita-kyushu and Fukuoka: A Survey in August 2004)*, Heisei 16nendo kagaku kenkyūhi hojokin kiban kenkyūA, Kadai bangou 16203022, Sangyō kurastā no chiteki kōdoka to gurobarizeishon, chousa report No.1. (2004 Grant-in-Aid for Scientific Research(A), JSPS Grant number 162030222, Up-grading Knowledge Intensive Cluster and Globalization, report no.1) (in Japanese).

Horaguchi, Haruo, Tomofumi Amano, Yongdo Kim, Yoshinori Konno and Hisashi Yaginuma (2005b), *Amerika, Silicon Valley Chousa Hōkokusho: 2004nen 9gatsu chousa (A report on Silicon Valley in the United States: A survey in September 2004)*, Heisei 16nendo kagaku kenkyūhi hojokin kiban kenkyū A, kadai bangou 16203022, Sangyō kurastā no chiteki kōdoka to globalization, Chousa report No.2 (2004 Grant-in-Aid for Scientific Research(A), JSPS Grant number 162030222, Up-grading

Knowledge Intensive Cluster and Globalization, report no.1) (in Japanese).

Horaguchi, Haruo and Seiki Yukimoto (2008), *Nyūmon keieigaku: Hajimete Manabu Hitono Tameni* (Introduction to Business Management: For Those who Learn for the First Time), Tokyo: Dōyūkan (in Japanese).

Horaguchi, Haruo, Seiki Yukimoto and Ruixue Li (2007), 'Chiteki kurastā sousei jigyō no nakano Toyama iyaku baio kurastā: Shin ketsugou no genba niha darega sankaku surunoka' (Toyama medical bio-cluster among the knowledge cluster initiative: Who participate in the spot of new combination?), *Innobeishon Manejimento (Journal of Innovation Management)*, **4**, 79–103 (in Japanese).

Horaguchi, Haruo and the Research Institute for Innovation Management, Hosei University (2008), *Daigaku Kyōiku no Inobeitā: Hosei Daigaku Souritusha Satta Masakuni to Meiji Nihon no Sangyō Shakai (The Innovator of University Education: Satta Masakuni, the Founder of Hosei University, and Industrial Society of Meiji Japan)*, Tokyo: Shosekikōbō Hayama (in Japanese).

Horaguchi, Haruo and Koichi Shimokawa (eds) (2002), *Japanese Foreign Direct Investment and the East Asian Industrial System: Case Studies from the Automobile and Electronics Industries*, Tokyo: Springer-Verlag Tokyo.

Horiba, Masao (2001), *Kodomo wo Shiawaseni suru Kyouikuron: 'Suki' ni Makasero (Pedagogy to make children happy: Let children do as they like)*, Kyoto: PHP kenkyūjo (in Japanese).

Huang, Kuan-Tsae (1997), 'Capitalizing collective knowledge for winning, execution and teamwork', *Journal of Knowledge Management*, **1** (2), 149–56.

Ijichi, Tomohiro (2000), 'Sangakukan no intāakushon ni kakawaru rieki souhan: Tokkyo deita ni yoru jittai bunseki oyobi manejimento ni kansuru shuyōkoku no genjō' (Conflict of interest among interactions between business and university: Empirical analysis by patent data and status quo of management in major countries), *Soshiki Kagaku (Organizational Science)*, **34** (1), 54–75 (in Japanese).

Ikegami, Takashi (2003), 'Jinkō seimei kara mita shūgōchi' (Collective intelligence from the perspective of artificial life), *Jinkō Chinō Gakkaishi (the JSAI Journal, the Japanese Society for Artificial Intelligence)*, **18** (6), 704–9.

Ikegami, Yoshihiro (2008), 'Linguistics and poetics of "Ego as Zero": The Japanese speaker's preferential choice of subjective rather than objective construal', a paper presented at the 12th International Conference of the European Association for Japanese Studies, September 2008, Lecce, Italy.

Inoki, Takenori (1985), 'Keizai to anmokuchi: Rōdō to gijutu ni kansuru ichi kōsatu' (Economy and tacit knowledge: An essay on labor and technology), *Kikan Gendai Keizai (Modern Economics Quarterly)*, Tokyo: Gendai Keizai Kenkyukai and Nihon Keizai Shinbunsha, **61** (April), 119–26, reprinted in Hiroyuki Itami, Tadao Kagono, Motoshige Itoh (eds), *Rīdingusu Nihon no Kigyō Sisutemu 3, Jinteki Shigen (Readings, Corporate System in Japan, 3, Human Resource)*, Chapter 4, Tokyo: Yuhikaku, 1993, pp. 104–25 (in Japanese).

Inoki, Takenori (1987), *Keizai Shisō (Economic Philosophy)*, Tokyo: Iwanamishoten (in Japanese).

Inoki, Takenori and Osamu Umezaki (eds) (2004), 'Murata Akira, Kabushiki Kaisha Murata Seisakujo Meiyo-kaichō, Ōraru Hisutorī' (Murata Akira, Honorary Chairman of Murata Manufacturing Co. Ltd. Oral History), National Graduate Institute for Policy Studies, C.O.E. Ōraru Seisaku Kenkyū Purojekuto, Heiei 16 nendo monbu kagakushou kagaku kenkyūhi hojokin tokubetu suishin kenkyū (COE) kenyū seika houkokusho, Kadai-bangou 12CE2002 (in Japanese).

Ishikura, Yoko, Masahisa Fujita, Noboru Maeda, Kazuyori Kanai and Akira Yamasaki (2003), *Nihon no Sangyō Kurasutā Senryaku: Chiiki ni Okeru Kyōsōyūi no Kakuritsu (Industrial Cluster Strategy of Japan: Establishing Competitive Advantage in Local Economy)*, Tokyo: Yuhikaku (in Japanese).

Jackson, Matthew O. and Alison Watts (2002), 'The evolution of social and economic networks', *Journal of Economic Theory*, **106** (2), 265–95.

Jackson, Matthew O. and Asher Wolinsky (1996), 'A strategic model of social and economic networks', *Journal of Economic Theory*, **71** (1), 44–74.

Kanai, Toshihiro (1994), *Kigyō-sha Networking no Sekai: MIT to Boston Kinpen no Kigyō-sha Kommunitī no Tankyū (The World of Entrepreneurship Networking: Inquiry into the Entrepreneur Community around MIT and Boston Area)*, Tokyo: Hakuto-Shobo (in Japanese).

Kenney, Martin (2000), *Understanding Silicon Valley: The Anatomy of an Entrepreneurial Region*, Stanford, CA: Stanford University Press.

Kitagawa, Fumi (2004), 'Chiiki inobeishon sisutemu no kouchiku ni mukete: Kokusai hikaku no shiten kara' (Towards the construction of local innovation system: From the viewpoint of international comparison) *Kenkyu, Gijutsu, Keikaku (Journal of Science Policy and Research Management)*, **19** (3/4), 159–71 (in Japanese).

Kiyonari, Tadao (1986), *Chiiki Sangyō Seisaku (Regional Industrial Policy)*, Tokyo: University of Tokyo Press (in Japanese).

Kiyonari, Tadao (1990), *Chūshō Kigyō Dokuhon (Readings on Small and Medium Scale Company)*, Tokyo: Toyo Keizai (in Japanese).

Kiyonari, Tadao (1998), *Kigyōka toha Nanika (What is Entrepreneurship?)*, Tokyo: Toyo Keizai (in Japanese).

Kiyonari, Tadao and Juro Hashimoto (eds) (1997), *Nihongata Sangyō Shūseki no Miraizō (Vision for the Future Japanese Industrial Agglomeration)*, Tokyo: Nihon Keizai Hyouronsha (in Japanese).

Knight, Frank H. (1921), *Risk, Uncertainty and Profit*, Frederick, MD: BeardBooks, 2002.

Kogut, Bruce and Udo Zander (1993), 'Knowledge of the firm and the evolutionary theory of the multinational corporation', *Journal of International Business Studies*, **24** (4), 625–45.

Koike, Kazuo and Takenori Inoki (eds) (1987), Jinzai Keisei no Kokusai Hikaku: Tounan Ajia to Nippon, Tokyo: Toyo Keizai (translated into English by K. Koike and T. Inoki (1990), *Skill Formation in Japan and Southeast Asia*, Tokyo: University of Tokyo Press).

Koike, Kazuo and Haruo Horaguchi (2006), *Keieigaku no Fīrudo Risāchi: Genba no Tatsujin no Jissen-teki Chōsa Shuhō (Field Research for Management Study: A Practical Guide by Research Master of Working Scene)*, Tokyo: Nikkei (in Japanese).

Kolstad, Charles D. and Lars Mathiesen (1991), 'Computing Cournot-Nash equilibria', *Operations Research*, **39** (5), 739–48.

Konno, Yoshinori (2007), 'Nihon jidōsha sangyō ni okeru sentan gijutu kaihatsu kyōgyō no doukou bunseki: Jidōsha maker kyoudou tokkyo deita no patent mapu bunseki' (Transition of the advanced R&D cooperation between automakers and suppliers in the Japanese automobile industry: Patent map analysis of joint patents), *Keiei Shirin (The Hosei Journal of Business)*, **44** (3), 29–56 (in Japanese).

Kotler, Philip (1999), *Marketing Management: The Millennium Edition*, 10th ed., Upper Saddle River, NJ: Prentice Hall.

Kotler, Philip and Gary Armstrong (1996), *Principles of Marketing*, 7th ed., Upper Saddle River, NJ: Prentice Hall.

Kotler, Phillip, Hermawan Kartajaya and Hooi Den Huan (2006), *Think ASEAN!: Rethinking Marketing toward ASEAN Community 2015*, Singapore: McGraw-Hill.

Kreps, David M. (1990), *A Course in Microeconomic Theory*, Princeton, NJ: Princeton University Press.

Krugman, Paul (1991), *Geography and Trade*. Cambridge, MA: MIT Press.

Kubo, Takao, Seiji Harada and Shin Sangyō Seisaku Kenkyūjo (2001), *Chishiki keizai to Saiensu Pāku (Regional Economy and Science Park)*, Chapter 8, Tokyo: Nippon Hyoronsha (in Japanese).

Kuhn, Thomas S. (1962), *The Structure of Scientific Revolutions*, Chicago: University of Chicago Press.

Le Bon, Gustave (1895), *Psychologie des foules*, (Bibliothèque de philosophie contemporaine), Paris: F. Alcan, uploaded by Wikisource France at: http://fr. wikisource.org/wiki/Psychologie_des_foules/Livre_ III (translated into Japanese by Sakurai, Naruo as *Gunshū Shinri*, Koudnsha Gakujutsu Bunko, 1993).

Lécuyer, Christophe (2000), 'Fairchild semiconductor and its influence', in Lee, Chong-Moon, William F. Miller, Marguerite Gong Hancock and Henry S. Rowen (eds), *The Silicon Valley Edge: A Habitat for Innovation and Entrepreneurship*, Stanford, CA: Stanford University Press.

Lee, Chong-Moon, William F. Miller, Marguerite Gong Hancock and Henry S. Rowen (eds) (2000), *The Silicon Valley Edge: A Habitat for Innovation and Entrepreneurship*, Stanford, CA: Stanford University Press.

Lee, Yew-Jin and Wolff-Michael Roth (2007), 'The individual/collective dialectic in the learning organization', *Learning Organization*, **14** (2), 92–107.

Le Roy, Frédéric (2003), 'Rivaliser et coopérer avec ses concurrents: Le cas des stratégies collectives « agglomérées »', *Revue Française de Gestion*, **143** (Mars/Avril), 145–57.

Liang, Thow Yick (2004), 'Intelligence strategy: The evolutionary and co-evolutionary dynamics of intelligent human organizations and their interacting agents', *Human Systems Management*, **23** (2), 137–49.

Marshall, Alfred (1920), *Principles of Economics: An Introductory Volume*, 8th ed., London: Macmillan.

Martin, Ron and Peter Sunley (2003), 'Deconstructing clusters: Chaotic concept or policy', *Journal of Economic Geography*, **3** (1), 5–23.

Martin-de-Castro, Gregorio, Pedro Lopew-Saez and Jose E. Navas-Lopez (2008), 'Process of knowledge creation in knowledge-intensive firms: Empirical evidence from Boston's route 128 and Spain', *Technovation*, **28** (4), 222–30.

Marx, Karl (1890), *Das Kapital: Kritik der politischen Ökonomie*, Erster Band, Berlin: Dietz Verlag Berlin, 1947 (translated into Japanese by Jiro Okazaki based on 'Karl Marx-Friedrich Engels Werke, Band 23–25' (Dietz, 1962–1964), published by Ōtsukishoten in 1972–75).

Matsushima, Shigeru (2002), 'Jidōsha sangyō to sangyō shūseki: Toyotashi shūhen no field work karano chūkan teki kousatu' (The automobile industry and industrial clustering: An interim examination based on fieldwork in Toyota city and its environs), *Keiei Shirin (The Hosei Journal of Business)*, **39** (1), 47–59.

Matsushima, Shigeru (2005a), 'Sangyō kōzō no tayousei to chiiki keizai no gankensa: Gunma ken Kiryushi, Ohtashi, Ohizumimachi no keisu' (Diversity of industrial structure and robustness of local economy: Cases of Kiryu-shi, Ohta-shi and Ohizumi-cho in Gumma prefecture), in Takeo Kikkawa and Rengo SōgōSeikatsu Kaihatsu Kenkyūjo (eds), *Chiikikarano Keizai Saisei: Sangyōshūseki, Inbeishon, Koyou Soushutsu (Economic Rejuvenization from Regions: Industrial Agglomeration, Innovation and Job Creation)*, Chapter 1, Tokyo: Yuhikaku, pp. 11–36.

Matsushima, Shigeru (2005b), 'Kigyōkan kankei: Tasōteki supplier system no kōzō: Jidōsha sangyō ni okeru kinzoku puresu buhin no niji supplier wo chūshin ni' (Inter-corporate relationships: Structure of multilayered supplier system: Focusing on secondary press-parts suppliers among automobile industry), in Akira Kudo, Takeo Kikkawa and Glenn D. Hook (eds), *Gendai Nihon Kigyō, Kigyō Taisei, Jou), (Modern Japanese Companies, Corporate System, vol. 1)*, Chapter 10, Tokyo: Yuhikaku, pp. 265–96 (in Japanese).

Matsushima, Shigeru and Konosuke Odaka (2007), *Kumamoto Yūzō Ōraru Hisutorī (Kumamoto Yūzō oral history)*, The Research Institute for Innovation Management, Hosei University, working paper, **27** (in Japanese).

Matsushita, Kounosuke (2001), *Matsushita Kounosuke, Yume wo Sodateru: Watashi no Rirekisho (Matsushita Kounosuke, Nurturing Dreams: My Biography)*, Tokyo: Nikkei Business Bunko.

McKendrick, David. G., Richard. F. Doner and Stehan Haggard (2000), *From Silicon Valley to Singapore: Location and Competitive Advantage in the Hard Disk Drive Industry*, Stanford: Stanford University Press.

Mikuriya, Takashi (2007), *Oral Hisutorī Nyūmon (Introduction to Oral History)*, Tokyo: Iwanamishoten (in Japanese).

Mintzberg, Henry (1973), *The Nature of Managerial Work*, New York: Harper & Row, Harper Collins.

Mione, Anne (2006), 'Les Normes comme Démarche Collectives', *Revue Française de Gestion*, **167**, 105–22.

Mishina, Kazuhiro (2004), *Senryaku Fuzen no Ronri: Manseiteki-na Teishūeki-no Yamai -kara Dou Nukedasuka (The Logic of Strategy Failure: How to get out of Chronic Disease of Low Profitability)*, Tokyo: Toyo Keizai (in Japanese).

Mishina, Kazuhiro (2006), 'Bubun to zentai: Case study wo dou tsukau noka' (Part and whole: How can we use case study?), in Kazuo Koikeand Haruo Horaguchi (eds), *Keieigaku no Fīrudo Risāchi: Genba no Tatsujin no Jissen-teki Chōsa Shuhō (Field Research for Management Study: A Practical Guide by Research Master of Working Scene)*, Chapter 3, Tokyo: Nikkei, pp. 69–88 (in Japanese).

Mitsuzawa, Shigeo (1996), 'Shūgō senryaku to kōkyō seisaku' (Collective strategy and public policy), *Doushisha Shougaku (The Doshisha Business Review)*, **48** (1), 331–53 (in Japanese).

Miura, Asako and Yasushi Kawaura (2008), 'Hito ha naze chishiki kyouyū community ni sanka surunoka: Shitsumon koudou to kaitou koudou no bunseki' (Why do people join Web-based knowledge-sharing communities?: Analysis on questioning and answering behaviors), *Shakai Shinrigaku Kenkyū (Japanese Journal of Social Psychology)*, **23** (3), 233–45 (in Japanese).

Miwa, Kazuhisa (2000), 'Kyōyū sareru ninchi kūkan to sougo sayou niyoru sōhatsu no shutsugen kanousei' (Realization possibility of emergence caused by shared cognition space and interaction), in Kazuhiro Ueda and Takeshi Okada (eds), *Kyodo no Chi wo Saguru: Sōzō-teki Koraboreishon no Ninchi Kagaku (Searching for Shared Knowledge: Cognitive Science of Creative Collaboration)*, Chapter 2, Tokyo: Kyoritsu Shuppan, pp. 78–107.

Miyahara, Junji (2001), 'Sōzōteki gijutsusha no ronri to pāsonatitī' (Logic of creative engineers and personality), Hitotsubashi University Institute of Innovation Research (ed.), *Innovation Manejimento Nyūmon (Introduction to Innovation Management)*, Chapter 8, Tokyo: Nikkei, pp. 218–44 (in Japanese).

Miyashita, Tadashi and Takashi Noda (2003), *Gunshū Seibutsu-gaku (Community Ecology)*, Tokyo: University of Tokyo Press (in Japanese).

Morita, Akio, Mitsuko Shimomura and Edwin M. Reingold (1990), *Made in Japan: Waga Taikenteki Kokusai Senryaku (Made in Japan: My Experiential Global Strategy)*, Asahi Shimbun Publications Inc. (translated from an English version, Made in Japan: *Akio Morita and Sony*, by Mitsuko Shimomura published in London: Harper Collins Publishers Ltd, 1987).

Murphy, Frederic H., Hanif D. Sherali and Allen L. Soyster (1982), 'A mathematical programming approach for determining oligopolistic market equilibrium', *Mathematical Programming*, **24** (1), 92–106.

Nakakoji, Kumiyo (2001), 'Collective creation no tame no kansei teki komyunikeisyon' (Emotional communication for Collective Creation), *System/Jōhō/Seigyo (System, Information, Control)*, **45** (6), 314–21 (in Japanese).

Namatame, Akira (2003), 'Fukuzatukei to shūgōchi: Shakai kagaku kara no chiken' (Complexity and collective intelligence: Knowledge from social science), *Jinkō Chinō Gakkai-shi (Journal of Japanese Society for Artificial Intelligence)*, **18** (6), 723–32 (in Japanese).

Nelson, Richard R. and Sidney G. Winter (1982), *An Evolutionary Theory of Economic Change*, Cambridge, MA: Harvard University Press.

Nikkei Microdevices/Nikkei Electronics (eds) (2005), *MEMS Tekunoroji 2006: Apurikeishon kara debaisu, souchi, buzai made (MEMS Technology 2006: From Application to Device, Equipment, and Material)*, Tokyo: Nikkei BP (in Japanese).

Nonaka, Ikujiro (1990), *Chishiki-sōzō no Keiei: Nihon Kigyō no Épistémologie (Management of Knowledge Creation: Epistemology of Japanese Firms)*, Tokyo: Nikkei (in Japanese).

Nonaka, Ikujiro (1991), 'The knowledge creating company', *Harvard Business Review*, **69** (6), 96–104.

Nonaka, Ikujiro and Takeuchi, Hirotaka (1995), *The Knowledge Creating Company: How Japanese Companies Create the Dynamics of Innovation*, New York: Oxford University Press.

Numagami, Tsuyoshi (1999), *Ekishō Display no Gijutsu Kakushin-shi: Koui-rensa Sisutemu toshiteno Gijutu (History of Liquid Crystal Display Technology)*, Tokyo: Hakutōshobō (in Japanese).

Odagiri, Hiroyuki and Akira Goto (1996), *Technology and Industrial Development in Japan: Building Capabilities by Learning, Innovation, and Public Policy*, Oxford: Oxford University Press (translated into Japanese by Takahiro Kawamata under the title of *Nihon no Kigyō Shinka: Kakushin to Kyoso no Dynamic Process*, Tokyo: Toyo Keizai, 1998).

Ohashi, Masao and Kaoru Sasaki (eds) (1989), *Shakai Shinrigaku wo Manabu, Shinpan (Learning Social Psychology, New Edition)*, Tokyo: Yuhikaku sensho.

Ohmukai, Ikki (2006), 'Web2.0 to shūgōchi' (Collective intelligence and Web 2.0), *Jōhōshori (IPSJ Magazine*, Information Processing Society of Japan), **47** (11), 1214–21

Okamoto, Yoshiyuki (2001), 'Coordinator towa nanika: Ōbei ni okeru coordination jigyō to sono kyoukun' (What is coordinator?: Lessons from coordination business in Europe and in the United States), in Takao Kubo, Seiji Harada and Shinsangyō Seisaku Kenkyūjo, *Chishiki Keizai to Science Park (Knowledge Economy and Science Park)*, Chapter 8, Tokyo: Nippon Hyoronsha, pp. 235–57.

Oliver, Christine (1988), 'The collective strategy framework: An application to competing predictions to isomorphism', *Administrative Science Quarterly*, **33** (4), 543–61.

Peirce, Charles S. (1868), 'Some consequences of four incapacities', *Journal of Speculative Philosophy*, **2** (3), 140–57.

Penrose, Edith (1959), *The Theory of the Growth of the Firm*, Oxford: Oxford University Press, with a new Foreword by the author, 1995.

Piore, Michael J. and Charles F. Sabel (1984), *The Second Industrial Divide: Possibilities for Prosperity*, New York: Basic Books.

Polanyi, Michael (1957), 'Problem Solving', *British Journal for the Philosophy of Science*, **8** (30), 89–103.

Polanyi, Michael (1958), *Personal Knowledge: Towards a Post-Critical Philosophy*, Chicago: University of Chicago Press.

Polanyi, Michael (1962a), 'Tacit Knowing: Its Bearing on Some Problems of Philosophy', *Reviews of Modern Physics*, **34** (4), 601–16.

Polanyi, Michael (1962b), 'The republic of science: Its political and economic theory', *Minerva*, **1** (1), 54–73, reprinted in *Minerva*, **38** (1), 1–21, 2000.

Polanyi, Michael (1965), 'The structure of consciousness', *Brain*, **88** (4), 799–810.

Polanyi, Michael (1966a), *The Tacit Dimension*, Gloucester, MA: Peter Smith, reprinted by New York: Doubleday & Company, 1983.

Polanyi, Michael (1966b), 'The logic of tacit inference', *Philosophy*, **41** (155), 1–18, reprinted in Michael Polanyi (1969), *Knowing and Being: Essays*, Marjorie Grene (ed.), Chicago: the University of Chicago Press, London: Routledge & Kegan Paul.

Popper, Karl R. (1957), *The Poverty of Historicism*, London: Routledge & Kegan Paul.

Popper, Karl R. (1974), *Unended Quest: An Intellectual Autobiography*, La Salle, IL: Open Court.

Porter, Michael E. (1980), *Competitive Strategy: Techniques for Analyzing Industries and Competitors*, New York: Free Press.

Porter, Michael E. (ed.) (1986), *Competition in Global Industries*, Boston: Harvard Business School Press.

Porter, Michael E. (1990), *Competitive Advantage of Nations*, New York: Free Press.

Porter, Michael E. (1998), *On Competition*, Boston: Harvard Business School Press.

Putnam, Robert D. (1993), 'The prosperous community: Social capital and public life,' *American Prospect*, **13**, 1–8.

Riesman, David. (1960), *The Lonely Crowd: A Study of the Changing American Character*, New Haven: Yale University Press.

Rogers, Everett M. (1995), *Diffusion of Innovations*, 5th edition, New York: Free Press.

Satō, Fusao. (1984), *Shizen no Sūri to Shakai no Sūri: Bibun Hōtēshiki de Kaiseki-suru I (Mathematics in Nature and Mathematics in Society: Analyzing by Differential Equations I)*, Tokyo: Nippon Hyoronsha, (in Japanese).

Saussure, Ferdinand de (1916), *Cours de linguistique générale*, Paris: Payot (translated into Japanese by Hideo Kobayashi under the title of *Ippan Gengogaku Kougi*, Tokyo: Iwanamishoten, 1972).

Saxenian, Annalee (1994), *Regional Advantage: Culture and Competition in Silicon Valley and Route 128*. Cambridge: Harvard University Press.

Saxenian, Annalee (2000), 'Networks of immigrant entrepreneurs', in Chong-Moon Lee, William F. Miller, Marguerite Gong Hancock and Henry S. Rowen (eds), *The Silicon Valley Edge: A Habitat for Innovation and Entrepreneurship*, Chapter 12, Stanford, CA: Stanford University Press, pp. 248–75.

Schelling, Thomas C. (1960), *Strategy of Conflict*, Cambridge, MA: Harvard University Press.

Schelling, Thomas C. (1978), *Micro Motives and Macro Behavior*, New York: W.W. Norton & Company.

Scherer, Frederic M. and David Ross (1990), *Industrial Market Structure and Economic Performance*, 3rd ed., Boston: Houghton Mifflin Company.

Schumpeter, Joseph A. (1926), *Theorie der Wirtschaftlichen Entwicklung*, Berlin: Duncker & Humbolt, 1997 (translated into English by Redvers Opie under the title of *The Theory of Economic Development*, Cambridge, MA: Harvard University Press, 1934, reprinted in 2012) (translated into Japanese by Yuichi Shionoya, Ichiro Nakayama and Seiichi Tōhata under the title of *Keizai Hatten no Riron (Theory of Economic Development)*, Iwanamibunko, 1977).

Schumpeter, Joseph A. (1939), *Business Cycles: A Theoretical, Historical, and Statistical Analysis of the Capitalist Process*, 1st ed., New York: McGraw-Hill (translated into Japanese by Shōzō Yoshida under the title of *Keiki Junkanron*, Tokyo: Yūhikaku, 2001).

Schumpeter, Joseph A. (1942), *Capitalism, Socialism and Democracy*, 3rd ed., 1949, New York: Harper & Brothers.

Segaran, Toby (2007), *Programming Collective Intelligence: Building Smart Web 2.0 Applications*, Sebastopol, CA: O'Reilly.

Sherali, Hanif D. and Joanna M. Leleno (1988), 'A mathematical programming approach to a Nash-Cournot equilibrium analysis for a two-stage network of oligopolies', *Operations Research*, **36** (5), 682–702.

Shinobu, Chikako (2003), *Post Lean Seisan Sisutemu no Tankyū: Fukakuteisei-eno Kigyō Tekiou (Inquiry into the Post Lean Production System: Corporate Fit toward Uncertainty)*, Tokyo: Bunshindō (in Japanese).

Shintaku, Junjiro (1994), *Nihon Kigyō no Kyōsō Senryaku: Seijuku Sangyō no Gijutu-iten to Kigyō Koudou (Competitive Strategy of Japanese Firms: Technology Transfer and Corporate Behavior in Mature Industry)*, Tokyo: Yūhikaku.

Simon, Herbert A. (1945), *Administrative Behavior: A Study of Decision Making Processes in Administrative Organization*, New York: Free Press.

Simon, Herbert A. and Glenn Lea (1974), 'Problem solving and rule induction', in H.A. Simon, *Models of Thought*, volume I, pp. 329–46, New Haven, CT: Yale University Press, 1979.

Smith, Adam (1776), *An Inquiry into the Nature and Causes of the Wealth of Nations*, Edwin Cannan, reprinted by Tokyo: Charles E. Tuttle Company, 1979.

Snowden, David (2002), 'Complex act of knowing: Paradox and descriptive self-awareness', *Journal of Knowledge Management*, **6** (2), 100–111.

Spencer, Herbert (1916), *The Principles of Sociology*, volume 1, New York and London: D. Appleton and Company.

Suehiro, Akira (2000), *Kyacchi-appu-gata Kōgyō-ka-ron: Asia Keizai no Kiseki to Tenbou (Catch-up Type Industrialization: Miracles and Visions of Asian Economy)*, Nagoya: The University of Nagoya Press.

Surowiecki, James (2005), *The Wisdom of Crowds*, with a new afterword by the author, New York: Anchor Books.

Takadama, Keiki (2003), 'Sougo-sayou ni umekomareta shūgōchi: Shūdan no soshiki level no kaiseki' (Embedded collective intelligence for interaction: An analysis of group in organizational level), *Jinkō Chinō Gakkaishi (the JSAI Journal, the Japanese Society for Artificial Intelligence)*, **18** (6), 704–9 (in Japanese).

Takayasu, Hideki (2003), 'Keizai butsuri kara mita shūgōchi' (Collective intelligence from the perspective of economic physics), *Jinkō Chinō Gakkaishi (the JSAI Journal, the Japanese Society for Artificial Intelligence)*, **18** (6), 684–9 (in Japanese).

Takekawa, Hiroko (2001), 'Shōshūdan katsudō no kigyō-nai iten ni kansuru kenkyū: Tounan ajia nikkei-kigyō wo jirei to shite' (A study on intra-firm transfer of small group activities: Cases on Japanese firms in South-East Asia), International Graduate School of Social Science, Yokohama National University, Doctoral dissertation (in Japanese).

Tarde, Jean-Gabriel (1895), *Les Lois de L'imitation*, Paris: Alcan (translated into Japanese by Shōei Ikeda and Mahoro Murasawa under the title of *Mohō no Hōsoku*, Tokyo: Kawaide-shobo shinsha, 2007).

Tarde, Jean-Gabriel (1901), *L'Opinion et la Foule*, Paris: Alcan (translated into Japanese by Michio Inaba under the title of *Yoron to Gunshū*, Tokyo: Miraisha, 1964).

Taylor, Frederick W. (1911), *The Principles of Scientific Management*, New York: Harper.

Teece, David J. and Gary Pisano (1994), 'The dynamic capabilities of firms: An introduction', *Industrial and Corporate Change*, **3** (3), 537–56.

Timmons, Jeffrey A. (1990), *New Venture Creation: Entrepreneurship in the 1990s*, 3rd ed., New York: Richard D. Irwin.

Tirole, Jean (1988), *The Theory of Industrial Organization*, Cambridge, MA: MIT Press.

Udagawa, Masaru and Sangyō Jōhō Center, Hosei University (eds) (1999), *Keisubukku: Nihon no Kigyōka Katsutdō (Casebook: Entrepreneurship Activities in Japan)*, Tokyo: Yuhikaku (in Japanese).

Ueda, Kazuhiro and Takeshi Okada (2000), *Kyōdō no Chi wo Saguru: Sōzō-teki Koraboreishyon no Ninchi Kagaku (Searching for Collaborative Knowledge: Cognitive Science of Creative Collaboration)*, Tokyo: Kyoritsu Shuppan (in Japanese).

Uekusa, Masu (2000), *Sangyō Yūgō: Sangyō Soshiki no Aratana Hōkō (Industry Fusion: A New Direction of Industrial Organization)*, Tokyo: Iwanamishoten (in Japanese).

Vandermeer, John H. and Deborah E. Goldberg (2003), *Population Ecology: First Principles*, Princeton, NJ: Princeton University Press.

Veblen, Thorstein (1899), *The Theory of the Leisure Class: An Economic Study in the Evolution of Institutions*, New York: Macmillan, reprinted by Oxford University Press, 2007.

Vernon, Raymond (1966), 'International investment and international trade in the product cycle', *Quarterly Journal of Economics*, **80** (2), 190–207.

Vives, Xavier (1999), *Oligopoly Pricing: Old Ideas and New Tools*, Cambridge, MA: MIT Press.

von Hippel, Eric (1994), '"Sticky information" and the locus of problem solving: implications for innovation', *Management Science*, **40** (4), 429–39.

von Hippel, Eric (2005), *Democratizing Innovation*, Cambridge, MA: MIT Press.

Walras, Léon (1874/1926), Éléments d'économie politique pure, ou théorie de la richesse sociale, Paris et Lausanne: Pichon et Durand-Auzias (translated by Masao Hisatake into Japanese in 1926 version, Iwanamishoten, 1983).

Waterson, Michael (1984), *The Economic Theory of Industry*, Cambridge: Cambridge University Press.

Watts, Duncan J. (2003), *Six Degrees: The Science of a Connected Age*, New York: W.W. Norton & Company.

Weber, Max (1919), *Die Protestantische Ethik und der Geist des Kapitalismus*, Tübingen: J.C.B. Mohr (translated into Japanese by Chikara Kajiyama and Hisao Ohtsuka under the title of *Purotestantism no Riron to Shihonshugi no Seishin*, Tokyo: Iwanamishoten, vol. 1, 1955, vol. 2, 1962).

Williamson, Oliver E. (1975), *Markets and Hierarchies: Analysis and Antitrust Implications*, New York: Free Press.

Williamson, Oliver E. (1985), *The Economics Institutions of Capitalism*, New York: Free Press.

Yamagishi, Toshio (1998), *Shinrai no Kōzō: Kokoro to Shakai no Shinka Geimu (The Structure of Trust: The Evolutionary Games of Mind and Society)*, Tokyo: University of Tokyo Press.

Yamakura, Kenshi (1993), *Soshiki-kan Kankei: Kigyō-kan Nettowāku no Henkaku ni Mukete (Interorganizational Relationships: Towards the Reformation of Inter-company Network)*, Tokyo: Yūhikaku.

Yamasaki, Akira (2003), 'Chiiki sangyō seisaku to shiteno claster keikaku' (Cluster scheme as regional industrial policy: Establishing competitive advantages in regions), in Yoko Ishikura, Masahisa Fujita, Noboru Maeda, Kazuyori Kanai, Akira Yamasaki (eds), *Nihon no Sangyō Kurasutā Senryaku: Chiiki ni Okeru Kyōsōyūi no Kakuritsu (Industrial Cluster Strategy of Japan: Establishing Competitive Advantage in Local Economy)*, Chapter 5, Tokyo: Yūhikaku, pp. 175–210 (in Japanese).

Yamasaki, Akira and Hajime Tomokage (2001), *Handoutai Kurasutā heno Sinario: Sirikon Airando Kyūshū no Kako to Mirai (A Scenario for Semiconductor Cluster: Past and Future for Silicon Island)*, Fukuoka: Nishinippon Shimbun (in Japanese).

Yamazaki, Hideo (2004), 'Posuto Nonaka-riron heno apurōchi ni kansuru shiron: Chishiki shakai ni fusawashii atarashii chishiki riron no kouchiku wo mezashite' (A tentative theory on post-Nonaka theoretical approach: Aiming for constructing knowledge theory suitable for knowledge society), *Narejji Manejimento Kenkyū Nenpo (The Annual Bulletin of Knowledge Management Society of Japan)*, **5**, 21–34 (in Japanese).

Yami, Saïd (2006), 'Fondements et Perspectives des Stratégies Collectives', *Revue Française de Gestion*, **167**, 91–104.

Yasuda, Yuki (2004), *Jinmyaku Zukuri no Kagaku: Hito to Hito tono Kankei ni Kakusareta Chikara wo Saguru (Science for Human Relationships: Searching for Hidden Power in Person to Person Relationships)*, Tokyo: Nikkei.

Name index

Subject index